Aesthetic Leadership

Aesthetic Leadership

Managing Fields of Flow in Art and Business

Edited by

Pierre Guillet de Monthoux,

Claes Gustafsson

and

Sven-Erik Sjöstrand

palgrave
macmillan

First published 2007 by
PALGRAVE MACMILLAN
Houndmills, Basingstoke, Hampshire RG21 6XS and
175 Fifth Avenue, New York, N.Y. 10010
Companies and representatives throughout the world

PALGRAVE MACMILLAN is the global academic imprint of the Palgrave
Macmillan division of St. Martin's Press, LLC and of Palgrave Macmillan Ltd.
Macmillan® is a registered trademark in the United States, United Kingdom
and other countries. Palgrave is a registered trademark in the European
Union and other countries.

ISBN-13: 978–0–230–51558–1 hardback
ISBN-10: 0–230–51558–4 hardback

This book is printed on paper suitable for recycling and made from fully
managed and sustained forest sources.

A catalogue record for this book is available from the British Library.

Library of Congress Cataloging-in-Publication Data
Aesthetic leadership:managing fields of flow in art and business/edited by
    Pierre Guillet de Monthoux, Claes Gustafsson and Sven-Erik Sjöstrand.
       p.   cm.
    Includes bibliographical references and index.
    ISBN-13: 978–0–230–51558–1 (cloth)
    ISBN-10: 0–230–51558–4 (cloth)
    1. Management. 2. Aesthetics. I. Guillet de Monthoux, Pierre, 1946–
    II. Gustafsson, Claes, 1941–   III. Sjöstrand, Sven-Erik, 1945–
    HD31.A324 2007
    658—dc22   2006051505

10   9   8   7   6   5   4
16   15   14   13   12   11   10   09   08   07

Printed and bound in Great Britain by
Antony Rowe Ltd, Chippenham and Eastbourne

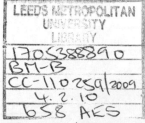

Contents

Part III   Conditions for new leadership: art and business

List of illustrations

List of figures

Notes on the contributors

Ivar Björkman is President of the University College of Arts, Craft and Design, Stockholm, Sweden

Helena Csarmann is Research Assistant at the Royal Institute of Technology, Stockholm, Sweden

Bertil González Guve is Assistant Professor at the Royal Institute of Technology, Stockholm, Sweden

Claes Gustafsson is Professor of Industrial Management and Organization at the Royal Institute of Technology, Stockholm, Sweden

Ann Sofie Köping is Assistant Professor at Södertörn University College, Sweden

Jenny Lantz is Research Assistant at Stockholm School of Economics, Sweden

Marcus Lindahl is Assistant Professor at the Royal Institute of Technology, Stockholm, Sweden

Katja Lindqvist is Assistant Professor at Stockholm University School of Business, Sweden

Stefan Meisiek is Assistant Professor at the Universidade Nova de Lisboa, Portugal

Pierre Guillet de Monthoux is Professor of General Management at Stockholm University, Sweden

Erik Piñeiro is Assistant Professor at the Royal Institute of Technology, Stockholm, Sweden

Alf Rehn is Professor at the Royal Institute of Technology, Stockholm, Sweden

Sven-Erik Sjöstrand is Professor of Management and Organization at the Stockholm School of Economics, Sweden

Emma Stenström is Assistant Professor at Stockholm School of Economics and CEO of Arts and Business, Sweden

Marja Soila-Wadman is Assistant Professor at Vaxjo University, Sweden

Jeanette Wetterström is Researcher at the School of Business, Stockholm University, Sweden

Acknowledgements

The editors wish to thank *Riksbankens Jubileumsfond* (Bank of Sweden Tercentenary Foundation) for its generous financial support, which made possible both the whole *Fields of Flow* research programme and this concluding editorial volume.

The editors would also like to thank *Andrew Sandrews stiftelse* (Andrew Sandrews' foundation) for its support for a research project on the movie business. In this volume part of that project has materialised as Chapter 4, 'Gendered Textbook Filmmakers'.

Finally, the editors would like to express their deep gratitude to the following members of its Advisory Board (with equal representation from the arts and business corporations in Sweden) for their strong encouragement and support to all researchers during the seven-year *Fields of Flow* programme:

Bertmar, Lars, Chair, *Carnegie*
Björkman, Ivar, President, *Konstfack* (University College of Arts, Crafts and Design)
Bonnier, Kerstin, Production manager, *Svensk Filmindustri*
Dalborg, Hans, Chair, *Nordea*
Johnson, Antonia Axson, Chair, *the Axel Johnson Group*
Kallifatides, Theodor, Author/Professor
Kåks, Olle, Artist/Painter
Holm, Staffan Valdemar, *Dramaten* (Royal Dramatic Theatre)
Lindencrona, Carl, CEO, *Svenska Musikförläggarföreningen* (Swedish Music Publishers Association)
Nitve, Lars, Director, *Moderna Museet* (Museum of Modern Art)
Rock, Yvonne, Producer
Tiveus, Meg, CEO, *Svenska Spel*
Weil, Robert, Chair, *Proventus*

Introduction

1
Leadership in fields of flow

Pierre Guillet de Monthoux, Claes Gustafsson and Sven-Erik Sjöstrand

Feeling a new kind of leadership

> *"Hi! Where are you from?" inquired the salesclerk. "Did you see the thing in the Park? What did you think of it?"*
>
> *The customer nodded. "I saw it on the weekend, and I liked it very much."*
>
> *"I bet you want to go through the Park," declared the taxi driver as he loaded the couple into his cab. "You are not the first today, you know!" As they reached Columbus Circle, he slowed his vehicle and motioned out the side window. "How do you like it? Cool, eh?"*

Here in the middle of a bleak February in 2005, Manhattanites who had never paid even a sound bite's worth of attention to the museum mile could not stop talking about the art exhibition going on in the Park. It had been played up on the front page of *The New York Times*, it had been featured on TV, and now it was the talk of the town: Christo and his wife and partner Jeanne Claude had just put up their Gates installation in Central Park.

Hundreds of guides were posted along the pathways to tell the backstage story of the event, the story of the more than 7000 gates, their making, their unfurling and their scheduled lowering and recycling all within a relatively short span of time. They distributed fact sheets about the quantity of steel and vinyl used and the way the gates were manufactured and tested. A volume detailing the history of the more than two decades-long project was soon sold out in the merchandising booths run by the city of New York and in the Met bookstore. Now and then, between speeches and dinner parties for celebrities and collectors, the Christos themselves strolled under the saffron curtains.

3

Within ten days, rumors were circulating that the costly project, which was entirely financed by the artists themselves, had broken even and that single paintings of the Gates fetched prices over $1 million. In a management seminar at the Guggenheim Museum, experts from Columbia University, Harvard Business School and Stockholm University drew on the Gates as a model for the marketing of Central Park and Manhattan, the financing of mega art projects and artful ways of organizing work in general.[1] By the end of the project, quite a press debate had fermented over the issue of just what the Christos' $21 million investment had actually covered (McIntire, 2005).

Just a few years back, it would not have crossed the minds of journalists, the audience or art connoisseurs that this spectacular piece of land art was simply an enterprise run by the Christo art firm.[2] A decade ago, artists as well as managers would have raised serious objections to such a connection between the fields of art and business. And 20 years ago, the Christos, now proudly posing in Central Park as the leaders of the Gates project, protested at being called entrepreneurs: 'That is precisely what our enemies call us!'

Times have changed, and the iron curtain between culture and the economy has rusted away. In an era when global capitalism has blurred public interest and private enterprise, a radical antagonism between moneymaking and culture seems tricky to argue. It takes more than just being a rational economic man to run a successful business, you know; managers are Janus-faced (Sjöstrand, 1997), rather than one dimensional. Further, managers with new products, who struggle to make an impact on markets, realize there is a lot to learn from the Christos' careful long-range planning, detailed preparation and astounding perseverance. Most enjoying the Gates project in February 2005 would think it both obvious and unproblematic for successful artists to enhance the aesthetic impact of their art by picking up a lesson or two from business. Furthermore, not only is artwork now acknowledged as the product of an art firm, more and more regular businesses also seem to be art-based in one way or other. We drive cars labelled Picasso, read books about Da Vinci, and travel to places with Guggenheim museums, for as French sociologists Luc Boltanski and Eve Chiapello point out, art and aesthetics are at the foundation of the new spirit of global capitalism.[3]

While art does indeed inspire products and services overtly, it operates covertly as well. For example, previously hidden aesthetic dimensions of work processes have today been discovered and appreciated as central to efficiency and creativity. Aesthetic competence is as little the exclusive business of art schools as knowledge of how to run a business is the privileged domain of management schools. The differences between not-for-profit culture and profit-driven business[4] have been thoroughly recounted; now there is a need to research similarities between doing art and running businesses. In light of the Christo experience, artists like Warhol, Beuys, and Pistoletto are at last seen as leaders too. We have no reservations about referring to the Christos and their like as real leaders in business as well as art, but the time has come to figure out why and how.

Mapping fields of flow

History offers plenty of instances of value-making in the art–business exchange. Groups of practitioners and scholars, as well as authors of inspirational literature, advocate forging creative links between art and business. Yet research-based knowledge reflecting authentic conditions for the emergence of new leaders operating in the art–business nexus is scarce. In response to this situation and in an attempt to paint an accurate portrait of these new leaders, a Swedish research programme called Fields of Flow was launched five years ago.[5] The anthology you are reading today is the result of work conducted through the programme. The 13 cases provided here report the findings of the research.

Fields of Flow was chosen as the name for the programme because the term describes the unique characteristic of its interest. To say, for example, that the people in the Park were satisfied or even impressed by the Christos' enterprise would be utterly inappropriate; they got a kick out of it and were euphoric about it. This kind of feeling, the extreme joy of an experience, seems to be something the new leaders are good at orchestrating, both on markets and for their collaborators. The concept of Flow alludes to this kind of aesthetic joy, and although the word Flow implies motion, energy and momentum in its literary sense, it also implies change and crossing of borders. In psychology, the concept of 'flow' has evolved to cover almost ecstatic experiences.[6]

In the case researched by Helena Csarmann, we are introduced to a roller coaster designer/builder handling thrilling flow in a business easily classified as an experience economy (Pine and Gilmore, 1999). Whether it is the sensation of an amusement park thrill that Csarmann talks about, or the feeling of becoming beautiful that Emma Stenström describes, or the sublime music-making in symphonic orchestras that Ann-Sofie Köping focuses on, or the visual feats of haute cuisine that Alf Rehn considers, flow is seen as a product of our bodily senses rather than being connected to our discursive intellect. Katja Lindqvist, in her chapter, explicitly identifies the dynamics of the leadership she studies as erotic.

Flow: an aesthetic phenomenon

The feeling of flow[7] is an aesthetic phenomenon, one that might just occur outside of what we usually consider art. The cases analysed in the chapters by Bertil Guve, Marcus Lindahl, Erik Piñeiro and Stefan Meisiek illustrate that aesthetic flow is also central to businesses like banking, power-plant construction, computer programming and home care organizations.

As it seems reasonable that all individual actions contain an aesthetic potential, there should be no question about the presence of this special form of sense-knowledge in the worlds of business and management. The new kind of leadership we want to understand seems grounded in the fact that beauty, harmony and the sublime dwell in factories, markets and offices, as well as in theatres, museums and concert halls. In the business world, aesthetics has long been suppressed and dismissed as 'irrational' and 'taboo,' an effect of the spirit of achieving scientific control over social life which dominated most nineteenth- and twentieth-century Western industrialized civilizations. This techno-economic rationality has reached such a prominent position – verging on hegemony in many Western societies – that it is often taken as a synonym for economic *rationality*.

Today, however, its privileged position has been challenged and is being recognized increasingly as a rather limited type of rationality, one associated with a certain era and a specific culture. By reintroducing aesthetics and flow as concepts central to the worlds of managers and leaders, we round out and fill in this incomplete perspective on rationality. How could we maintain that agents, managers or artists acting outside strict technical rationality are irrational and that all humans are merely victims of their interests or prisoners of historical conventions reflected in the limited concept of economic rationality? To the rather narrow and technical idea of a 'rational rationality', a wider 'rational irrationality' that does not discard flow as irrational but instead supports flows of emotions, intuition and feelings as sources of aesthetic knowledge affords a healthier perspective (Gustafsson, 1994; Sjöstrand, 1997).

The aesthetic flow concept applied here is not primarily a question for psychology. Flow, as the quality experienced by many of us wandering under the Gates, is an organizational phenomenon orchestrated under the leadership of the Christos. This kind of art depends on collaborative, organized and managed artistry, and that is why we speak of it as Fields of Flow.

Fields: organizational space

The fields concept assumes the presence of many different and rather unexplored arenas where actors produce and reproduce norms and develop habits as well as specific tasks. Many studies addressing activities and organizations in the art field have neglected to take into account the social space in which those who produce the works and their value are situated. This is the site of the art firm and its aesthetic play. As early as the 1980s, sociologists contended that it was not possible to understand art without also examining the socio-economic system in the society in which it was embedded. In studying art management it is absolutely necessary to consider how art firms are organized, including peripheral external aesthetic players like technicians, critics and audiences. Using the art firm approach (Guillet de Monthoux, 2004), the authors in this anthology apply both organizational and aesthetic readings to get a handle on the various fields of artistic production. This results in mapping different arenas for leadership. For example, the Gates case might be described in this context as taking place in the public arenas of Central Park and the City of New York, as well as in the private arenas of art markets or the construction sites of the Gates themselves.

Jeanette Wetterström's chapter demonstrates how over time the Swedish Royal Opera has moved between such arenas, specifically from the courtly performance to the realm of modern cultural policy. In Ivar Björkman's account of beautiful business, the case of Grythyttan rests upon combining different kinds of organizations into new fields where flows emerge and generate aesthetic value. Katja Lindqvist talks about leadership as a dance between different spaces and atmospheres. Jenny Lantz approaches the phenomenon from a negative side; she observes and deplores the gendered practice of restricting fields, which may as a result force closure on possible flow in the traditional film industry.

The concept of Fields is not necessarily identical to that of organizations or institutions, however. As a concept, Fields is a little fluid and vague. In the 1990s, precedents were set that changed control modes and organizational structures in a way that had seldom been seen before. Organizations are no longer formalized action-protective hardware. Instead of hierarchies' tying people and organizations together, we now all swim in a broth of networks, alliances, partnerships, heterarchies and holarchies.[8] Moreover, in relation to increasingly attentive consumers, products and services have acquired distinctiveness through aesthetic rationales also, and through the organizational rhetoric software, these rationales have often earned positive connotations.

Product marketing is also comprised of immaterial values and experiences to a greater extent. Business now seems to happen in networks and floating structures; it has escaped the classical walled realities of factories or offices. This is something Erik Piñeiro comments on in his discussion of open system programming. Art today has become free floating; not all artists have the defined production site of a symphonic orchestra or opera company. They have to explore and invent new spaces and contexts, as Katja Lindqvist and Ivar Björkman point out in their chapters.

Thirteen cases for grasping new leadership

In the spirit of ethnographic open inquiry, we have investigated the everyday realities of curators, actors, film directors, haute-cuisine chefs, opera-house managers and conductors of symphonic orchestras, as well as of engineers, programmers, film producers, financial analysts, weight watchers and regional tourist developers. Part I of our study focuses on artistic production, while Part II treats art-connected phenomena in business. In Part III, our researchers look at cases riding the fuzzy border overlapping art and business.

Art

Ann-Sofie Köping's chapter addressing creativity in symphony orchestras begins the first part, and she discusses both the planning of musical projects and the strong institutional control involved. The concert hall is described as an arena where standardized instruments, scores and skilled musicians meet to perform under the very special leadership of conductors.

Chapter 3, written by Jeanette Wetterström, presents an historical tale of institutional conditions affecting opera management. She discusses how operatic enterprise over three centuries has shifted from being embedded in the body of the kingdom to being a cultural project in state public policy, a development present in many European countries. Her focus is on the changes in the way operas have been governed and controlled, on the management principles applied by various stakeholders over time.

Jenny Lantz's Chapter 4 explores constructions of the film producer and the film director, and their intersection with constructions of gender conveyed in the textbooks used by graduate students in a leading American film programme. She conducts a study of the interplay of the dichotomy between cultural and economic capital, and that between femininity and masculinity. She shows how producers and directors tend to become typecast as readymade representatives of two basically male opposing rationales, namely the calculating *homo oeconomicus* and the creative *homo ludens*.

Marja Soila-Wadman's Chapter 5 pictures how film workers – primarily technicians and actors – cooperate in highly interactive processes. She spotlights the role of the director and challenges the construct of her or him as a kind of heroic creator. In her account of the anti-hero leader, she points out that filmmaking is concrete, almost physical, with blood-sweat-and-tears ingredients.

Business

The second part of our book focuses on business production. The first of its five chapters is written by Emma Stenström. In this chapter 'Body Business', the Weight Watchers organization constitutes the empirical setting. She considers the new 'body consciousness' or so-called 'bodily turn' in a reassessment of the importance of the concrete embodiment of human action. Chapter 7 by Erik Piñeiro addresses technical development in software producing firms, deploring particularly how production processes that aim at generating beautiful products struggle in the squeeze between creativity and control. In Chapter 8, Bertil Gonzaléz Guve introduces us to the managerial task of judging investment risks in the world of a Swedish investment bank. Drawing from his own experience as an investment analyst, he argues that investment assessment involves something more than just calculative rationale and tradition-based norms. Guve contends that it involves aesthetics.

Chapter 9, written by Helena Csarmann, acquaints us with a true entrepreneur operating in an environment framed by two strong opposing rationales: commercial business versus technical safety standards. She describes how this entrepreneurial leadership navigates between science and technical conventions and the tradition of safety standards to produce extraordinary aesthetic thrills in the form of roller-coaster rides.

Chapter 10, written by Marcus Lindahl, shows how industrial projects use playfulness and improvisation to cope with technical crises such as standstills and breakdowns. Lindahl shows how improvisation-leadership breaks out of the deadlock by doing something exceptional while still preserving established norms.

Art and business

The third part of our study begins with Stefan Meisiek's chapter on a rather common topic: what to do when changing the way an organization works becomes problematic. In this case, traditional solutions, like bringing in management consultants or enforcing the institutionalized hierarchical control, have failed. In Meisiek's study, management tried asking a theatre company for help. The artists were informed that the first goal was to improve communication skills among the workers, particularly in relation to their clients; the second was to increase job satisfaction. Even though the meeting between workers and artists did not solve the two basic managerial problems, it still had some useful consequences, such as opening up communication between the workers and between the workers and management. The intervention of the theatre company also provided a way for management and the workers to jointly reconsider the way that the vertical processes in the home care organization were executed.

In Chapter 12, Katja Lindqvist presents four European examples to illustrate her attempt to account for success and failure in curating projects. She describes the making of an exhibition as a process where visions and ideas are transformed into, and interpreted through, material form and artefacts. The basic question raised in her chapter is how such a translation should or could be managed. She addresses the question primarily through examples of *mis*management and through the suggestion of a metaphor for the forces and wills inherent in exhibition realization processes in general.

Alf Rehn's Chapter 13 looks at how food becomes refined and thereby becomes a part of high culture. He spotlights a chef who manages innovation and value production. Since food is a primary phenomenon both in the economy and in the upkeep of the human body, he claims that aesthetic values do enter in at a fundamental stage. Rehn develops his topic by studying the work of a particular entrepreneur – an inventor of *haute cuisine* – who actually succeeds in changing basic institutions.

Ivar Björkman's Chapter 14, the last of the empirical chapters, maintains that marketing today has to convert a product or service into an ultimate 'beauty experience'. The empirical setting is a place in Sweden named Grythyttan, and Björkman characterizes it as a 'beautyscape' that specializes in providing the customer with a unique aesthetic experience. Björkman analyses how a regional entrepreneur makes it possible to combine a business rationale with an aesthetic one, making Grythyttan both a strong brand and a kind of mini-society, complete with an inn, a university branch, a research unit, a museum, a theatre, and wine and food businesses.

Chapter 15, our wrap-up discussion, draws general conclusions from the implications of the 13 research projects. Then, in one final stroke, we take up our brushes and attempt to paint an accurate portrait of the new aesthetic leader, building our palette from pieces scattered all over our Fields of Flow.

Notes

1. Conversations across Cultures, a seminar organized by Ruth Bereson and Graeme Sullivan of Columbia University and held at the Guggenheim Museum, 19 February 2005.
2. An 'art firm' is the idiosyncratic way of organizing and managing art. See Guillet de Monthoux (2004).
3. In *The new spirit of capitalism* (2005), their study of contemporary capitalist ideology, Boltanski and Chiapello imply that artistic criticism has now taken over the role of social criticism as the main source of capitalist criticism and inspirer of reforms of the economic infrastructure. The fact that the co-authors have a background in the study of cultural organizations and art management has probably facilitated the discovery of this important societal trend.
4. The work of French sociologist Pierre Bourdieu was the uncontested vanguard for such attempts. The second most important influence is most certainly the Marxian Frankfurt School of which Adorno is the main culture-critical reference.
5. Through five years of research grants, the Tercentenary Foundation of the Swedish National Bank financed Fields of Flow. During joint seminars, conferences and meetings, the Fields of Flow team was encouraged to work in tune with some keynote texts by senior members of the team. See Sjöstrand (1997); Björkegren (1996); Guillet de Monthoux (2004); and Gustafsson (1994). Professor Gustafsson of the Royal Institute of Technology introduced the concept of play and frivolity as a theme in the usually rather austere study of management of technology; Professor Sjöstrand emphasized both problems and opportunities of rationality and irrationality cohabiting in organizational reality; and Professor Guillet de Monthoux shared work done by his European Centre for Art and Management at Stockholm University. In addition, Fields of Flow urged its members to take part in international encounters between business communities and art worlds. The research programme staged two international meetings in France and Germany. Our objective was to support crossovers while keeping high standards of management scholarship. Fields of Flow has been carried out in a spirit close to that of Antonio Strati, who in *Aesthetics and organization* (1999) advocated an aesthetic awareness among those investigating organizations. Strati and Guillet de Monthoux also edited a special issue of *Human Relations* (2002, 55, 7), gathering contributions treating methodological aspects such as aesthetic awareness that have been essential to contributors of this book. In addition, a video documentary, *Masters of Business Art, a Fields of Flow movie* (Guillet de Monthoux 2006), visually presents

the project. A CD, *Liedership, a Fields of Flow Musical* (Guillet de Monthoux 2005), poetically explains what aesthetic leadership is all about.

6. The psychological concept was minted by Mihaly Csikszentmihaly and is treated by him in a managerial context. See Csikszentmihaly (2003).

7. Csikszentmihaly defines flow as a feeling of clear goals, with immediate feedback, in a balance between opportunity and capacity that deepens concentration, where only the present matters, where control is no problem, the sense of time is altered and that finally provokes a loss of ego (42–6).

8. See, for instance, Sjöstrand (1997).

References

Björkegren, D. (1996) *The culture business*. London: Routledge.

Boltanski, L., and E. Chiapello (2005) *The new spirit of capitalism*. London: Verso.

Csikszentmihaly, M. (2003) *Good business, leadership, flow, and the making of meaning*. New York: Viking.

Guillet de Monthoux, P. (2004) *The art firm: Aesthetic management and metaphysical marketing*. Palo Alto, CA: Stanford University Press.

Guillet de Monthoux, P. (2005) *Liedership, a Fields of Flow Musical* (CD). Stockholm: Arvinius Förlag.

Guillet de Monthoux, P. (2006) *Masters of Business Art, a Fields of Flow Movie* (DVD). Stockholm: Arvinius Förlag.

Gustafsson, C. (1994) *Produktion av allvar, om det ekonomiska förnuftets metafysik* [Production of seriousness: On the metaphysics of economic reason]. Stockholm: Nerenius och Santérus förlag.

McIntire, M. (2005) Enough about 'Gates' as art: Let's talk about that price tag. *The New York Times* (5 March).

Pine, J., and J. Gilmore (1999) *The experience economy*. Cambridge, MA: Harvard University Press.

Sjöstrand, S.-E. (1997) *The two faces of management. The Janus factor*. London: Thomson.

Strati, A. (1999) *Aesthetics and organization*. London: Sage.

Part I

Conditions for New Leadership: Art

2
The creative compost: playing and conducting musical events

Ann-Sofie Köping

Creativity is a concept that almost universally carries positive connotations. In a society where repeating yourself or staying in one place too long is frowned upon, creativity delivers us from regression and boredom. But how about an organization that has not changed much in the last two centuries, an organization where the people who are part of it are part of it for decades? Should this organization automatically be labeled uncreative and dull? It certainly repeats itself in its outreach and its programme. And its members are encouraged to stay put and continue contributing to the organization until they are ready for retirement in some cases. Perhaps instead of trying to squeeze this organization into a handy concept, it is time to expand our thinking about how creativity operates and what goes into the creative process.

The organization we have just described is a symphony orchestra; it operates as a collective or team. While the musicians produce immensely beautiful sound, the process of getting there is often anything but attractive. So how does it all come together? How does an orchestra manifest its creativity? Drawing upon an ethnographic study of everyday life in a concert hall in Sweden (Köping, 2003), this chapter uses a relational perspective to focus on the collective interplay that takes place in the production of that glorious sound. The interaction between the musicians and their conductor, for example, referred to in this chapter as relational attainments, provides some thought-provoking challenges to preconceived notions about creativity.

Collaborative artistry

Musicians who play symphonic music must be extremely disciplined. They have scores, a conductor and one hundred other musicians to follow and adapt themselves to. As a result of these conditions, some raise the question of whether music reproduced in this way is really creative. The answer of course depends on what is being used as a definition of creativity. Since the middle of the twentieth century, companies and organizations have often used the concept of creativity as a tool for doing things no one else has done before. Sveiby (1992) defines a creative idea or product as one that is new, useful and elegant. Creativity is a tool for helping a company build new business areas, invent new items for production, and generate new ideas about services or organization. Employing and encouraging creative personnel is a major challenge facing all organizations.

The musicians in an orchestra do not actually do anything new, their playing is not very useful and their performance sometimes does not quite reach a level of elegance. While their interpretation may give the impression of being a smooth and easy collaboration, it represents a compromise or rather a negotiation between a lot of wills, skills and ideas. Is the only real creator in this context then the composer who wrote the score? Or in the process of each run through, does the orchestra create a new interpretation of the work, one that may indeed be quite elegant from time to time?

A machine cannot replace an orchestra by any stretch of the imagination. When the musicians under the direction of their conductor and in response to the audience come together in a work, something is added to the music. Even what this something is, is negotiated in the process of interpretation and playing. This very delicate situation with a specific score, one hundred musicians, sometimes a soloist, and always a conductor provides a very special form of the creative process for study. It differs in some ways from other creative processes, but maybe not as much as many musicians and managers would like to imagine.

The idea of the genius originated historically as a man inspired by God. Today we often assume that the genius is creative, and I use the concepts *genius* and *creator* synonymously. By early definition, the genius was always a man. According to Skoglund, the Romans believed that every man had a guardian spirit, a 'genius' that was also connected to male reproduction; the corresponding female was called 'juno'. This is probably one reason why the majority of people who have been considered 'geniuses' have been men and still are today. Females – though equally intelligent and/or talented – work harder to earn the label. In the Romantic era, a creative person was described as a strange and somewhat mad man driven by depression and anxiety and using his mysterious imagination as the force. During the last century, the creative person turned out to be a man who created by hard work and invented by serendipity and flashes of genius and inspiration.

These stereotypical ideas about creativity still prevail in some places. Some believe artistic creativity develops in the autonomous mind of talented and inspired (spirited) men, often during or after periods of depression. Researchers are often viewed as hardworking men who sometimes accidentally find solutions to big problems. Using a systems theory perspective, Csikszentmihalyi (2001) points out that creativity is not only a mental process inside human minds but also a cultural and social phenomenon. The creative process is part of a cultural domain and social field as well as an individual form of play. This line of reasoning suggests that studying creativity and creative processes should include the societies and expertise that foster or fail to foster genius.

It has been a long time since symphonic music was considered creative and new, but it was something of a revolution during the eighteenth century. In contrast to the aristocrats who ran the opera, the audience and the financiers were the new private bourgeoisie. In fact, it was a period of newness: a whole new musicology was born and new instruments were invented. Even the old instruments were upgraded. The music of the new orchestra had no words; it was autonomous and instrumental. Composers and virtuoso players became famous, publishing houses enjoyed their glory days, and the music debate in papers and books flourished. It was *the new thing* in many respects.

Today symphony orchestras are classified as living museums and cultivators of musical tradition:

> Orchestras, although they are still important civic and national symbols, are no longer central to the display of social power and authority. Compared to football teams, presidential inaugurations and space stations, orchestras seem old-fashioned – representatives of outmoded tastes, values and authority. Even more, perhaps ideas about authority and social control have changed. (Spitzer, 1996, p. 254)

Despite this shift in power, the metaphor of the conductor is still popular and commonly used by managers and leaders (Stenström, 2000). There is still something that thrills managers about this potentially chaotic crowd of people producing wonderful music that has been around for centuries and promises to be around for centuries more. Perhaps the music is not new, but each new rendering of the music produces a re-creation each time it is performed. If not, it would be enough to listen to a single recording of each musical piece to get the whole picture. This chapter investigates how the orchestra, the soloists and the conductor all add this something new to the score.

The orchestra

Preparing

The process of creativity in a first-class symphony orchestra of course requires tremendous technical skill, time both for practicing and performing, a concert hall with good acoustics and, finally, an audience. The interplay and interaction among the musicians propel the process.

The work of the musicians can be catalogued into three different phases. First, the individual rehearses on her own. Since many musicians begin their music studies in early childhood and have attended or graduated from conservatories or music schools, they are motivated, highly educated and do most of their concert preparation alone. Second, the musicians join in a collective rehearsal with the conductor and the soloists for three to four days to rehearse and agree upon an interpretation of a piece. During the final phase, the musicians present the concert, which adds an audience to the mix. Each of the three phases increases the individual and collective competence and skill of the orchestra, and each of the phases has its own features. Some musicians claim that the rehearsals are often more important than the actual concert, while others emphasize the importance of the concert and the communication with the audience. One musician raved: 'I like Paavo Berglund [a seasoned Finnish conductor] rehearsing because it is like a lecture in the core elements of the orchestra. When he says something, you find out that – Hey, this is really what it is all about!' And another declared: '[A]nd of course the best part of all this is to have the audience in front of you. The communication with the audience is what is most important.'

Like the various opinions, the creation of the interpretation takes place on many different levels and in many different places: in the mind of the musician, including the conductor, and between the musicians, the score and the audience.

Narcissism

According to Swedish psychiatrist Cullberg (1992), author of a book on the crisis of creation,[1] one phenomenon that favours the act of creating is a form of 'grandiose narcissism'. He stresses that this is not a form of pathological narcissism but the type of narcissism that every human being must possess, the measure of self-love necessary for survival.

[E]verybody is depending upon the appreciation of others in order to keep their self-love alive. All human beings also have a more or less well-hidden grandiose fantasy of themselves, as well as experiences of violation of their self-esteem. Grandiosity and self-hatred – shame – are two sides of the same coin. (p. 112)

This opinion corresponds with the relational perspective that the individual is a social product, as George Herbert Mead's theories champion as well (see, for example, Habermas, 1992; von Wright, 2000). Consequently, the musician and his/her self-esteem as a musician depend on his/her relationships with and the judgement of other musicians. Unfortunately in a huge collective like an orchestra, opportunity becomes an issue. There are not many, if any, occasions where musicians can openly and candidly comment on or give feedback about each other's playing. Typical rules of orchestra behavior include not looking at players performing solos, not turning around if someone is playing incorrectly, and not making comments about fellow orchestra members; these are attitudes that rest upon long-held traditions. Goffman (1967) calls this kind of behavior *avoidance ritual*.

One way musicians get more feedback on their playing is to become part of chamber groups or smaller ensembles. In this way, they feed their self-esteem and grandiose narcissism in other places and other contexts than in the symphony orchestra. Of course the audience and critics offer their judgment, but this does not concern the individual orchestra member specifically. He or she has to be his/her own judge and biggest fan, a difficult task at best.

Compost

Being an artist means exposing your skill and talent and giving others the opportunity to challenge your own grandiose fantasy. Every artist takes a personal risk when performing. In the words of Danish dramaturg Frans Baunsgaard[2]: 'As an artist you risk your identity – in a way you are naked. You have to expose your own self. If not everybody in a (theatre) ensemble does that, there will be an imbalance. It is not rewarding to work in a context where some just sit.' The same goes for the orchestra as well. The term for a person who 'just sits' in the orchestra is 'pension-musician,' a player who minimizes his or her risk-taking and does not commit himself or herself to the task at hand.

The core of creation in a symphony orchestra is the active musical meeting of score, instrument and player. The musicians act and react to the sound of their colleagues' instruments, to the directions of the conductor and to the body language of other musicians (see also Koivunen, 2003). In this process they expose their artistic convictions and run the risk of making mistakes. In a Danish study of symphony orchestras, Nielsen (1989) points out that typical strains in the harmony of the orchestra include the fear of making audible mistakes, the difficulty of constantly interpreting ambiguous information like a conductor's conflicting words and gestures, and the concern about criticism from the conductor. Many of these worries are never addressed, and musicians are left frustrated, uncertain and self-deprecating, sometimes to the point of depression.

Cullberg calls this kind of ambiguity and immanence 'the creative compost'. This form of melancholy or light depression is another element in the creative process – one of the not-so-beautiful elements. What an observer might interpret as silence and suspicion among the musicians might actually be the concentration, immanence and sometimes even destructive moodiness that is part of this creative compost.

This sensitivity is evident in rehearsals but is especially evident at concert time. The musicians find different ways of coping with nervousness and stage fright. Many of them go through personal rituals, some use beta blockers, and others argue that nervousness stems from having the wrong focus, like worrying more about what people will think about you than concentrating on the actual concert. Smith and Carlsson (1990), researchers in creativity, explain that what makes a creative person different from a not-so-creative person is the ability to cope with anxiety: 'Creative people are ready to confront very diverse aspects of their private worlds, the dark as well as the bright. Obviously, these people are tolerant of the anxiety likely to be aroused by such confrontations. Without this tolerance their freedom to exploit new paradoxical aspects would be impeded' (p. 213).

Nervousness or anxiety takes place both inside and between the musicians, the conductor and the audience. It is not always pleasant. It can be aggressive as well as depressive, and it seems as if the creative compost is needed to transform ambitions, ideas and fantasies into the audible artistic interpretation of the music.

Imagination

Instrumental music is non-verbal. As we listen to music, we often analyse and interpret it into feelings and logical understanding. Langer (1957) argues that music communicates insight not statements:

The imagination that responds to music is personal and associative and logical tinged with affect, tinged with bodily rhythm, tinged with dream, but concerned with a wealth of wordless knowledge, its whole knowledge of emotional and organic experience, of vital impulse, balance, conflict, the ways of living and dying and feeling. (p. 244)

Our feelings and understanding of music, our aesthetic experiences, are personal, according to Langer and others, such as Sandelands and Buckner (1989). In order to render music in a creative way, musicians are both personally affected and technically synchronized with the collective. Cullberg argues that 'one of the prerequisites of creation is to be able to intermediate between reality and imagination/daydreaming. To be in this state or condition implies openness to the laws of playing and dreaming' (1992, p. 174).

Musicians have endured a long education and share a musical language, which give them the tools they need to fantasize and daydream together. According to Starobinski (in Liedman, 2001, p. 29), imagination is 'a distance capacity that makes us able to create a picture of the distant things and to distance from the present.' Imagination allows us to play with reality and realize new possibilities and new constellations. Ricoeur argues in a similar way that imagination consists of ideological and utopian functions (in Kristensson Uggla, 1994). This implies that the social imagination constitutes a sort of mutual reality: '[T]he most fundamental ideological function of social imagination consists of keeping order, of confirmation, of preserving the identity in a group or society, while the most fundamental utopian function is to be an instrument for exploring the impossible and discover new possible worlds' (p. 368).

The challenge for the collective imagination in a symphony orchestra is two sided: musicians must keep the score of a musical composition together while simultaneously experimenting and playing with the ideas of the composer. In a group of 100 musicians, there are always some who are interested in exploring or discovering 'new worlds'. Every now and then, there are moments or even whole concerts that the musicians remember and talk about for years or maybe the rest of their lives. Something – inspiration or a visit from the muse of music – has happened. Many prefer to talk about it in terms of flow or collective virtuosity.[3]

Flow

Dependence and the need to adapt to each other[4] are challenges as well as rewards for the committed musician. Individual performance is not enough; musicians have to rely upon each other – like it or not – and when a perfect understanding of the music unfolds, indescribable emotions arise. According to an orchestra member in the Stockholm Royal Philharmonic:

> One of the great things about being in such a huge collective is that – you see sometimes it can be a lot of hard work and quite heavy on rehearsals and touring with all the travelling – but in the very moment you come in and start playing and you recognise that "fooogh"! It's such an incredible feeling. It may sound naive, but you really forget all the rest. It is almost indescribable. It is some kind of ecstasy of joy. (Köping, 2003, pp. 100–1)

Csikszentmihalyi (1990) described this kind of happiness as an experience of flow, a situation when you lose yourself into a sort of new reality where the feeling of time and space becomes invalid and self-doubt disappears.

> When the self is regained after having been lost and absorbed in the object, one's senses and imagination have explored new possibilities of the world, and these possibilities have become part of the self. This regaining of self is associated with accounts of feeling freedom from routine, personal delight, new knowledge, clarity and a sense of acquaintance with reality or truth. (Marotto, Victor and Roos, 2000, p. 9)

These experiences can make changes individually or in a group. Marotto, Victor and Roos call this act 'collective virtuosity', by definition 'an aesthetic experience in a group that is transformed by *its very own performance*' (p. 3, italics mine).

Both ethical and aesthetical standpoints must be considered in groups or collectives like a symphony orchestra. Musicians communicate ongoing aesthetic judgments about the composition, but they must also consider what others in the orchestra are communicating both audibly and visibly in the composition as well. Since many of the musicians are unable to hear or see their colleagues, someone must act as collective eyes and the ears for the group, someone who can both control and contribute. This is where the conductor comes in.

The conductor

Leadership

Few professions are as exposed and mythical as the profession of conductor. Some people harbor rather romantic notions of a conductor as a hero bringing light, enthusiasm, inspiration and order into this creative chaos of ideas and convictions. More accurately, the conductor in this study was vulnerable, humble, considerate, dependent, charismatic, inspirational...and quiet. In the creative process going on between the orchestra and the conductor, the most conspicuous characteristic was mutual dependence and adaptation.

Koivunen (2003, 2004) has examined in depth how the sense of hearing affects a conductor's leadership. Listening is one core element in conducting. As one Swedish female symphony orchestra conductor put it:

> [Y]ou have to listen – partly if they play something wrong that you have to correct. Partly you have to listen to intonation and balance between the parts. But you also have to listen to what actually these people sitting in front of me present to me according to their musicality and their ideas of the piece. I have to trust their musicality and know where my baton ends and their music rendering take over. (Cecilia Rydinger-Alin in Köping, 2003, p. 158)

I have labeled this kind of reciprocal acting *relational attainments*, or in other words, attainments or skills that two or more humans share. I have identified several relational attainments/skills that I have described in terms of listening and adaptation; feeling ('Einfühlung'), empathy and 'performativity'; trust and deference.

Circular response

According to Mary Parker Follett (in Kolb, Jenson and Shannon, 1996),[5] possible conflicts may be handled in three different ways: domination, compromise and integration. Probably the most common idea of the role of the conductor is that he/she dominates the orchestra and forces or entices its members to come along. Even though this statement expresses an over-simplification, the creative process of playing music should not be seen as a compromise either. That would suggest that every part gives up something for the benefit of the other parts. The most creative process is a situation where all the ideas are integrated into a new interpretation, a 'third' way. In this process the conductor operates as a consultant or negotiator. 'Success in integrative negotiation is achieved when parties can identify their respective interest and revalue them in light of the other's response, so that both can see where their interests fit into each other and that all may find some place in the final solution' (Kolb *et al.*, 1996, p. 154). The authors call these final solutions *creative resolutions*. Neither the conductor nor the musicians try to put themselves into the other's situation; according to Follett, they all change in the creative process:

> Rather than having a vision of autonomous individuals who come together for the purpose of meeting their individual needs, she sees interaction as the site for connection where the self is affected and changed. 'Through the circular response, we are creating each other all the time...I never react to you but to you-plus-me...That is, in the very process of meeting we both become something different'. (In Kolb *et al.*, 1996, p. 156)

In rehearsal and performance, the musicians, including the conductor, do not speak or argue with words; rather they respond by playing and reacting to each other's sound and body language. Their instrumental/visual argumentation resembles a kind of reflection rather than a conviction. The sounding music then is *not* the sum of individual playing but rather a unity or a whole; it is a relational process. In Follett's words,

> [T]he essence of a group...lies in the exercise of a particular type of process – 'an acting and reacting, a single and identical process which brings out differences and integrates them into a unity'; it is in this way that we evolve the collective thought and the collective will. (In Tonn, 1996, p. 172)

Follett refers to this as a 'group idea', which in the case of a symphony orchestra finds its expression in the musical interpretation of a composition. The conductor is one of many musicians but has a very special instrument and a special role. The instrument of the conductor not only sounds, but thinks and acts with a will of its own. It is human and needs a special kind of relational attainment.

Deference

In order for the circular response to take place, people need to relate to each other authentically and sincerely. That of course can be accomplished in many different ways. Conductors of the past used to scare orchestra members by shouting at them and used their power and position to force the other musicians to obey.[6] Today that kind of attitude does not win any admirers, especially not in an orchestra where the members themselves choose their principal conductor and invite the guest conductors.[7] When the interaction between the orchestra members and conductor functions well, what happens is *symmetrical deference*. Goffman (1967, p. 59), instead of conceiving deference 'as something a subordinate owes to his superordinate', argues that there is a form of symmetrical deference that social equals owe each another. And even if there still is a clear difference in professional status between the orchestra members and the conductor, they are usually considered equal. Conductors who get up on their high horse are usually brought down to earth rather quickly. The power of the orchestra members is obvious; they can always choose not to consider or care about the conductor's direction and do their own thing. Orchestra members do not like conductors who are self-absorbed. According to Goffman's theory, self-absorption is an example of alienated interaction. Orchestra members prefer a conductor who has a professional attitude and focuses on the music. The optimal work situation is characterized by a relationship of mutual trust and symmetrical deference between the conductor and the orchestra members. The Russian conductor Gennadi Rozhdestvensky explains conducting like this:

[I]t is an important thing not to disturb the orchestra. Just to have a feeling that they must do their best. And they must understand that they can play without the conductor. In reality it is of course an opposite situation. [laughter] So the connection between the conductor and the orchestra is a very, very complicated thing. It's a psychological process, and it is nothing with moving your hands here and there. You cannot move at all and conduct sometimes... [You conduct] with your soul, with your eyes, with understanding your musicians. When I come to a new orchestra, which I have never conducted before, I immediately find the persons with whom I can communicate. (In Köping, 2003, p. 144)

Rozhdestvensky's statement may be interpreted as a statement of deference... or manipulation. To see it as manipulative implies an individualistic/tentative interpretation, however, and this chapter considers the issue from the very different reciprocal relational perspective.

The orchestra members' opinions of Rozhdestvensky's conducting were divided. Half of the orchestra seemed to love his conducting style while the others argued that he often left the orchestra to meet its own destiny. This is a good illustration of differing opinions among the musicians. Regardless of the difference of opinion, however, conductors must be careful not to insert themselves into the playing of the orchestra members. Very seldom do conductors speak, and they usually do not correct. They just go over the part that was weak or incorrect until it improves. They usually do not make suggestions on how to think or interpret. Conductor Esa-Pekka Salonen made an exception during one of his rehearsals. During a Witold Lutosławski selection, Salonen was dissatisfied with a short bassoon solo. He suggested that the musician see the bassoon as a single individual in a great babbling crowd. Afterwards I asked him if he had achieved what he wanted with the metaphor:

> Actually I am not very anxious about drawing these kinds of parallels between life and music, since my opinion is that music should function within its own system. And I think that you actually destroy something when you start giving these kinds of images. Because you have already cut out a lot of other possible imaginations. And furthermore I cannot be sure that my images are more valid than anybody else's. (In Köping, 2003, p. 291)

After a pause he changed his metaphor to the babbling cousin of Donald Duck, which turned out be much more successful in this particular case.

Deference is a behaviour that means keeping a distance and not violating the recipient's 'ideal sphere' (Goffman, 1967, quoting Simmel). It can take many forms; for example, Goffman calls one form of deference *presentational rituals*. These 'rituals encompass acts through which the individual makes specific attestations to recipients concerning how he regards them and how he will treat them in the oncoming interaction' (p. 71).

Orchestras are large-scale organizations and it is easy for the individual orchestra member to disappear, especially in a large section like the string section. In order to still feel like a member whose contribution is important, everybody needs to be noticed in some way. Salutations, invitations, compliments and minor services are forms of presentational ritual evident in society as well as in the orchestra. The conductor is the only person who is supposed to speak during rehearsals; he[8] greets the orchestra first thing in the morning and tries to have eye contact with all the musicians. He signals to them when it is time for them to step into the music and when to use different dynamics and tempo. He smiles or nods his head to show his appreciation, and he helps orchestra members out in difficult places or bars of the piece. Thus the conductor is not only passively listening, he is also actively representational. Maestro Lutosławski indicated that every single member of the orchestra was important and that it is his job to make him or her realize that:

> I think that we should feel very strongly that we are all artists. We have a common task. I'm not a sergeant and they are not soldiers. And even if not a single word is said about it – they feel it! And I think it's just psychological. After all they are all important people. They must know that I consider them important. (in Köping, 2003, p. 126)

This feeling of importance develops in the interaction between the orchestra members and the conductor. It originates from the values and convictions of each actor/player and is manifested through actions and rituals of both avoidance and presentation. A feeling of importance is one of the core elements of the creative process and an absolute condition for collective virtuosity.

Defining the *role* of the conductor also draws upon differing perspectives and views. One can see roles as structures adopted by actors in a play, for example, or by people in a specific social context. A relational perspective on roles, however, states that the role is created not by a given structure or screenplay but that it develops in the interaction with others; it is never a property of a single individual. '[R]ole describes one's social situation relative to other people at any moment and to the part one plays in that situation. This conception emphasizes the reciprocity of roles' (Burr and Butt, 2006).

The role of the conductor is dependent upon the role he/she gives to the orchestra members, and vice versa. It is a true circular response. Since the conductor is the representational person, he/she has a special responsibility for creating a favorable setting for grandiose narcissism, risk taking, imagination and collective virtuosity to flourish. Finnish conductor Leif Segerstam agrees. He describes the relationship of the conductor to the orchestra in this way:

> It should be a harmonious relation, a stimulating relation and especially an inspiring and creative relationship. Because actually the conductor is an ambassador for the composer. The conductor is representing the person who made the decision that at a special moment there was a feeling of motivation why you should try to capture in notes something, which when this moment is recreated, makes the music sound like it sounds when it should sound... And how do you reach this true sound during the rehearsals? It should be through a stimulating,

creative and very harmonious interaction with the huge collective. (In Köping, 2003, p. 148)

The conductor has an active part in this harmonious interaction and is also in a position where he can be actively involved with this task. He is the one being representational and not only avoiding. Marotto *et al.* claim that the sizable challenge for leaders of collective virtuosity is to create a context where 'people feel safe and trustful of one another to act spontaneously and candidly' (p. 20).

Concerting

All musicians involved in a performance should remember that not even the composer has the ultimate right to decide how a composition should be interpreted. As Maestro Lutosławski explains:

> I try not to feel like the composer who is presenting his own works. Because it would have been very embarrassing to me. I always imagine myself as a conductor who performs the works of his younger colleague. I know probably more than any other conductor. And it's always a question of performing, of giving a form of expression and of course technically an insurance of an accurate rendering of the piece. So I try to think not so much about presenting my own work. Rather I concentrate on rendering the work as it is. Because after all, when a piece is finished, it's finished! It doesn't belong to the composer's life anymore.... I must learn my own pieces in order to conduct. (In Köping, 2003, p. 129)

Every situation is new, and all relations have to be reconsidered and reconstructed. The creative process does not rest upon one person's having a blueprint and that person telling the others what to do. A truly collective creative process is a circular response, a relational process of action and reaction.

Relational perspective

During the seventeenth and eighteenth centuries, a mechanical and individualistic ontology gained a foothold and promoted the idea that society was built up by sovereign and autonomous individuals representing only themselves and who joined other people in order to gain certain advantages. One of the theorists of this view was Thomas Hobbes:

> Hobbes argues that society is an unnatural state for selfish creatures such as human beings and that it exists only as an expedient order coerced by sovereign authority. Where it exists, society is the fruit of self-interest and power ... In these accounts society is a network of economic actors, a logical product of self-interest in the marketplace. (Sandelands, 1998, p. 7)

This is also one of the most common paradigms found in mainstream management literature. Employees are viewed as bearers of certain traits that the talented leader uses in a fruitful way.

Hosking (1995) calls this view 'entitative' or 'possessive individualism' and argues that another way of viewing individuals and organizations is relational. Since this is an alternate ontology and epistemology, we have to interpret common situations and concepts in a new way. For example, the concept of inter-subjectivity becomes something different depending on whether you have a relational or individualistic perspective. In a relational perspective inter-subjectivity is the only kind of subjectivity that actually exists since the individual becomes through meeting and relating to 'the other'. In an individualistic perspective, inter-subjectivity can be reduced to the interaction between two autonomous subjects (von Wright, 2000).

From an individualistic perspective, leadership is seen in a person who possesses certain kinds of traits or knowledge, like the power to influence others. In a relational perspective, leadership becomes a process of negotiation where by using verbal or non-verbal communication it comes into being.

This chapter on the creative process in artistic work – in this case the process between the conductor and orchestra members – rests on a relational perspective of organization. The individual and society are processes of relationships. Individuals, groups and organizations are not autonomous and fixed entities; they are constantly coming into being and constantly interacting. The process of creativity is a process of social interaction and social expectations, not the product of a number of great ideas and skills added together in a 'creative way'. The relational perspective challenges traditional ideas in organizational behaviour and organizational theory (see, for example, Hosking, 1995, 2004; Koivunen, 2003; Köping, 2003; Soila-Wadman, 2003). It seems obvious that organizational researchers should redirect their focus from internal psychological processes to what actually happens between people in organizations. Or as Goffman sums it up: 'Not, then, men and their moments. Rather moments and their men' (p. 3).

Notes

1. He studies the crises of two authors, August Strindberg and Stig Dagerman, during their writing careers.
2. At a conference on 'Aesthetics and Enterprise' at Stockholm Business School in 1996.
3. See Chapter 3 in this book and Soila-Wadman (2003).
4. See Wennes (2002) for a study of paradoxes in art organizations.
5. Another concept similar to Follett's circular response is the Swedish social anthropologist Johan Asplund's (1987) 'social responsivity'.
6. Elias Canetti (1960) (in Nielsen [1989]) argues that there is no more obvious expression of power in our society than the performance of a conductor. And I agree that all the rituals during a concert could point in that direction, but the rehearsals and the attitudes of the conductors I have interviewed say something else.
7. The orchestra is run as a union with general meetings, voting and different committees.
8. 'He' since the conductor is still a 'he' in almost all symphony orchestras!

References

Asplund, J. (1987) *Det sociala livets elementära former*. Göteborg: Bokförlaget Korpen.
Beardsley, M.C. (1982) Aesthetic experience. In M.J. Wreen and D.M. Callen (eds), *The aesthetic point of view: selected essays of Monroe C. Beardsley*. New York: Cornell University Press. In Marotto, M., Victor, B., & Roos, J. (2000) *Collective virtuosity: the aesthetic experience in groups*. (Working Paper). Lausanne, Switzerland: Imagination Lab.
Burr, V., and T.W. Butt (2006) The relational nature of leadership. In D.M. Hosking and S. McNamee (eds), *Social constructionist alternatives to organisational behaviour*. Malmö: Liber. Retrieved 30 January, 2004, from <www.geocities.com/obkook2002/bookoutline>
Collinson, D. (1992). Aesthetic experience. In O. Hanfling (ed.), *Philosophical aesthetics: an introduction*, pp. 111–78. Milton Keynes: The Open University.
Csikszentmihalyi, M. (1990) Att uppleva flow. In M. Odman (ed.), *Om kreativitet och flow*. Stockholm: Brombergs.
Csikszentmihalyi, M. (2001) A systems perspective on creativity. In Jane Henry (ed.), *Creative management*. London: Sage Publications.
Cullberg, J. (1992) *Skaparkriser. Strindbergs inferno och Dagermans*. Stockholm: Natur och Kultur.
Follett, M.P. (1918) *The new state*. Retrieved 1 March 2004, from <www.sunsite.utk.edu/FINNS/Mary_Parker_Follett>.
Follett, M.P. (1924) *Creative experience*. Retrieved 1 March 2004, from <www.follettfoundation.org/writings.htm>
Goffman, E. (1967) *Interaction ritual. Essays on face-to-face behaviour*. New York: Pantheon Books.

Habermas, J. (1992) Individuation through socialization: on George Herbert Mead's theory of subjectivity. In *Post-metaphysical thinking: philosophical essays*. Cambridge: Polity Press.

Hosking, D.M. (1995) *Management and organization: relational alternatives to individualism*. Aldershot: Avebury.

Hosking, D.M. (2006) Organizations, organizing and related concepts of change. In D.M. Hosking and S. McNamee (eds), *Social constructionist alternatives to organisational behaviour*. Malmö: Liber. Retrieved 30 January 2004, from <www.geocities.com/obkook2002/bookoutline>

Koivunen, N. (2003) *Leadership in symphony orchestras. Discursive and aesthetic practices*. Tampere, Finland: Tampere University Press.

Koivunen, N. (2006) Auditive leadership culture: lessons from a symphony orchestra. In D.M. Hosking and S. McNamee (eds), *Social constructionist alternatives to organisational behaviour*. Malmö: Liber. Retrieved 30 January 2004 from <www.geocities.com/obkook2002/bookoutline>

Kolb, D.M., L. Jenson and V.L. Shannon (1996) She said it all before, or what did we miss about Ms. Follett in the library? *Organization* 3 (1), pp. 153–60.

Köping, A.-S. (2003) *Den bundna friheten. Om kreativitet och relationer i ett konserthus*. Stockholm: Arvinius Förlag.

Kristensson Uggla, B. (1994) *Kommunikation på bristningsgränsen. En studie i Paul Ricouers projekt*. Stehag: Symposion.

Langer, Susan K. (1957) *Philosophy in a new key. A study in the symbolism of reason, rite and art*. Cambridge, MA: Harvard University Press.

Marotto, M., B. Victor and J. Roos (2000) *Collective virtuosity: the aesthetic experience in groups*. Working Paper. Lausanne, Switzerland: Imagination Lab.

Nielsen, J. (1989) *Organisationskultur i en kulturorganisation. Symfoniorkestret – den spaltede organisation*. COS Forskningsrapport 7/1989. Center for Organisation og Styrning. Handelshøjskolen i København.

Sandelands, L. (1998) *Feeling and form in social life*. Lanham, MD: Rowman & Littlefield.

Sandelands, L., and G.C. Buckner (1989) Of art and work: aesthetic experience and the psychology of work feelings. In L. Cummings and B.M. Staw (eds), *Research in Organizational Behaviour*, 11, pp. 105–31.

Skoglund, C. (1987) Några föreställningar om kreativitet och skapandegenom tiderna. In G. Berfeldt (ed.), *Barns skapande lek*, pp. 10–31, Stockholm: Centrum för barnkulturforskning.

Smith, G.J.W., and I. Carlsson (1990) The creative process. A functional model based on empirical studies from early childhood to middle age. In G.J.W. Smith and I. Carlsson (eds), *Psychological issues*. Monograph 57. Madison, CT: International Universities Press.

Soila-Wadman, M. (2003). *Kapitulationens estetik*. Stockholm: Arvinius Förlag.

Spitzer, J. (1996) Metaphors of the Orchestra – The Orchestra as Metaphor. *Musical Quarterly*, 2: pp. 234–64. G. Schirmer: New York.

Starobinski, J. (1970) L'empire de l'imaginaire. In S.-E. Liedman (2001), *Ett oändlig äventyr. Om människans kunskaper*. Stockholm: Albert Bonniers Förlag.

Stenström, E. (2000) Konstiga företag. Doctoral dissertation. Stockholm School of Economics.

Sveiby, K.-E. (1992) *Chef i Kreativ miljö*. Stockholm: Svenska Dagbladets Förlags AB.

Tonn, J.C. (1996) Follett's challenge for us all. *Organization*, 3 (1), pp. 161–79.
von Wright, M. (2000) *Vad eller vem? En pedagogisk rekonstruktion av G H Meads teori om människans subjektivitet.* Göteborg: Daidalos.
Wennes, G. (2002) Skjönnheten og udyret. PhD dissertation, Norwegian School of Economics, Bogen.

3

Aesthetic institutions: three centuries of judgement and management in the Royal Swedish Opera

Jeanette Wetterström

The movie *Les Enfants du Paradis* (1945) transports the viewer into the dynamic world of nineteenth-century theatre. The setting is the streets and stages of Paris in the 1830s. In the theatre, the audience is noisy and messy, and in the street, public life is just as theatrical – a *comédie humaine*, in Balzac's terms.

The scene mirrors backstage life at a second-rate theatre. The director of the comedy, an entrepreneur unfamiliar with Shakespeare's tragic character Romeo, explains the circumstances of his theatre to a visiting gentleman. 'They [the grand and serious theatres] consider us a threat', he boasts. Then, without missing a beat, he turns to a third person, the stage director, who is trailed by an actress and has just entered the scene. He barks an instruction: 'Barigni shall be fined two francs for drunkenness on stage.' The stage director nods and hurries on.

Turning back to the visitor, the manager continues. 'My theatre is ravaged by hatred and envy. It's a volcano.' He rolls his eyes and throws his hands into the air to punctuate his statement. 'Emergence and disappearance like in real life. Kicking and punching just like reality.' He lets his sentence hang for a moment, and then sweeping his arm magnanimously toward the crowd, he declares, 'What an audience, though. They are worth their weight in gold. Look up there, in 'paradise ['the gods']!' He grabs the man by his arm and points at the crowd in the gallery beneath the roof. The camera lens silently depicts the crowded playhouse, a simple, unadorned auditorium. People look down on the stage; they hang on the edge with their legs in the air.

Suddenly the two actors on stage begin to quarrel loudly. They call for help from their personal supporters backstage: 'Barignis, come! All Debureaus!' People race in from all directions. A heated fight breaks out, a real comedy of combat, and the audience shouts and screams in excitement. The theatre manager panics.

'*Rideau! Rideau!*' he screams, but no one pays attention. '*Rideau! Rideau!* You are all fined three francs. *Rideau!*'

Greenblatt (1988) has written that there can be no art without social energy. The stage and the street share a reciprocal relationship; the arts rely especially on places where people collide and spaces where they move around. Art depends on the social network of practices that govern the circulation of money, ideas and items. It is in these networks that collective beliefs and experiences are shaped, moved from one medium to another, concentrated in a manageable form and offered for consumption.

Institutional development from stage to street

For some years now, business scholars have paid attention to art and the aesthetic dimensions of management. Aesthetic judgement suggests, for example, that managers are guided by an aesthetic point of view in their actions, such as having an appreciation for the beautiful. To Dobson (1999), they are true 'aesthetic managers.'

Researchers often draw from the ideas of phenomenology and philosophical aesthetics when they study the relationships between art and business. As most of the authors of these studies begin by considering contemporary managerial aspects, they often fail to recognize the historical constitution of an aesthetic consciousness. This chapter instead presents a 'return to history' as a way of illustrating the temporality of the aesthetic consciousness.

Institutional time

This temporality in the aesthetic makes itself known in the social activities occurring in art worlds. Within the arts, we find a steady shift of styles as the social fabric of transformations is demonstrated by praxis. When we become familiar with aesthetic perception during different historical periods, we recognize the effect of time on the act of seeing, listening and perceiving. Understanding is altered and appears different in each historical period. As Heidegger (1926/1962) claims in his writings on temporality, 'understanding is never free-floating but always goes with some state of mind' (p. 389).

Perception changes further with spatial arrangement and specific social milieu and atmosphere. If when we turn to the long history of leadership in theatres we learn that distinct transformations of practices do happen, we are then able to recognize *how* managers, artists and audiences change their mode of paying attention. A shift in the dominating form of perception has a direct influence on shifts in artistic and managerial practices. This modification in understanding may actualize new dispositions and directions. A specific mode serves as a pathfinder that guides attention to – or indeed overlooks – the phenomena that managers encounter in their work.

Theatre managers change their aesthetic consciousness through experience and over time. When awareness emerges, it conducts and governs new ways to act and reach conclusions in making judgements. Shifts in focus and concentration occur. Furthermore, time, space and history all affect consciousness on both personal and collective levels.

Institutional costs

In large arts organizations such as theatres and opera houses, a dynamic interplay of judgement and management takes place. In addition to artistic choices, many other factors influence managerial judgement. The stewardship of the theatre's financial resources, including concern for increasing costs, could be a major influence, for example. Furthermore, in practical everyday situations it is hard to distinguish between different kinds of judgements. An historical analysis, however, identifies and clarifies the ideas that guide actions in organizations. Historically, judgement was the most prominent feature of a theatre manager's work during the nineteenth century; now we also face the consequences of increased functional managerialism in the arts.

At the official archive of the Royal Swedish Opera, I had the opportunity to look over detailed documents describing administrative practices going back to the 1770s. I analysed qualitative and quantitative data produced by general managers at the opera, including series of memos, statements, regulations, personal diaries and annual reports. I also accessed public and official reports and investigations (Wetterström, 2001).

During my examination, I uncovered what Michel Foucault once termed the 'discontinuity' of history, a premise contrary to the old idea of tradition and universal continuity (Wetterström, 2001). Tracking the history of artistic and managerial practice in the opera house revealed the emergence of crises and movement. We are able to 'really grasp both the discontinuity of events and the transformation of societies' (Foucault, 1998, p. 431).

The act of transformation is a complex phenomenon in itself. What we are dealing with are different types of events and different types of duration that appear in administrative routines. Through a thorough empirical work of tracing, following carefully what managers and artists have actually done and do in their practices, we recognize an essential difference between how an aesthetic judgement and a management evaluation work. For example, duration in a managerial procedure may cause a shift in artistic practices, or vice versa. An essential shift in attention occurs when investors – the public owners – replace their interest in judgement with that in cost accounting. The owner then begins to apply statistical data to evaluation processes and proclaim a certain 'cost awareness' at theatres run by public subsidies. The intention is to follow up public expenditure in a monetary form as well, because of expense and its reference to cultural politics. This requires firm administrative methods for auditing, for monitoring and for keeping tabs on artistic activities likely to generate cost. Necessary administrative mechanisms include identifying the type of cost, implementing procedures that estimate costs and being able to assign the origin of costs to specific cost centres.

This implies that the work of today's manager in a public theatre is governed by principles of quantitative evaluation as well as by aesthetic judgements regarding the quality of performances. Managers guided by managerial ideals change their attention. Due to their new awareness, they come to different solutions for the problems they perceive. While the owners expect managers to be able to identify phenomena that trigger costs, managers in turn must invent systems and routines that make graphic the cost-effectiveness of the theatre. The eye is slowly cultivated and becomes trained to perform the task of cost-hunting. Moreover, costs sometimes become symbolic instead of staying technical in administrative character. According to Yakhlef (1998), we 'construct accountable worlds.'

To be a manager in a public theatre is to be in the public eye and to be judged and evaluated by the public. In their 1995 article 'Civilization, art, and accounting', Mouritsen and Skærbæk note that throughout history managing the Royal Danish Theatre is a task closely linked to effectively managing the whole Danish state. Similar sequences of state administrative situations happen in Stockholm, too. In the managers' statements at the Royal Theatres in Stockholm, a tension between judgement and evaluation occurs repeatedly. With the rise of a more functional administration, various methods are used for collecting the 'facts' that periodically indicate the financial status of the theatre. These are practical techniques based on evaluation and quantitative standards instead of aesthetic and intersubjective values.

Throughout the history of managing the Royal Opera, a distinct discourse claims that a diffusion of taste and judgement is beneficial when forming common 'civility'. Thus in legitimizing the high cost of running the national opera in Sweden, the directors, stage directors, and artists became involved in the process of forming taste, judgement, and behaviour in public urban space. The owner regarded investments in the Stockholm opera as serving a wider purpose of maintaining social order in the streets. This arrangement appears as social artwork in itself. As Sennet (1977) put it, the theatre shared many of its problems, not with society in general, but with organizing urban space in the great modern cities. The city was a theatre (see also Czarniawska and Solli, 2001).

Pacing management practices

History illustrates a dynamic relationship between management evaluation and aesthetic judgement. Gradually, abstract quantitative standards for a functional cost evaluation were introduced at the theatre. They transformed former practices inherited by aristocratic households and oriented toward concrete sense perceptions. That managerial attention was aesthetic response to qualitative values.

National theatres

With the rise of national theatres and opera houses, the ownership balance slowly changed and turned from the royal court to a political and public arena. A new audience demonstrated the emergence of the modern onlooker, and administrative practices reflected this principle of intense looking. Looking is an activity where perception happens on an aesthetic level. As Genette (1999) writes, 'seeing' is merely an attentional fact, whereas 'looking' is an intentional mode of behaviour with a definite end purpose (p. 115). It would be possible to counterpose 'hearing' and 'listening' in the same way.

During the eighteenth century, the architectural style of theatres developed into spectacular auditoriums carefully designed and inspired by the great halls of the noble palaces. The upper classes were apt to visualize an impressive quality of decoration and extravagance in costs.

Inside a theatre, the spatial arrangement of the auditorium accommodated the social atmosphere between the actors and spectators. At an aristocratically owned theatre of high rank, the architecture was able to support a specific type of gaze, and the buildings were often designed for centralized observation. The *modus operandi* at the royal court theatres was the eye of royal power, the king or the emperor. The king's seat was in a central position in the auditorium where he could best experience the *mise en scène* as long as linear perspective and the vanishing point were still used in the scenery.

At these aristocratic theatres, the arrangement of space followed an aristocratic perception of the world, how the social world *ought* to be according to aristocratic ideals of reality. For this reason, theatre architects arranged the interiors according to *sight* rather than sound. The music and serious opera performed were linked to social rites in court life.

Ultimately, a lively interest in establishing national theatres like the Comédie Française in Paris began to emerge. Several European theatres changed from court theatres to national theatre institutions. The Emperor reorganized the old Burgtheater built in Vienna in 1741 into the Hof-und Nationaltheater, where they even performed a national opera in 1778. Other national theatres were established, and resid-ence theatres opened in Copenhagen in 1746, in Warsaw in 1765, in Hamburg in 1767, in Prague in 1784 and in Stockholm in 1772. Theatres performed German national opera in Weimar in 1773 and in Mannheim in 1777 (Senelick, 1991).

These attempts at nationalism connected theatre architecture and opera management to the societal problems of population and urbanism. Before this time, performances had manifested power and might, but from this time on, theatrical life was arranged according to the idea of public urban space.

Institutionalization of theatre practices had an effect on the executive management of theatres, and many European groups went through innovations in managerial forms. The independent entrepreneurs, men of the theatre, who earlier had been contracted by the courts, met obstacles when attempting to break into the large institutions run by privilege and by a different body of managers. Power relations also shifted as structural changes to an early modernity expanded the public sphere. This course reached its peak with the construction of the grand opera houses in nineteenth-century cities where this type of perform-ance became the style.

The founding of the Royal Swedish Opera in the 1770s was meant to create a Swedish grand opera and an opera system. These were ideas linked to a call for a critique, for public 'enlightenment' and for the form-ation of taste and judgement. The noun 'civility' later became the noun 'civilization' and signified the whole of the Swedish nation. 'Civiliz-ation', 'moral culture', and *Bildung* [Swe: *moralisk kultur* and *bildning*] were concepts used in discourse for legitimizing the costs of the Royal Swedish Opera during the nineteenth century.

In Stockholm during the early days of the century, opera managers associated the concepts of 'national wealth' and 'population' with the arts. They referred to the prosperity of the nation and to the symbolic value that the opera had to the capital city of Stockholm, at least in the 'travelling foreigners' eyes'. Financial investments in the opera institu-tion, a director maintained, aimed at 'cultivating taste, language, and manners.' Continuing his argument, he raised the issues of the public need for opera and its effect on social order. Then he compared annual costs at other 'foreign theatres':

In Copenhagen / only opera comique 82,000 R.B. annually
In Berlin / 10–12 presentations per year 108,000 R.B. annually
In Petersburg / the court spectacles 396,000 rubles
In Paris, before the Revolution, 1 million livres or 166,000 R.B.
In London 350,000 R.B., and so forth.

These theatres, except for the one in Copenhagen, were more expensive to run than the Swedish one; therefore, he alleged, Stockholm really ought to raise its monetary support to cover increasing costs and salaries for the fixed ensemble.

The expression 'moral culture' meant tasteful behaviour in public, although aristocratic preferences still remained and were supposed to be spread to the lower classes. The existence of the opera, managers claimed, served the purpose of maintaining social order, keeping people occupied and avoiding 'anarchy', 'disorder', and 'riots' in the streets.

Apart from the burden of theatre censorship, the royal theatres held an exclusive monopoly in Stockholm between 1795 and 1840. Despite the royal privilege, taxation of travelling theatre companies and strolling players all over the country was used to help finance the Royal Opera in the capital city. Since 1818, the Swedish government has regu-larly transferred money to cover the annual costs of running the royal theatres.

The current Stockholm opera house opened in 1898. It was a gift from an influential local financier, who constructed a 'consortium', built the house, and left its ownership to the state. Even though the state owned the house, a group of entrepreneurs held the risk of running it. The opera was reorganized into a privately owned joint-stock company that

3.1 Civility under construction? The new opera house in Copenhagen is a $1.5 billion gift from Maersk McKinney Møller. The opening event happened in 2005; until then, the architect carefully followed the instructions that came with the private cheque. The building is situated across the water from the royal Danish castle. Anyone willing to pay for a new opera house by the waterfront in Stockholm?

remained until 1975. By then, the state had slowly taken over company control and the majority of shares. In addition, it covered decades worth of its losses. Today, the opera is a public joint-stock company, a form of association comparable to an American not-for-profit organization.

Household management

During the nineteenth century, court theatres were not yet autonomous entities. Roselli (1984) is quite right in using the Italian term 'administrazione economica' in the old sense of 'economy' as 'household management'.

Although the Stockholm opera was open to the public, it was organized for a long time within the framework of the royal household. Until the 1880s, staging opera performances was an activity closely linked to the social energy and atmosphere at court. The king usually picked a suitable manager from his own staff.

Administration of the theatre was listed as a task of 'internal housekeeping', and part of the manager's task was to supervise bodily movements within this observable space. All actions backstage were conducted as if they occurred onstage. Instruction and supervision were proper tasks for an aristocratic character, and until 1858 the managing director was always a nobleman. Artistic skill was the responsibility of a specialized master, and the stage, ballet, choir and music masters had places in the hierarchy of the formal organization.

When the opera house opened in 1782, the king changed the institutional environment by displacing court entertainment and the Royal Orchestra. Certain administrative housekeeping routines already in use at court were brought along. In addition to observation, regulations firmly controlled behaviour within the theatre's physical environment and settings.

In 1786, an updated written regulation that included instructions for 'the opera theatre' and the Royal Academy of Music was put into practice. The articles of the ruling copied verbatim the French regulations of 1714 for L'Académie royale de musique in Paris.

As the opera institution was a jurisdiction, theatre directors had the power to judge artists. They could impose a fine or even sentence an artist to prison. One of the articles declares that the direction of the opera shall follow royal commandments and that artists shall follow the commandments given by the directors of the opera. The director in charge, according to the regulation, must 'write a state', meaning that he must draw up a budget. Costs were not very specific, however.

These laws were a precise method of supervision that had long been in use in the administration of the court. Using court articles was an old and widespread administrative technique for managing and controlling the social and economic order of the household. In the Swedish court, 'observation' was an old control procedure with accurate inventories aimed at reducing consumption (Persson, 1999).

A problem arising at this point of crosswise influences is that of text. Court administrations relied on memoranda to preserve their routines; written documents, articles, journals, records and classifying titles were sorted with care and kept in archives. Written instructions were used for regulating the 'actor's state', meaning the estimation and settlement of expenditures for various titles in the artistic community.

The demand for documents began to complicate the skilled experience of actual stage praxis. Court societies had always had an eagerness for arranging spectacular and entertaining events for their members. Now at the permanent theatre, a general repertoire given during regular seasons replaced many of those events. With the introduction of theatre censorship in 1785, the censor's permission to perform was based on a moral and aesthetic judgement of a dramatic text beforehand, and this made it risky to use improvisation *in actio*.

In Russia, Catherine II reorganized the court theatre in 1763 and 1764. It became national and incorporated in the overall power structure administering the Russian state. As Borovsky (1999) notes, a new written statute was introduced at the theatre with the intention that the living experience praxis be forgotten and replaced by the new Western European grammar. By the late eighteenth century, regulations were a current phenomenon at national theatres.

Although its praxis developed over the years, the final theatre regulation was repealed in Stockholm in 1974. As a public investigator wrote, the articles had turned into 'parodical antiquated official documents' by then.

Style, space, and bodily movements

In the 1780s, the opera manager was occasionally a 'sur-intendant'. The managerial tasks – the superintendence – at the royal theatres were described in words that express a hierarchical position, a bodily movement or a direction. It signified the social order.

When Armfelt, the close protégé of Gustavus III, made a note on his task as a manager at the opera in the 1780s, he wrote: 'I know little or nothing about theatre, but the king is directing me.' This statement illustrates the managerial mechanisms at work at that time. Being a manager was not yet thought of as a profession but as the outcome of a specialist's task. It was an ability to fulfill the king's volition, to be guided by his will and to supervise subjects. Artists were labeled 'sujet', a precise translation of the French word for subject, *le sujet*. The word *subject* is derived from the Latin words *sub*, meaning *under*, and *jicere*, meaning *to throw*. The subjective status of the artist was this 'thrownness' under a sovereign power. When governing the institution, royal power functioned like taste; it was visible and supposed to trickle down like a stream of energy through a social stratum.

Elias (1983) describes the exercise of royal power during *l'ancien régime* in energetic terms and as interactions within spatial arrangements. The closer you got to the royal body of power, the less energy was put into an action. The king's effort in carrying out an action was merely to give it lip service or to make a gesture; others actually performed the actions.

The role of a court functionary was to translate words and gestures into deeds. Kantorowicz (1957) makes us familiar with the king's two bodies: the physical body and the body politic. The king embodied the major kingdom, using an analogy between the social and the human body in the monarchic power structure. The collective body of the people was incomplete without its head, in this case the king.

Swedish regal law had made a similar distinction between *regalia majora* and *regalia minora*. Economic issues belonged to the minor realm. For a long time, *economy* was associated with the king's physical body and his right as a noble man to own and manage estates; it was a king's right to give royal mercantile privileges.

An effort in governing the opera was to keep its diverse 'states' well ordered. Several of the concrete nouns used to describe the fiscal condition of the theatre referred to the human body and its conduct, or to be more precise, to the royal body of power, like 'head', 'hand', 'eye', 'Crown', and 'corpse', in contrast to the common public. The 'public', one critic wrote, 'is everywhere a dark body in its nature, and its enlightenment is only in the beginning just a vague reflection of the original and pure light that certain rare geniuses possess' (Wetterström, 2001).

At the opera, quarterly accounting routines were called 'head accounts'. At first most of the income came from the king's personal assets and his 'hand money'. The financial situation was reported in terms of spatial relationships and by words expressing motions and positions: 'inside', 'above', 'below', or 'in between' (as in *entre*-preneur). A manager discussing finances hopes that the theatre would be able to 'carry its own cost'.

Obviously, the economic and managerial manner followed a sensorial technique, a form of immediate organizational control. Gestures and vocal responses came as instant expressions from the human body. The ability to manage was still a form of sensory knowledge. Later, we find a parallel to Bentham's *panopticism* at work at the 'spectacle-house'. It was this similar *principle of visibility* in order to control that introduced new administrative routines at the opera institution and guided attention in a calculable way. Running public operas became a functional task.

This eye, this voice, this gesture

Gestures had the function of 'pointing there'. Managing the theatre was not yet detached from that of having a purely local presence or from a concrete way of perceiving. It is important to understand that spoken words and visualized gestures pointing in a direction did perform a concrete commanding function within the social context by that time. Words, gestures and written regulations were 'speech acts', that is, they were powerful and direct forms of communication.

Conceptual knowledge and theory, on the other hand, surpass such a first sensory immediacy. They are a transition from a physical to a conceptual grasping of things in a process of representation. Compared to other means of expression like singing or playing music, the spoken sound is far more capable of articulation.

The articulated language, this spoken sound, is a truly human activity in the ordering of the social world. While it is possible to transfer a panoramic view of an organization into a written form, a precise articulation is essential in order to divide activities and arrange cost-auditing routines. Administrative techniques of writing make it possible to present a generalized view of the present status of a theatre. Such acts of inscribing are necessary for representing various events that happen at a theatre and to simplify this complex social reality to put it in place in a balance sheet. Events become periodic activities that may recur in the coming fiscal years, and this inscription provides evidence for building macro-theory.

From the 1850s on, the general managers at royal theatres accomplished their tasks by following certain modernized administrative manners. Detailed text documents lay bare the routines and new methods practiced. A functional quality of attention became the method of management, not traditional authority. Activities had been administered rationally, with costs calculated and work organized in a specialized division of labour. Now managers relied on an abstract notion of administrative continuity.

This was a turning point, a clear transformation of practice and the unfolding of an evaluative style of conduct. This disciplinary functionalism was accused of being 'bureaucratic', and the conductor was renamed 'foreman for the Royal Orchestra' (1858). Since the texts were so practical, they controlled routines for a long time to come and called for a professional attitude towards administrative tasks.

Aesthetic response

This shift in terms of aesthetic attitude was a transition from mere response to reflective judgement. At first, the form of judgement that the opera managers expressed followed *simple perceptions* [*perceptio*]. This may be termed an aesthetic response to an aesthetic feeling. Stimuli from outer phenomena arouse sensational *impressions* like a *pleasure* in beauty. Taste became subjective. Intuitions and representations were subject to outer appearances only; the musical pleasure at a performance is a simple avoidance of displeasure. Stage performances appealed to the eye and to the ear first, and the aesthetic relationship was direct.

Enjoyment and admiration of beauty occurred immediately in front of an object and referred to the property and the quality of things. This was valid either if it was in front of the shape of a beautiful young performer or the beauty of the virtuosity of musicality. It was primarily a moral impulse.

In judgements of taste, Armfelt regarded theatre performances to be 'good' at Versailles, where the visual impression was clearly enlightened, conspicuous and extravagant. Another notation moralized about the less impressive visual and material quality of performance that small companies in the provinces were capable of showing off.

Taste judgements covered the skill and behaviour of actors and spectators, the staging, the plot and characters, and the less impressive playhouses where they performed. Performances were spectacles and exciting experiences. Words used to describe the aesthetic feeling after a pleasurable experience were 'admiration', 'agreeable', 'affection', 'satisfaction', 'attention', and other affirmative terms. The directors regarded the performance's effect on the spectator to be a major aspect of quality, and so the quality of performance, its lavishness, had a *direct* influence on the cost of running the theatre. These judgements still followed the characteristic noble preferences of court life and were moral. The term 'self-knowledge' implied the ability to conduct, observe and adjust oneself to outer rules and to the social norms of the court society, like court etiquette or becoming a 'nobleman' and a 'Swede'. Accordingly, the typical aristocratic play with social roles – masks, faces, disguises, appearances and masquerades – is evident as well.

As taste was social, the pleasure found in beauty had reference to its *communicability*. Taste was not yet considered *generally valid* as a judgement, however; it was just aesthetic response, like reacting to the mere sight of the solely amusing beauty of stage settings. On the other hand, we cannot expect to find a more sophisticated aesthetic attitude at work in early theatre administrations. In his lectures in 1770, Kant was not even able to distinguish the occurrence of pleasure in the beautiful from the reflection of this pleasure that was necessary to make a judgement in taste.

By this time, the philosophical problem of taste lay in the lack of a clear distinction between aesthetic response and aesthetic judgement. As Guyer (1997) points out, only a distinction between the conditions of the occurrence of a feeling of pleasure and the conditions for judgement of such a feeling could solve the problem of taste. Then there is a clear recognition that the fact of its intersubjective validity plays a role in the assessment of pleasure that leads to a judgement of taste. It is such a distinction that underlies Kant's argument in the *Critique of Judgement* (1790) 20 years later (Guyer, pp. 24–25).

Kant passed that threshold, and his critique opened the possibility of a philosophical aesthetics based on a general critical attitude and a conscious reflection. To Kant, taste was not just judgement of an aesthetic feeling, but the *feeling of judgement* in taste or *Urteilsgefühl*.

Aesthetic judgement

During the nineteenth century, a form of judgement appeared that proves a genuine critical and aesthetic judgement. Taste in the beautiful then gave rise to a form of judgement based on conscious perception [*apperceptio*]. Considered here are intelligible aspects in the experience of a performance. From the perspective of the audience, it was no longer merely an aesthetic response to an aesthetic feeling, but a reflective judgement that happens with awareness of certain artistic aspects or an experience. Taste then concerned internal self-awareness, a genuine personality and a reflective attitude in making judgements. It was important to the formation of a more sophisticated critique and judgement with an intersubjective validity. When a free press emerged, as Habermas describes, critics gained a position from which they could argue and proclaim their ideas in public. Critics were men and women who had read widely on philosophical and aesthetic issues.

By the middle of the nineteenth century, the press could express a public opinion against royal privilege and monopoly. Entrepreneurs called for a national theatre independent of the royal court. Societal change produced new debates, reflections and discussions of public expenses. At the opera, early twentieth century entrepreneurs tried to implement a Tayloristic programme with 'modern' principles for observing and guarding costs. The programme recommended electric 'light' directed at the stage and 'rational' techniques for a 'faster change of scenes'. There was an attempt to adopt business methods in the running of the arts. Today, some economic theories confirm the 'chronic cost disease' of the performing arts. In brief, the rise of the national economies and their theatres had the flavour of a theory of their own.

Voices from far away

Throughout the long history of managing the Royal Opera in Stockholm, directors perceived the cost situation as an overwhelming problem, and they acted upon this dilemma in different ways. At first, managers were creative in finding ad hoc solutions when financial difficulties came up. When the ownership structure changed, administrative methods at the theatre became abstract, continuous and functional in form. In the eye of the public, managers needed to look for costs. As Genette (1999) writes, 'I see an object because it is in front of me, I look at it in order to see it better' (p. 115).

Today an unknown public owner claims the necessity of 'cost awareness' and 'cost responsibility' among artists and theatre managers. What was still a moral and aesthetic requirement in the nineteenth century has transformed into a cultural economic discourse today. We have learned, however, that those macroscopic voices speaking and looking at costs are from a more distant place than that of a speaking person appearing on stage and in the flesh.

Interplay of management and judgement: an institutional model

These historic examples signify a general interplay of judgement/ management in large arts organizations, but they also apply to many of today's human activities. The following dynamic model suggests their key differences. The model is an energetic contingency tool. We are interested in understanding the movements and rhythm within all the diverse practices that embody an organization. Within practices, there are energies of formation, and we regard the apparent form in each situation. There is a double movement of progression–regression. Each concept serves as a possible transformer of energy. Brought into a managerial context, it is as follows:

Transformers of Energy When Managing Artistic Practices
Regression _____ *Progression*

Here we must abandon the idea that artistic creation is freedom from binding rules. There is always a reciprocity between these two dimensions: regression is necessary for progressive forces to occur, and progressive forces for the regressive to occur. By putting ourselves in the background and viewing the practices apart from what we personally prefer, we may see its present status of difficulties and possibilities.

1. When regression dominates, management forms come forward. Management usually appears in terms of functional and durable 'methods' for controlling activities. We found, for example, an eagerness to administer and control expenditure by applying methods that 'look after' costs. On the bottom line then, acts of cost evaluation and the request for 'savings' always embrace an ethics. As management is regressive, it may be *regulative* or *suppressive*.

MANAGEMENT
Regressive Forces (perception)
Regulative _____ *Suppressive*
Control Methods: Rules, Normalization and Quantitative Evaluation

Regulative forces may be *legislative* and concern the explicit laws and rules in a society or institution. Once it was theatre censorship; today it is *normative* and deals with the financial aspects of the organization. Its forms are often programmes, norms and standards for calculation or behaviour. Such control routines may block flows of aesthetic energy.

Suppressive aspects concern the critical choices of artistic expression. It could be steady artistic norms in a society, a restraining bureaucracy, or market and consumption conditions. The cancelled grand festivals in Avignon and Aix-en-Provence in July 2003 are examples of temporary events hitting durable structures. A celebrity system can be suppressive if it drives up the costs of contracts and makes it difficult to engage artists. Suppression may be subtle and internal if exercised by a charismatic leader in small groups of people (rehearsals).

2. *Judgement works differently and acknowledges aesthetic aspects. This is a nonfunctional quality of attention.*

JUDGEMENT
Progressive Forces (apperception)
Provide with Capital _____ *Facilitate Flow and Intensity*
Aesthetic Modes: Communicability, Cooperation and Aesthetic Values

A judgement is not likely to come from following a method but from a certain *modus*, a 'mode' of approach to a particular organizational situation. And modes shift. Depraz, Varela and Vermersch (2002) help explain acts of 'becoming aware' and changing attention. Acknowledging an aesthetic judgement is a matter of *re-directing* our attention: we turn our attention away from the spectacle of the world (*perception*), and return to an interior world and a self-reflection (*apperception*) pertaining to pragmatism. Then we change our attitude toward the world and release our *control* over things – and are released from their grasp. As Depraz *et al.* put it, you go from 'looking for something' to 'letting something come to you'. Changing our quality of attention and acknowledging aesthetic judgement in our everyday activities involve moving from an active search to an accepting 'letting-arrive' attitude. We move our attention from looking for costs toward letting the aesthetic event – the performance – surprise us and move us ahead. We let ourselves accept our sense-experience, become aware and let this feeling of judgement guide us in a pragmatic situation, apperception.

Visions, tacit skills and intuitive aspects may guide a judgement, but how do managers overcome difficulties threatening the artistic process? A manager should have a creative mind with an ability to find temporary or ad hoc solutions. Managers should know *how* to facilitate necessary aesthetic energy. It could be to protect and support the flow and intensity in the artistic work, provide it with care, attention or resources. Managers must pay attention to problematic processes that require special support in the organization. Traditions and routines may block the circulation of items, ideas or money. An important task of the manager is to provide opportunities for collaboration and temporary teamwork.

In a way, this is the dénouement of the drama. The word itself comes from the Old French *desnouer*, to untie, plus *nodus*, the knot. Solutions rest on our own experience and ability to overcome a restraining obstruction at work and to untie its bound force. Guillet de Monthoux (2004) suggests the insightful point that art firms driven by aesthetic missions actually employ 'negative management' in their way of doing, management in the form of negation. I disagree, though, that the aesthetic style of Dionysus is preferable in every situation. It would be hard to run theatres in a total lack of Apollonian light, planning and clear-cut routine. When management and judgement are in balance, managers are true aesthetic managers.

References

Borovsky, V. (1999) Theatre administration at the court of Catherine II: the reforms of Ivan Elagin. *Theatre Research International*, 24 (1).

Czarniawska, B., and R. Solli (eds) (2001) *Organizing metropolitan space and discourse*. Malmö/Oslo: Liber Abstrakt.

Depraz, N., F. Varela, and P. Vermersch (eds) (2002) *On becoming aware – A pragmatics of experiencing*. Amsterdam: John Benjamins.

Dobson, J. (1999) *The art of management and the aesthetic manager: the coming way of business*. Westport, CT: Quorum Books.

Elias, N. (1983) *The court society*. Translated by E. Jephcott. Oxford: Basil Blackwell.

Foucault, M. (1998) Return to history. In J. Faubion (ed.), *Aesthetics, method and epistemology*, vol. 2. Translated by Robert Harley. New York: New Press.

Genette, G. (1999) *The aesthetic relation*. Translated by G.M. Goshgarian. Ithaca, NY: Cornell University Press.

Greenblatt, S. (1988) *Shakespearean negotiations – The circulation of social energy in renaissance England.* Oxford: Oxford University Press.

Guillet de Monthoux, P. (2004) *The art firm – Aesthetic management and metaphysical marketing.* Palo Alto, CA: Stanford University Press.

Guyer, P. (1997) *Kant and the claims of taste.* Cambridge: Cambridge University Press.

Heidegger, M. (1926/1962) *Being and time.* New York: Harper & Row.

Kant, I. (1790/1988) *The critique of judgment.* Oxford: Oxford University Press.

Kantorowicz, Ernst H. (1997) *The king's two bodies.* Princeton, NJ: Princeton University Press.

Mouritsen, J., and P. Skærbæk, (1995) Civilization, art and accounting: The Royal Danish Theatre. In *The institutional construction of organizations.* London.

Persson, F. (1999) *Servants of fortune – The Swedish court between 1598 and 1721.* Lund: Wallin and Dalholm.

Roselli, J. (1984) *The opera industry in Italy from Cimarosa to Verdi: the role of the impresario.* Cambridge: Cambridge University Press.

Senelick, L. (ed.) (1991). National theatre in northern and eastern Europe 1746–1900. In *Theatre in Europe – A documentary history.* Cambridge University Press.

Sennet, R. (1977) *The fall of public man.* Cambridge University Press.

Wetterström, J. (2001) *Stor opera, små pengar.* Bjärnum: Carlssons.

Yakhlef, A. (1998) 'Construction of accountable worlds.' *Organization,* 5 (3).

4
Gendered textbook filmmakers

Jenny Lantz

Drawing on Pierre Bourdieu (1984, 1993), Yvonne Hirdman (1988) and other social constructionist thinkers, this chapter stresses the importance of not mistakenly considering dichotomies as existing in 'reality' instead of in our conceptual frameworks. By challenging two taken-for-granted dichotomies – the construction of gender and the construction of economic and cultural capital – this discussion explores the constructions of the film producer and the film director as conveyed in a quartet of film school textbooks.

Gender power structures that subordinate women to men are well-documented in organizations in the economic field (see, for example, Kanter, 1977; Game and Pringle, 1984; Walby, 1986; Brown and Pechman, 1987; Acker, 1988; Adler and Izraeli, 1988; Wahl, 1992; Wahl *et al.*, 2003). In the cultural field, however, which is conceptualized as an 'economic world reversed' due to its dissimilar principles of legitimacy[1] (Bourdieu, 1993), one might expect different gender structures and assume that more women would occupy key positions in this field.

In his study of the creative industries, Caves (2000) distinguishes between 'creative' and 'humdrum' workers, arguing that the former really care about artistic achievement, while the latter are just in it for the money. Positions in the cultural field generally are constructed in these dichotomous terms with emphasis on either cultural or economic capital (see Bourdieu, 1993). Accordingly, the top positions in the film team – the director and the producer – are constructed dichotomously: 'The role of the producer is chiefly financial and organizational' (Bordwell and Thompson, 1993, p. 11f). In other words, the construction of the producer stresses economic capital, while 'the director is considered the single person most responsible for the look and sound of the finished film' (Bordwell and Thompson, 1993, p. 12ff). The construction of the director then underlines cultural capital.

In western society, femininity and masculinity are also constructed as a dichotomy, masculinity being the norm and femininity being the deviant (Hirdman, 1988). Considering the concurrent dichotomy of 'creative' and 'humdrum' labor – cultural and economic capital– characterizing the cultural field, one could expect greater opportunities for women in certain top positions in this sector of the economy. Stenström (2000) argues that constructions of femininity are closely related to constructions of art and artistic work. Thus, given the role descriptions of the film producer and the film director, it is possible to imagine a construction of the producer as a breadwinner (that is, a construction of masculinity), and a construction of the film director as a sensitive aesthete (that is, a construction of femininity). Conversely, but equally feasible, is a construction of the film producer as a nurturer (that is, a construction of femininity), and a construction of the director as a visionary (that is, a construction of masculinity). Film industry statistics reveal the same type of gender structures permeating the economic field and its organisations (see Hirdman, 1988; Wahl, 1992), however, belying the notion of the cultural field as a place offering women better career opportunities.

In 2002, women accounted for only 7% of all directors and 26% of all producers working on the top 250 films in the United States (Lauzen, 2003). In 2004, Sofia Coppola became the first woman director ever to win an Oscar. Furthermore, despite its reputation for being progressive in terms of equal opportunity, Sweden's corresponding figures do not deviate greatly from those of the United States. A Swedish Film Institute report on gender equity in the Swedish film industry[2] shows that in 2000, men held 72% of producer credits and 76% of director credits in the films produced. The same pattern emerges in the top 20 films between 1993 and 2002: 16 films had male producers, and 17 films had male directors.[3]

The gender power structures manifested in these observations may be reproduced in many ways (see Hirdman, 1988; Wahl, 1992, for general overviews and Vinterheden, 1991; Hermele, 2002, for the film industry more specifically). Certainly, one arena for the construction of gender and the film professions is the film school.

Students being educated and trained to enter the film industry acquire some of their role- and industry-specific knowledge in school, that is, their *secondary socialization* (see Berger and Luckmann, 1966). Further, despite the variety of professions involved in a film production and the clear division of labour, film training is almost exclusively provided by art schools (Bordwell and Thompson, 1993; Mackaman, 1997). As a result, the business and organizational aspects of the education probably receive little attention; the curriculum is most likely framed from an artistic perspective.

How the film producer and the film director are constructed certainly influences the attitudes of crew members towards them and their tasks; in addition, these constructions also affect the individual roles of the film producer and the film director, respectively, and their sense of worth in the film team as well. Constructions can also serve as impediments to career advancement for people who do not match them (see, for example, Wahl, 1992; Collinson and Hearn, 1996; Holgersson, 2003).

One way to find out the prevalent constructions is to study the textbooks used at film schools. These texts written by people familiar with the industry become required reading for the men and women aspiring to enter the field.

This chapter explores constructions of the film producer and the film director and their intersection with constructions of gender as conveyed in the textbooks used by graduate students in a leading American film programme.[4] In other words, it is a study of the interplay of the dichotomy between cultural and economic capital, and that between femininity and masculinity. I endorse a social constructionist perspective. Based on the syllabi of the graduate programme in film at New York University's Tisch School of the Arts, four books were selected: *Alternative Scriptwriting* (2nd ed.) by Ken Dancyger and Jeff Rush; *Film Directing Shot by Shot. Visualizing from Concept to Screen* by Steven D. Katz; *Directing. Film Techniques and Aesthetics* (2nd ed.) by Michael Rabiger; and *Directing the Documentary* (2nd ed.), also by Rabiger.

My interest lies not in the possible textual interpretations by student readers. Instead I focus on the texts themselves, and thus what I present here is my interpretation – or my construction – of the constructions of the film producer and the film director. These are important in two respects. First, the authors of these books claim to base their texts on their experience in the film industry. Therefore, the textbooks may capture widespread constructions of these film professions. Second, textbooks often constitute the basis for interaction in an educational setting. Consequently, the predominant constructions in the textbooks may serve as constraints for the actors (i.e., students). Of course, student interaction may also center on a range of other things, e.g. student projects, films, lectures, and everyday experiences.

Four thematic categories

This study considers textbook content in four thematic categories: *the position of the textbook author, crew members (skills, personalities, and hazards), careers,* and *the industry*. The first section deals with the position the author takes in relation to the reader. Texts that fall under the second heading, *crew members*, illuminate relationships between crew members. Also, the filmmaker is introduced to crew development, an activity frequently described in directing books for the beginner 'filmmaker'. This vague designation of 'filmmaker' accommodates the reader as one who has not yet chosen an area of specialization and gives the content a general applicability. Also highlighted in this section is a seemingly essentialist view of human nature appearing in the texts, one expressed through emphasis on 'personality traits'. The *career* theme encompasses texts that explain the industry and describe the skills and personality traits necessary to succeed in it. These texts also advise the young filmmaker about how to break into the industry. Finally, the *industry* section highlights assumptions regarding the film business. After discussion of the treatment of the filmmaker in film school textbooks, I identify textbook constructions of the film producer and film director. These ideas are then framed according to Bourdieu's (1984) concepts of economic and cultural capital. Finally, I complete the chapter by addressing how these constructions intersect with constructions of gender.

Position of the textbook author

The textbook authors often write in the first person singular, and they frequently give examples from their own professional life as film directors/editors, crew members, or scriptwriters. Not one of these authors refers to a background as a film producer. The fact that the authority of the authors hinges on their practical experience in the industry confirms the construction of film professions as practical crafts. The legitimacy of the author rests on the number of films to her or his credit. Katz, author of *Film Directing Shot by Shot*, and Rabiger, author of *Directing*, both stress the craftsmanship of filmmaking. Summarizing this construction, Rabiger remarks, 'you are what you have done and what you can show' (p. 491). In these texts, writing style is not academic; the authors do not spend a lot of time hedging their claims. Rather, the tone is personal and reminiscent of self-help literature, an impression further enhanced when the author takes on the role of advisor.

Crews

Crew members appear in the texts in three different contexts. At the centre of the texts are constructions of the different skills corresponding to the various professions in the film team. The authors also present desirable personality traits for crew members and, drawing on these personality traits and skills, identify potential hazards materializing in certain crew members. These three elements together point to the constructions of filmmakers in general. I regard these constructions as normative expectations for each profession, as well as constraints for people presently in the professions and for people who seek to join a specific part of the crew. The most thorough presentation of the crew members is found in *Directing* by Rabiger (1997). In this passage I highlight the relationship between, and the dichotomous constructions of, the director and the producer.

Skills

Rabiger (1997) assigns desirable qualifications and skills to different crew positions, always with the reservation that in real life 'some of the best practitioners will be the exceptions' (p. 325). The texts repeatedly emphasize the importance of the director's education in the arts, as well as his or her relationship to and understanding of the other members of the crew. The Rabiger text constructs the director as the artist by stressing the necessity of developing one's artistic identity if one wants to direct. While no mention is made of the director's ability to stick to the budget, the ideal producer is described as a project enabler and supplier of vital resources. This again stresses the dichotomy of the two positions. The producer has the task of nourishing the work of the artists and craftspeople and should only engage in the film's artistic process if he or she is 'a person of taste' (Rabiger, 1997, p. 325). This seems to be a rare occurrence, however.

In *Alternative scriptwriting*, the producer is represented as conservative, reading 'with an eye on emulating the latest greatest success at the box office' (Dancyger and Rush, 1995, p. 259). According to the textbooks, the producer does not need an MBA or any other business degree, and an advanced education in the arts is not brought up as a critical advantage. Certain hazards may surface in relationships with members of the crew, Rabiger points out. Producers unfamiliar with the film business sometimes transfer to their new environment the 'dirty tricks' they used in the financial arena. The call for producers with an artistic foothold is greater than for those with a strong business background; experiences from the 'sub-world' of finance are obviously not highly valued.

The ideal producer seems to be an individual with long experience in the film industry. Rabiger draws several conclusions about producers, in fact. 'These men and women were the professionals – true leaders with a long history of deserving survivorship' (1997, p. 326). Continuing, he declares, '[B]ecause they control money, producers have a great deal of power, and some, especially the inexperienced, assume that because artists and technicians are subordinates, their work and values are subordinate too' (Rabiger, 1997, p. 325). Finally, he endorses the ideal production manager: '[G]ood PMs make good producers' (Rabiger, 1997, p. 332).

While Rabiger admits that artists and technicians are formally subordinate to the producer, he also points out that they can attempt to 'educate the producer'. This is a rather revealing assertion for it implies that the knowledge of the artists and technicians is considered more essential than that of the producer. Moreover, the artists and technicians are advised to exercise some caution when it comes to particularly 'unscrupulous' producers.

Personality traits

The personality traits of the director and the producer are described in great detail. The traits are presented as mere 'facts' about the people who hold different professional positions in the film team, thereby fostering a non-interactionist, idiosyncratic view of these traits. This perspective favours psychological (or essentialist) explanations over social constructionist ones. To succeed, a director must be instinctive and emotional as well as having a lively and inquiring mind. Rabiger's text illustrates this perspective in the section that begins:

> The truth is that directing a reflection of life is a heady business. The person responsible for making this happen is living existentially; that is, fully and completely in the moment as if it were the last. The pressures of directing a movie usually make all this happen whether you like it or not. Especially is this true after an initial success, thereafter you face failure and artistic/professional death every step of the way. Like stage fright, the dread and exhilaration of the chase may never go away. But surely the portent of any worthwhile experience is that it makes you more than a little afraid. (1997, pp. 327–8)

Additionally, the *good* director is portrayed as a curious, flexible, articulate, patient and people-loving person who can make just decisions and who respects team members and their knowledge. The production process, however, also frequently gives rise to 'signs of acute insecurity (depression, manic energy, low flashpoint, panic irresolution)' in the director. This state of 'acute doubt and anxiety' may be coupled with unsurpassed amounts of energy and fortitude (Rabiger, 1997, p. 327).

According to Rabiger, developing an artistic identity is said to rest on the individual's ability to 'live life courageously and fully' (1997, p. 492), and a few lines later he comments that most people's lives are so dull that they do not have anything to say. These statements are recurrent in the texts, constructing the director as an exceptional person, someone who knows more about life than 'ordinary' people do. It seems as if the authors give themselves the right to determine what is mundane and who lives ordinary lives.

The ideal producer is described as 'a cultivated, intelligent, and sensitive business person whose goal in life is to nourish good work by unobtrusively supporting the artists and craftspeople hired to produce it' (Rabiger, 1997, p. 325). Obviously, the ideal producer is constructed as a nicer-than-usual type of business person (from the perspective of the artists) endowed with an adequate amount of cultural capital (see Bourdieu, 1984). The perfect producer evidently lives life supportively through caring about other people's artistic fulfillments, not by living 'courageously and fully' like the director.

Hazards

These constructions of the director and the producer testify to the greater risk associated with the role of the producer. The drawbacks endemic to the typical director are presented as 'negative traits that make even good directors decidedly human', while the negative characteristics of some producers are portrayed as pretty fatal:

> Anyone with access to money can call himself or herself a movie producer, for access to money is the prime qualification. In the last three decades I recall working for producers who were, variously, an insurance man, a real-estate developer, a gentlemanly hood, and a playboy draft-dodger. For one or two of them, hell already has room reservations. While the funds assembled by these people made production possible, their congenital distrust, crassness, and megalomania made the crews' lives into a tragic-comic rollercoaster ride. Using threats, sudden dismissal, and humiliation, such people survive only because filmmakers depend on financing to survive. (Rabiger, 1997, p. 326)

Accommodation in hell has supposedly already been arranged for these producers, and the consequences of having one of them on a project may be substantial. *Bad* producers dote on their bags of 'dirty tricks', which include

- trying to play people off against each other,
- looking aggressive and competent when the opposite is true,
- trashing anybody or anything in a vulnerable position,
- replacing anyone who witnesses the producer's imbecilic perform-ance, and
- claiming personal credit for other people's work whenever possible. (Rabiger, 1997, p. 326)

According to the text, a bad producer is much more devastating for the film project than is a bad director. The shortcomings of directors involve a tendency to work in an idiosyncratic manner, an antisocial personality, an inability to make choices and decisions, a disproportionate time allocation between actors and crew, and a 'sensory overload'.

These constructions of the producer in relation to the director also affect the thematic subcategory of career. In closing, I would like to stress that art is certainly predominant over industry in the larger crew context when the producer is included. Textbooks exclusively addressed to one of the more artistic professions involved in filmmaking, for example, the scriptwriter or the documentary director, often highlight market and financial aspects as well, a theme I resume in the section on the industry.

When addressing the director of the documentary, Rabiger points out that

[a]ll this emphasis on becoming known and fitting in may seem like the slipway to destructive compromises. It doesn't have to be. After all, the films on which we were raised were produced for a profit, and some were good art by any standards. Almost the entire history of cinema has its roots in commerce, with each new work predicated upon ticket sales of the last. If cinema and capitalism go hand in hand, this marriage has a certain cantankerous democracy. Tickets are votes from the wallet that prevent cinema from being irrelevant or from straying too far from the sensibilities of the common man. (1992, p. 329)

Such advice seems to be kept from the eyes and ears of the producer. It seems as if adhering to the primacy of artistic professions in the team is a requisite for being part of the *Gemeinschaft* in this subworld, at least for the producer.

Careers

Most of the advice concerning career issues is addressed to the aspiring 'filmmaker', a general term designating the director, the producer or the cinematographer, or all three of them at once. When claiming that everyone who enters film school wants to direct, however, the text does in fact hint that the aspiring director is the main addressee. *Alternative scriptwriting* is, however, explicitly written for prospective scriptwriters.

The vaguely defined filmmakers, and those interested in documentary in particular, are prompted to keep an eye on the market:

> By all means watch what other people are doing and what distributors seem to buy. Go through catalogues of available films, giving partic- ular attention to your own areas of interest. If you make a list, you will certainly find gaps. Not only will you find significant holes in what is available, but you will also get an idea of what the distributors are offering and what presumably they are renting or even selling outright. By doing your own market study, you can decide where your interests might fit into the existing commercial structure. ... It is said that nothing succeeds like success, and people with judgmental responsibilities often seem most impressed by prizes and honors they know nothing about, preferring to add to one person's honors rather than take a chance on an outsider. (Rabiger, 1992, p. 330)

Once again, the industry and market aspects are highlighted when speaking to the general filmmaker assumed to aspire to directing. In this context, the view of the market is not as harsh as when the producers are described.

The young aspiring 'filmmakers' are told to be realistic about them- selves in terms of what kind of person they 'really are'. Only the ones with 'ideas and leadership' as well as self-confidence are fit for directing. Again, echoing a non-interactionist, individualist perspective, people are assumed to have qualities that either suit a certain film profession or not. However, individuals may obtain the appropriate characteristics by their own will, independent of the social environment:

> Developing an artistic identity is not easy and rests on your ability to live life courageously and fully. The resistance to your advancement may seem to lie with those higher up in your film school or higher up in the film/television industry, but really it lies within yourself.

> Most people's lives are centered on mundane matters and they have
> nothing original to say. When this changes, you will know it and you
> will be driven to express it. Your identity will be sensed and implicitly
> recognized by others seeing your work. (Rabiger, 1997, p. 492)

Accordingly, the would-be filmmakers are advised to prepare themselves for a challenging future where they may have to specialize in a
particular craft. Only if they have a fat enough résumé to prove their
skills will they get a job in the industry after film school. Filmmaking
is a practical business, and recognition and reward are only gained over
time, warn the authors. Would-be directors should spend all their money
and spare time on film projects with like-minded friends 'whose values
they share'.

> The committed professional is the person who puts the good of the
> project before everything. . . . If you consistently do good work, on
> time, and within the agreed parameters, then your reputation will
> slowly spread through the grapevine, and you will naturally rise.
> Make a costly mistake, and you will fall back. There are no reliable
> shortcuts to recognition and reward, for filmmaking is a long, slow,
> pragmatic business. Like any art form it will only gratify those who
> value the process as much as the product. (Rabiger, 1997, p. 493)

Not surprisingly, the authors all seem to be in favour of film school,
emphasizing the possibilities to experiment and the importance of an
education in the arts. Referring to it as a place where failures are not so
costly, they seem to regard film school as a place where one can learn
techniques more efficiently than on the job.

This message is rather ambiguous. The textbook authors support film
school education, but the rationale for doing so is not exactly clear:

> You are what you can show. A film degree is nice (indicating that
> you are educable and committed) but more than anything you
> need a portfolio of your work that demonstrates your capabilities to
> prospective employers or money backers. (Rabiger, 1997, p. 495)

Current norms in the industry regarding prestige and career tracks are
taken as an objective reality. The textbooks seem to propose film school
as a shortcut to the experience harmonious with the present norms of
the industry. After all, it is film experience that counts and nothing

else. Prior experience in other fields of work or study is not considered relevant.

The industry

The text directed to the scriptwriter underscores the constraints of the economic context the most:

> Unlike a novel that can be published modestly, or a play that can be produced locally, a film requires an infrastructure for production, distribution, and exhibition. Consequently, the economics of production preclude the production of the vast majority of screenplays. With producers, distributors, and exhibitors all eyeing audiences to determine what will sell, screenwriters are constantly pressed to do this as well. The results are screenplays that are strongly influenced by current issues – social, political, economic. Almost any personality or event that has significantly captured the public's interest, even for an instant, merits screen consideration. (Dancyger and Rush, 1995, p. 260)

Though emphasizing the economic aspects, the author seems to forget the institutional aspects inherent in film on all levels: the narrative structure of the film, working conditions, norms as to what skills are rewarded, and constructions of the ideal director and producer. All are constraints that do not derive from economic structure alone.

The scriptwriter is advised to apply a personal perspective to issues that may interest the public, to develop a personal style and to be innovative since 'the audiences today are very media-wise and they tire of repetition'. Once again a marketing perspective is applied to one of the artistic professions. In *Film directing, shot by shot*, Katz suggests directors use visualization as a means of eliminating some of the risks associated with the high cost and complexity of filmmaking. This casts the director's role in the light of budget considerations.

> More than anything else, live-action film is unpredictable. This is a creative virtue and a logistical liability – a virtue in that the unexpected is exciting for the artist and ultimately the audience; a liability because the expense and complexity of filmmaking can become a tremendous obstacle when things do not go as planned. Visualization is one way to reduce the obstacles even if the filmmaker takes his work to the edge. By developing ideas and planning their execution before shooting, the filmmaker is able to free his time and attention

so that he can respond to the unexpected opportunities that arise throughout the production from the first days of writing to the final cut. (Katz, 1991, p. 97)

Embedded in the career-related advice are 'objective facts' about the industry. 'Everyone entering film school wants to direct', claims Rabiger (1997, p. 491). By constructing directing as the ultimate goal for the film school student, he may raise the status of that particular profession at the expense of the other professions. The author thus reproduces a construction of the director as the most important individual in the film team and in the subworld of the film industry.

The industry will show an interest in you once you are fascinating enough in terms of artistic identity and lifestyle, writes Rabiger (1997, p. 92). In advocating originality, the author seems to overlook the fact that originality is also a construction. As Durkheim remarks, even when we transgress rules, we follow the rules of transgression (1895/1982). Therefore, only certain forms of originality are appreciated.

The industry context is mentioned several times. For example, film-makers are encouraged to establish contacts with the industry at film school. While one statement (Rabiger, 1997, p. 92) serves to convince the reader that experiencing resistance to your own advancement lies within yourself, another chapter includes a critical description of the professional structure within the film industry and a suggestion that this structure holds people back from teaching apprentices:

> In the freelance world, know-how and experience are earning power so workers systematically *avoid* enlightening their juniors.... Most employers live pressurized lives and do not consider preparing the individual for more responsibility any part of their job. That individual is either prepared through prior schooling to assume more complex duties or must somehow devise an education for herself while serving as the company peon. (Rabiger, 1992, p. 318)

This is as close to an interactionist, sociological perspective that one gets in these textbooks. One reason for the norm of filmmakers' living harried lives and lacking time to introduce novice film workers to the job could be that the organizations constituted by the film team are temporary; they lack organizational memory. No particular organization will thus gain from investing in training the individual, only the individual and the industry as a whole (DeFillippi and Arthur, 1998).

Having emphasized the importance of industry contacts, Rabiger assures the reader that such contacts do not necessarily imply having to make compromises (see citation on p. 58). Certainly, there is an underlying belief that engaging in matters related to the organizational and industrial context of filmmaking will eventually lead to artistic compromises. This belief is both challenged and reproduced by the author. Only when he addresses the reader as someone who primarily wants to become a director (that is, not a producer) does he attempt to convince the reader that the 'marriage between cinema and capitalism' has not been too bad. Furthermore, the sections in the book where the author takes a stand for the business or 'capitalist' side of film production are in the 'Getting Work' chapter. Elsewhere, Rabiger (1997) conveys an image of filmmakers as people 'who usually lack all flair for capitalism, and are only too aware of their dependency upon financial operators' (p. 326).

*   *   *

The two sides of filmmaking, the artistic and the business, are evident in all the texts. The authors seem to have a continuous and stable relationship with the artistic side but, depending on subject and addressee, vary in their relationship with the business side of filmmaking.

I will now outline these textbook constructions of the producer and the director in terms of cultural and economic capital and then discuss how these constructions can also be read as constructions of gender.

Constructed producer/director dualism

The constructed dichotomy of the director and the producer may serve as an impediment to the exchange of experiences and knowledge and, by extension, to the wider development of the industry. Furthermore, these constructions may also function as a barrier for women. At any rate, these constructions do become constraints for the actors.

The construction of a perfect match between personalities and professions is an essentialist, non-interactionist perception that assumes that some people are just made for certain jobs, regardless of the social context. Consequently, a widespread construction contends that the obstacle to one's career advancement lies within oneself. Ignoring the fact that some people are ascribed certain qualities in interaction with the social context, this construction serves to legitimize those presently holding these positions.

The textbooks convey a picture of a rather neglected film producer. Despite the fact that the producer is officially in charge of the film team, the professional superiority of the director is emphasized over and over again. It is the director who feels the urge to 'educate' the producer, not the other way around. The producer's main task seems to be that of providing money and nurturing the artistic vision of the team, yet the education, knowledge and skills of the producer are not conveyed as something other crew members should admire or try to emulate.

In fact, the performances of other crew members are not evaluated in economic terms. A director of photography – despite doing an excellent artistic job – may have spent four times as much money as projected and still receive plenty of awards and look forward to a splendid career. Warnings about the risks involved in having the 'wrong' producer on the team also point to the relative subordination of the producer to the director. The film producer is portrayed as cynical, dishonest and aggressive, a person who does not always trust other people's expertise. Since access to money is submitted as the key requirement for working as a film producer, the success of the latter is constructed as being independent of talent and skills. On the other hand, the ideal producer should have long industry experience.

Persistently mystified in the texts, the director is presented as someone who has something interesting to tell, whose life is not 'centered on mundane things', and whose job 'everyone who enters film school' aspires to. Without reservation, the director's line of work earns the highest status in the crew. Constructed as an emotional person, the director may be everything from curious, social and articulate to very insecure and depressed.

I would like to call attention to the authors' positions when analysing these constructions of the producer and the director in terms of Bourdieu's capital concepts. The authors all lean toward the cultural capital pole of the film field. In other words, their experience as directors, scriptwriters and crew members – but not as producers – implies that they belong to 'creative' rather than 'humdrum' labour. Bourdieu (1993) argues that the principle of legitimacy characterizing the cultural capital pole of the cultural field is autonomous; it refers only to internal demands. Consequently, the people whose position in this particular field hinges on the cultural capital principle of legitimacy have acquired their position through their accumulated experiences within the field. From their perspective, then, not much weight is given to experiences in other fields, like a producer's experience in the financial arena. Claiming that the producer can only be involved in the artistic process if he or she is a 'person of taste', one of the authors suggests a difference in cultural capital between the two leaders of the film team. The principle of legitimacy that rests on economic capital is heteronomous; it is based on external factors. To reiterate, textbook authors claim that anyone with money from anywhere can become a producer. Obviously, the dichotomous construction of the director (the cultural capital) and the producer (the economic capital) sets up an ongoing competition between the two, and these constructions seem to be a result of this continuing rivalry. Writing art school textbooks may be the only way for a director (the cultural capital) to fight back against the producer (the economic capital).

The whole business of filmmaking, expressed in the texts in terms of unstoppable production processes and the like, is somewhat mystified. Emphasis is on the practical qualities of filmmaking, implying both explicitly and implicitly that experience is far more important than education.

The presentation of the 'bad' producers as crass capitalists is, however, followed by an altered and seemingly more nuanced depiction of the industry side of filmmaking in the discussion of career-related issues. One of the authors temporarily abandons the individualist perspective in stressing the role of professionalism in filmmaking, as well as the structural problem of protectionist behaviour to which it gives rise.

Before moving on to the discussion of the gendering of the filmmaker, I wish to draw attention to the fact that economic capital is emphasized in the section on the industry. One interpretation of this is that the authors may be more comfortable ascribing importance to economic capital when it is not linked to the status of the producer but rather to the industry/field at large.

Gendered filmmakers

At this point, consideration of how the two dichotomies intersect will shed more light on the issue of gendered filmmakers. Inasmuch as the director and the producer are constructed as a dichotomy of the artist and the businessperson, and femininity and masculinity are also constructed in dichotomous terms, I would like to argue that the director and the producer are both constructed as male.

In their role as advisors to students, the authors of the texts write from their experience in the film industry. As part of a traditionally male-dominated industry, the authors help produce and reproduce the prevalent constructions of the filmmakers as male. Since gender is left unproblematized in all of the books, it is reproduced as something insignificant, while at the same time the male-norm is reinforced (Wahl, 1992). Katz, for example, consistently uses the pronoun *he*.

The construction of the producer as a man is most evident in certain descriptions. For example, Rabiger typifies the disastrous producer as 'an insurance man', 'a gentlemanly hood', and 'a playboy draft-dodger'. These examples all speak for themselves. I adopt a sociological perspective and refer to the social context of the authors as a basis for the gendering of the filmmakers, but one could also come to the same point by deconstructing the descriptions of the producer and the director in very much the same way as deconstruction has revealed the entrepreneur as gendered male (see Ahl, 2002).

Since femininity and masculinity are constructed dichotomously, one could have expected at least one pole of the cultural field to be gendered as female. Despite the two principles of legitimization (economic and cultural capital), however, women hold very few top positions. How then can the gendering of both the business and the artistic side of the film field as male be interpreted?

Return to the fact that the more emotional director is constructed as superior to the more rational producer. In terms of gender, the dichotomous construction of gender implies that masculinity is constructed as the norm and femininity as the deviant (Hirdman, 1988). For example, a dominant discourse constructs masculinity in rational terms (Bologh, 1990), and femininity is discursively constructed in irrational terms. However, despite the use of certain words typically associated with femininity, such as 'instinctive', 'social', 'non-hierarchical', 'insecure' and 'patient', the construction of the emotional director is a man. A study on gender in an advertising agency (Alvesson and Köping, 1993), where the work was constructed in feminine terms while the organization was still markedly male dominated, allows for several interpretations of the gendering of the director as male. The director is not solely portrayed in 'feminine' terms. Other characteristics mentioned in the texts are more vaguely gendered, for example, 'curious' and 'articulate'. In addition, many characteristics are rather unflattering, for example, an 'antisocial personality', an 'incapacity to make choices and decisions', and sometimes afflicted with 'acute doubt and anxiety'. Furthermore, the male authors and the men who presently dominate the film industry have the prerogative of interpretation when it comes to determining who 'lives life courageously and fully'.

As the construction of the film producer somewhat coincides with that of the business executive (see Holgersson, 2003),[5] its gendering as male is not particularly remarkable. However, writing from a position closer to the cultural capital pole of the cultural field, the authors construct the film producer as subordinate to the film director. This subordination could explain why, relatively speaking, more women call themselves film producers than film directors. Moreover, the prerequisite to becoming a producer is very transparent; a producer must have access to money. Therefore, women may more easily enter the industry as producers. A 'competent director', on the other hand, seems to be defined more vaguely (for example, in terms of someone who lives life courageously and fully), thus paving the way for the men who presently occupy positions of power (*and* the prerogative of interpretation) to continue identifying men as the most competent directors.

One way of interpreting the construction of both the film director and the film producer as male despite the dichotomous construction of the artist and the business person, is what Höök (2001) refers to as 'the privilege of the norm'. Being part of the norm allows for great differences within the group while still constituting an entirety. It could be argued that alliances unite men of both economic and cultural capital due to the common interest of maintaining the present division of labour in the film field. Hartman (1981) showed these alliances between men from the working classes and the capitalists. Women are then constructed as either complementary or deficient (Wahl, 1996; Höök, 2001; Holgersson, 2003).

The rivalry between the director and the producer mentioned earlier may constitute an important reproduction process. Typified through a list of personality traits, the ideal director may be described as a phantom (see Lindgren, 1999) against which aspiring male filmmakers evaluate themselves. Although the ideal producer is not as celebrated by the textbook authors, he may still serve as a phantom figure for people rich in economic capital. These two phantoms may then function as the basis for a homo-social game (see Lindgren, 1996; 1999) between the producer and the director. They constantly compete with each other, a struggle that results in their not only being confirmed but also strengthened by each other.

Abrahamsson (2002) argues that the construction of masculinity is continuously modified to encompass what is considered important in modern organizations. Along similar lines, Holgersson (2003) found that while women who hold positions as personnel, accounting, marketing or information directors are denied further career advancement in the organization, men with similar backgrounds are not excluded from recruitment processes for CEOs. Concomitantly, the gendering of the film director as male may be regarded as an adjustment to requirements in this particular field. Although it is likely that no major change regarding requested 'personal traits' has occurred throughout the history of the film industry – since male dominance has remained constant – one could argue that the circumstances/the social context determine what is to be included in the construction of masculinity. In fact, the director is a field-specific construction of masculinity.

To reiterate, since economic profit is not the only objective of film production (see Moran, 1996), film has two principles of legitimacy: economic and cultural capital (see Bourdieu, 1984). Consequently, besides economic profit, the struggles in the film industry also involve doing 'art for art's sake' (Bourdieu, 1984) to some degree. The director is constructed as male from the perspective of the cultural capital pole, to which the whole crew, except for the producer but including the authors, supposedly belongs. Also, from the same perspective, the producer is gendered male, viewed as someone – a business person – from the economic capital pole. As the producer most often does not meet the requirements for positioning and struggling in the cultural field, he or she is degraded in the cultural field. However, by profiting from the 'privilege of the norm', men can occupy both types of position and thus remain very different while still constituting an entirety. Hence, these two constructions of masculinities exclude women who want to enter film production from either pole. Further, these gendered constructions are reinforced by the homo-social game that takes place between them and which is evident throughout the textbooks in the authors' descriptions of the two protagonists in the film team.

Given the current and past male dominance in the film industry, the constructions of the filmmakers reflected in the textbooks are ubiquitous in the film industry. As texts may be seen as part of everyday practices that form social relations (Berger and Luckmann, 1966), and also gender relations (see Smith, 1987), the gendering of the film director and producer, as well as the hierarchy of the two of them, may be a central element in the reproduction of the gender power structures in the film industry.

Notes

1. Structured along two poles, the autonomous pole based on cultural capital – prestige (taste), consecration and artistic celebrity – and the opposite pole based on economic capital, the field of cultural production is an 'economic

world reversed', according to Bourdieu. This is so because the cultural pole has a positive connotation while the economic pole is marked negatively. All cultural practices are situated anywhere between these two poles (or principles of legitimacy). Moreover, he regards these principles of legitimacy as autonomous and internal (cultural capital) and heteronomous and external (economic capital). Thus *high* art, such as classical music and serious literature, are based on internal principles of hierarchization, whereas mass culture or popular culture is based on external principles of hierarchization.

2. These figures include a wide range of films: documentaries, children's films, feature films and short films; all are films that have been shown in movie theatres in Sweden. Women directors dominate the children's film section.

3. Statistics from the Swedish Film Institute's home page: www.sfi.se

4. The small scale of Swedish film education has made Swedish textbooks in production-oriented courses a rarity (G. Burstedt, School of Photography and Film at Göteborg University, e-mail interview, 29 August 2000). Consequently, an examination of US-based educational programmes and their accompanying textbooks provides a resource for this study which centres on the graduate programme in film at the Tisch School of the Arts, New York University. For many years, Tisch has been ranked by US News and World Report as the best film school in the United States (Mackaman, 1997). Students completing the Tisch programme earn a Master of Fine Arts (MFA) in film and television. I assume that textbooks used in the film programme of a top-ranked school are influential in film education elsewhere too.

5. However, the construction of the business executive is here seen from the perspective of the cultural field rather than the economic field.

References

Abrahamsson, L. (2002) Just när det blev viktigt blev det manligt. *Kvinnovetenskaplig tidskrift*, 1, pp. 37–52.

Acker, J. (1988) Class, gender and the relations of distribution. *Signs*, 13 (3), pp. 473–97.

Adler, N., and D. Izraeli (eds) (1988) *Women in management worldwide*. Armonk, NY: M.E. Sharpe.

Ahl, H. (2002) The making of the female entrepreneur: A discourse analysis of research texts on women's entrepreneurship. Unpublished doctoral dissertation, Jönköping International Business School.

Alvesson, M., and A.-S. Köping (1993) *Med känslan som ledstjärna: En studie av reklamarbete och reklambyråer*. Lund: Studentlitteratur.

Berger, P.L., and T. Luckmann (1966) *The social construction of reality. A treatise in the sociology of knowledge*. New York: Doubleday.

Bologh, R.W. (1990) *Love or greatness: Max Weber and masculine thinking: a feminist inquiry*. London: Unwin Hayman.

Bordwell, D., and K. Thompson (1993) *Film art: An introduction*. New York: McGraw-Hill.

Bourdieu, P. (1984) *Distinction: a social critique of the judgement of taste*. Cambridge, MA: Harvard University Press.

Bourdieu, P. (1993) *The field of cultural production: essays on art and literature.* New York: Columbia University Press.

Brown, C., and J.A. Pechman, (eds) (1987) *Gender in the workplace.* Washington, DC: Brookings Institution.

Caves, R.E. (2000) *Creative industries: contracts between art and commerce.* Cambridge, MA: Harvard University Press.

Collinson, D., and J. Hearn (1996) Breaking the silence: On men, masculinities and managements. In D. Collinson and J. Hearn (eds), *Men as managers, managers as men: critical perspectives on men, masculinities and managements,* pp. 1–24. London: Sage.

Dancyger, K., and J. Rush (1995) *Alternative scriptwriting.* 2nd ed. Newton, MA: Butterworth-Heinemann.

DeFillippi, R.J., and M.B. Arthur (1998) Paradox in project-based enterprise: the case of filmmaking. *California Management Review,* 40 (2), pp. 125–39.

Durkheim, E. (1895/1982) *The rules of sociological method.* New York: The Free Press.

Game, A., and R. Pringle (1984) *Gender at work.* London: Pluto.

Hartman, H. (1981) The unhappy marriage of Marxism and Feminism. In L. Sargent (ed.), *Women and revolution.* Boston: South End Press, 1–41.

Hermele, V. (ed.) (2002) *Män, män, män och en och annan kvinna.* Stockholm: Svenska Filminstitutet.

Hirdman, Y. (1988) Genussystemet – reflektioner kring kvinnors sociala underordning. *Kvinnovetenskaplig tidskrift,* 3, pp. 49–63.

Holgersson, C. (2003) *Rekrytering av företagsledare: en studie i homosocialitet.* Stockholm: EFI.

Höök, P. (2001) *Stridspiloter i vida kjolar.* Stockholm: EFI.

Kanter, R.M. (1977) *Men and women of the corporation.* New York: Basic Books.

Katz, S.D. (1991) *Film directing, shot by shot. Visualizing from concept to screen.* New York: Michael Weiss Productions.

Lauzen, M. (2003) *The celluloid ceiling: Behind-the-scenes and on-screen employment of women in the top 250 films of 2002.* Retrieved 25 September 2003 from <http://www.5050summit.com/stats2003.html>

Lindgren, G. (1996) Broderskapets logik. *Kvinnovetenskaplig Tidskrift,* 1 (4), p. 14.

Lindgren, G. (1999) *Klass, kön och kirurgi. Relationer bland vårdpersonal i organisationsförändringarnas spår.* Malmö: Liber.

Mackaman, J. (1997) *Filmmakers' resource. The Watson-Guptill guide to workshops, conferences, artist colonies, academic programs.* Watson, NY: Guptill Publications.

Moran, A. (ed.) (1996) *Film policy: international, national and regional perspectives.* London: Routledge.

Miles, M., and Huberman, M. (1994) *Qualitative data analysis.* London: Sage.

Rabiger, M. (1992) *Directing the documentary.* 2nd ed. Newton, MA: Butterworth-Heinemann.

Rabiger, M. (1997) *Directing. Film techniques and aesthetics.* 2nd ed.. Boston: Focal Press.

Smith, D. (1987) *The everyday world as problematic.* Boston: Northeastern University Press.

Stenström, E. (2000) *Konstiga företag.* Stockholm: EFI.

Vinterheden, K. (1991) *Om kvinnor i svensk filmproduktion.* Stockholm: Svenska kvinnors filmförbund.

Wahl, A. (1992) *Könsstrukturer I organisationer.* Stockholm: EFI.

Wahl, A. (1996) Företagsledning som konstruktion av manlighet. *Kvinnovetenskaplig Tidskrift,* 1, pp. 15–29.

Wahl, A., K. Regnö, P. Höök, C. Holgersson, S. Linghag, Y. Svanström and A. Karlssson-Stider (2003) *Mansdominans i förändring: Omledningsgrupper och styrelser. SOU,* 16. Stockholm: Fritzes.

Walby, S. (1986) *Patriarchy at work. Patriarchal and capitalist employment.* Minneapolis: University of Minnesota Press.

In addition, course syllabi for Directing; Production management; Producing the documentary; Writing the feature (New York University: The Tisch School of the Arts).

5

Can art be a leader? Beyond heroic film directing

Marja Soila-Wadman

The aesthetic event

It is dark, hot and smoky in the studio. Beeswax has been heated in a frying pan to manufacture smoke, and the smell in the studio is so bad it has given someone a headache. The set is crowded. Cameras, electric cables and lighting equipment are everywhere. People dash around between takes and everything is chaotic.

Actors arrive on the set for rehearsal. An older man points a gun at a younger man's head. The A and B photographers measure the distance between the camera and the heads of the actors while the director listens to the dialogue going on between them. The sound technician tries to find an appropriate place for the microphone and then checks the sound. Two of the actors sit close together on the set, and the makeup person dabs glycerin on the neck of one actor to give the impression of sweat.

Good camera angles are hard to come by. The director and the photographer decide to shoot the scene over and over again. The director complains that someone has brought coffee into the room and has jeopardized the equipment in the cases. He yells at the assistant who replies with the frying pan.

The director calls out, 'Silence! Action! Camera!' and his words cause an instant transformation. It is as if everyone begins concentrating all at once. Although the atmosphere is supercharged, everything is still except for the moves of the actors and the camera rolling. Time and time again the actors have to perform the same movement, express the same words and display the same emotion with feeling. It is a tough scene as far as content and emotion go.

The script person wonders if any earlier take has been good enough. The photographer wants one more. The new one is no good, and the photographer asks for another. The director sighs. Even though the photographer wants to do one more, the director is for going with what they have. The photographer says s/he's not trying to mess with anyone, but getting a good shot is difficult when s/he has to move the camera. They cannot be certain that any of the takes is good. They change the camera objectives several times. The photographer and director talk about different angles. Should the camera follow the first actor's look at the other actor's neck? The light technician makes a suggestion. The photographer wants to change the background light. The actor wonders whether or not the light closest to her or his head could explode. The electrician says it won't.

The actors laugh and joke between takes. The assistant director remarks that the actors always joke a lot. It's a way to keep your nerves under control. The director decides he needs more sweat drops on the neck of the actor. The makeup person dabs more glycerin. The director wonders if the actor's cap should be dirtier and asks the photographer his opinion. The photographer doesn't want to have an opinion. The director makes the decision that the cap must be more soiled. The makeup person dirties it further.

Stress. Problems with the camera angle. Smoke is needed, but the beeswax is not in place. Fetch. Wait. The script person and the makeup person play paper, rock, scissors. Someone trips over the frying pan. Sweat drops are needed on the neck of the actor again. The glycerin sponge looks disgusting. The photographer wants to discuss how they are to complete the rest of the day's scheduled work. The associate producer wants to know if they can reduce the number of takes and complete the most important ones first. S/he fears they might not have enough time for all the takes. The producer wants to know how much film has been used. 'Not that much', say the photographer and the director. There is enough to complete the shooting.

One actor must be shaved before the next take. The director is irritated because the producer has not anticipated what that will mean in terms of time. The director is also annoyed that the assistant has forgotten to spray some surfaces that are to appear wet. The director groans and wonders if s/he really has to think of everything. The photographer says it is all too much right now. Then things cool down. Time for the next take. 'Silence! Action! Camera!'

Eventually, they didn't live happily ever after. (Should they have?) A shooting is such a chaotic mixture of angst laced with solidarity, intimacy, playfulness and jocularity.

Management or magic

These episodes are part of an ethnographic study of the shooting phase of a film project; the study focuses on the leadership and organizational processes in filmmaking (Soila-Wadman, 2003b). These scenes take only a few minutes on the screen, but shooting them ate up two days.[1]

Making a film is a risky business. It involves expression, organization and, not the least, economics. While part of the film director's role is to manage the uncertainty and the consequences of that uncertainty in a film project, the question is whether or not it is even possible to manage an uncertain art-creating process. This question is provoked by normative project management literature in which one proceeds from the dream that a project is realized through an explicitly planned goal achieved by means allocated in advance and within a specified time. It is the 'superman' that is desired in the leadership role of a project.

In Swedish film production the director has the authority to make the 'final cut'. That means that the director has the right to decide what the final film text – the aesthetic product – is going to look like. This chapter explores some aspects of filmmaking organization and leadership. Questions to be considered include: How are organization and leadership constructed in the everyday professional activity of filmmaking practice? How does an effective film director act in order to lead/manage[2] the artistic process in a film team when the script is created in a film form? Other questions have been raised about a leader's judgment and decision-making activity also.

In addition to the ethnographic study, this chapter is based on interviews with various professionals in film production; these include two Swedish female film directors Christina Olofson (Soila-Wadman, 2003a) and Marianne Ahrne. This research is a reading of a 'foreign culture' of film projects (Law, 1994; Geertz, 1973; Czarniawska, 1997) from a platform of business administration and organization theory but without traditional managerial jargon. By participant observation and by listening to actors in film production talk about their everyday working conditions, the aim has been to find out how filmmaking takes place *in practice*.

Although interest in business administration in the context of film production has increased (Jäckel, 1998; Björkegren, 1994,

1996; De Fillippi and Arthur, 1998; Jones, 2001; Alvarez *et al*. 2002), little research material is currently available. Several biographical reports of filmmaking exist, written by practitioners in the field, but in theoretical cinematic literature, extensive research about the filmmaker as a project leader with connections to the creative working process on a production (Jerselius cited in Soila-Wadman, 2003b) has not been made part of the literature.

Interest in film science and post-Second World War film directors has centered on a debate on the *auteur* theory. Since the 1950s, the dominant view has been to consider a specific film as manifesting an individual artistic will, and the director has been viewed as an 'auteur' or author of the film. Eventually the film began to be viewed as a product of several people's work, where the director could not be ascribed control over the final film text (Andersson, 1999; Bordwell and Thompson, 1997; Hollows, 1995; Koskinen, 2000; Lapsley and Westlake, 1988). This debate has connections to the long-time discussion about the role of an artist and art and has given some inspiration for the reasoning in this chapter.

Since the film product is an aesthetic one, creating an understanding of the leadership and organizational dynamics in a film project must include the aesthetic slant as well. The aesthetic approach in organizational analysis has gained attention in recent decades (Barrett, 2000; Gagliardi, 1996; Guillet de Monthoux, 1993, 1998, 2000; Lindstead and Höpfl, 2000; Ramirez, 1991; Strati 1996, 1999, 2000). In this approach, the rational analysis of the organization is problematized, and essential aspects like emotions, intuition, improvisation and fantasy are emphasized. Several authors have also criticized the phenomenon of disembodiment in organizational writings and point out the importance of noticing that organizations, art-creating or other, are populated by persons with a material body (Strati, 1999; Ropo and Parviainen, 2001). For instance, some situations in a film project show expressions of strong feelings; sensitive issues surface when the director and the actor search for a correct expression or when the director and photographer try to find the optimal camera position.

Further, what about the magic an observer feels when studying a group of people in action around the camera? The director calls out 'Silence! Action! Camera!' and everything becomes quiet. The focus is on the actors' performance and the camera rolling. In this type of situation, who holds the decision-making responsibility? Is it the director? What type of leadership is evident here?

Relational leadership

One take on leadership goes back to Stogdill's 1950 definition. This perspective is still common among several researchers: 'Leadership may be considered as the process of influencing the activity of an organized group in its efforts toward goal setting and goal achievement' (p. 3). The goal for the director, actors and team is to give a filmic form to the story in the manuscript, and through this to create an artistic product. As the Swedish film director Olofson describes it:

> You have a manuscript in your hand, a story. What you want then is to be able to raise it from the paper, to turn it into something with feeling and life, together with a photographer and the actors, who on their part give life, body, and soul to the parts they create in the film. You want to create a feeling of authenticity, something that can affect the audience. (Cited in Soila-Wadman, 2003b, p. 86)

5.1 Shooting the film Happy End, 1998. From left: actors Stefan Norrthon and Harriet Andersson with director Olofson. According to Olofson, when a director shoots a film, one of her or his most important tasks is to create relationships of trust with the actors

(Still photographer Joakim Strömholm)

Searching through earlier research in the empirical and theoretical fields to find models for understanding both organization and leadership raised doubts about the traditional narratives of leadership in business administration – planning, coordination, governing and controlling – and the narratives of leaders as charismatic heroes, where the leader is assumed to be in full control of the course of events. Consequently, as a result of these doubts, looking at less mainstream discussions on leadership viewed in a relational perspective (Dachler and Hosking, 1995) turned out to be more rewarding. The epistemological position this perspective is based on is that knowledge and meaning are negotiated by 'multiloguing' in conversations where more voices than just the leader's or author's voice participate in the exchange.

The advocates of relational leadership are critical of the view of human beings in traditional management literature and term it entitative or possessive individualism (Dachler and Hosking, 1995). From the traditional point of view, leaders have certain qualities that make them suitable for their role. They are, for example, superior to their co-workers in terms of knowledge. They are heroes with 'charisma'.[3]

According to the traditional perspective, the goals and interests of the leader are considered privileged compared to those of people subjected to this leadership. In this model the leader is presented as the subject, and the co-workers are like objects. The central problematic here is how the leader/subject is to make the co-workers/object think, speak or act so as to reflect the leader's perspective. As far as social relationships go, the subject exploits the object in order to achieve knowledge and influence over other people and groups. Relationships are viewed as instrumental. The assumption is that the hero-leader is in control of the course of events.

Conversely, Dachler and Hosking (1995) want to focus on a relational perspective in organizational theorizing. Leadership seen from the relational perspective poses questions about the social processes within which a specific leadership model has been and is continuously being construed. Leadership is seen as dispersed in an organization. The leader shares responsibility with others in the construction of this understanding and, in the long run, in its execution. The leader is just one of many voices.

In the relational perspective, leadership cannot be defined by how successful or unsuccessful a leader is or by what special qualities she or he has. The main question is rather how the leader and those s/he interacts with are responsible for the type of relationships they jointly construe. The differences that exist within an understanding of oneself, the other and the state of things should be noticed and negotiated. The leader's attention will then focus to 'multiloguing, negotiating, and networking', as well as other social narratives dealing with the meanings in individual and collective activities. Doing this in practice means engaging in small talk, on both formal and informal levels. Though these conversations may seem trivial at times, it is in these communications that emotions and ambitions are expressed, and ideals, norms and rules are created, interpreted and re-interpreted (Gustafsson, 1994; Sjöstrand *et al.*, 2001; Ekman, 2001). Rather than isolating leadership and organizing as separate phenomena, they can be viewed as mutually constructing each other in human interactions.

Of course the overriding question is how these ideas about organizing and leadership apply to an art-creating field? Should the character of the artistic work be taken into account when talking about which kind of leadership theory does justice to art-creating organizations? Further, does the discussion concerning whether or not art work is similar to work of any other kind have connections to the nineteenth-century notion of the role of an artist as a romantic, lonely genius (Becker, 1982; Wolff, 1993)?

As mentioned earlier, the director has the right to the 'final cut' in Swedish film production. This compares to the practice in much of the European film industry and contrasts with the producer-ruled Hollywood film industry. 'It is the director who owns the film', one interviewee said in describing the ownership of the artistic contents in a film. Bordwell and Thompson (1997) report that according to several cinema researchers, the role of the director is the one coming closest to having an overall grasp of filmmaking in the shooting and editing phase. This is not to imply that the director can influence every decision but that the role of the director synthesizes the whole process and gathers the recorded contributions of the actors in the editing phase.

In director-ruled filmmaking, a spirited entrepreneurial drive is needed not only for shooting and editing but to propel the process forward as well. According to a popular story, Swedish film director Bo Widerberg started his projects only if he had a vision and will to tell the story. It was of little concern that the finances might not necessarily be in order or that the manuscript might exist only as some sheets of paper on the floor.[4] A portrait of the film director Werner Herzog indicates that nothing could have stopped him when he was making a film about transporting a steamship over a mountain in the Amazon jungle (Bjerkman, 1992; Brännberg, 1996). In this kind of filmmaking, the artistic vision organizes the whole process that leads to the creation of a final product.

As Laurent Lapierre puts it:

> For the creator, the most important thing is to follow through on an idea, an image or the theme that haunts him; for the designer – artist (conductor, choreographer, director, decorator, lighting designer), it is to offer his personal interpretation of a new or existing work; and for the performer (soloist, concert artist, dancer, actor) it is to recreate the work, score, or role by relying not only on his technical skill or virtuosity but more importantly, on his artistic sensibility and intelligence. The mission of the arts organisation is rooted in art, not in the market perceived as a business opportunity to generate wealth for individuals or for a group. The mission of the arts organization has its source in the creators and performers who have made art the focus of their professional and personal life. For these individuals, art is a way of seeing and creating, a means of self-fulfilment and of relating their times. The very fact of creating a work of art implies a desire to communicate. (2001, p. 5)

The next question then is: Is a single artist, like a film director, really a leader in the creation of her artwork? The field notes for this ethnographic study illustrate a thesis where art itself – not some kind of heroic leader – is the true organizer. The artistic expression-in-becoming in filmmaking practice is bringing out, bursting out, organizing itself in an ongoing negotiation process between the involved actors in the film team in front of the camera and behind the camera. In the collaborative team, members are testing varying camera angles, lighting, actor interpretations, positions and sound. They are thinking, watching, feeling, acting. They are talking about how to find solutions. For example, what is the solution for a situation when you have hail when, according to the script, you should have sun? Or the house – which should be burned down in the shoot tomorrow – happens to be on fire today? These are incidents that can increase the cost for the project on a large scale. Actors in film production use 'circus' or 'battlefield' to describe the turbulent characteristic of a shooting phase of a film project.

All this transforms a director from being a hero to being 'a vulnerable bulldozer', a description given Swedish film director Marianne Ahrne in her director role. In spite of the fact that careful plans and preparations are made before shooting, one must be prepared for change and improvisation all the time. Ahrne concludes:

On the one hand you must be a commander, who manages the pitched battle that a shooting is like. On the other hand you should be the artistic leader, who catches the moods and creates a secure platform for the actors. In all creation, courage is needed and the actor needs a secure relation to her/his director. It is only then you are capable of tearing away your mask and showing your naked soul. In front of the camera, in spite of all the chaos surrounding you – with people, electric cables, lighting equipment. (Cited in Soila-Wadman, 2003b, p. 72)

A great deal of flexibility and improvisation is necessary as the artistic/creative expression is emerging in a new film. The concept of improvisation is used here to describe a process which involves an openness to emerging possibilities and an ability to act in unexpected situations during a shooting. Gustafsson and Lindahl (2002) emphasize especially that improvisation should not be seen as some kind of amateurism.

Improvisation in a film project concerns both the interaction between the actors themselves and the interaction between the director and the actors. Director Ahrne was looking at a documentary of a shooting with Ingmar Bergman as the director. A situation had come up where an actor was blocked, and Ahrne was impressed by the skill with which Bergman solved the situation:

There is a set where the actor Halvar Björk should have a long monologue in a specific place in a room. Björk gets totally blocked and can't manage it. Bergman goes to Björk, he puts his long arm round Björk's shoulders. He is taking a walk around the room. He gets Björk to tell a story when Björk in the film 'Badarna' acted with Ingrid Thulin whom he would seduce in a hay-barn. Ingrid Thulin had two pairs of panties on her and Halvar should take off one pair of them, meanwhile he was blowing up an airbed with his right foot, and so forth. Everyone who had met Halvar Björk had heard this story, presumably also Bergman. But he gets Björk to tell the story as if it would be for the first time. Bergman looks like there isn't anything in the whole world which could be more important than the story. Thousands of crowns are ticking away, but it doesn't matter. When Björk comes to the point, he is, of course, just on the spot where the monologue would take place. Bergman bursts out into his rumbling laughter, then stops abruptly, and says 'camera!' And, how come, the whole team is there, ready for the take, the camera is rolling.

Björk reads his monologue, relaxed. It is a perfect take. (Cited in Soila-Wadman, 2003b, pp. 84–5)

In addition to being needed in front of the camera, improvisation is also needed when solving the practical problems that arise during the shooting. In order to continue the creative process, if the smoke machine crashes, the smoke must be manufactured by heating beeswax in a frying pan.

Clearly the script is a starting point, and the task for the team is to turn it into a filmic form. The process may be likened to starting an adventure, to seeking something new, to feeling one's way, to undertaking an experiment, to taking a leap into the unknown. When writing about how to understand the process of creating something new, Chia and King (1998) argue for seeing the creative process in the perspective of becoming, viewing it as a flow, as something in motion.

How is it possible to learn this spontaneity that is part of improvising? There are parallels between filmmaking and jazz improvisation. In jazz, according to Barrett (2000), the point is to learn the technique through listening and imitating the playing of the old masters so that improvisation will come automatically. Then it is time to begin with new combinations in different contexts. To be able to avoid routine, one needs to throw oneself into new, unexpected, provoking situations, to take risks. Mistakes should be considered with curiosity as possibilities for something new to break through.

Several professionals who were interviewed emphasized the value of unexpected, even troublesome, situations in film making, to accentuate artistic expression. The challenge is being able to 'keep your cool'. Professionalism and experience are important qualities for the whole team to have in order to tackle troublesome situations; they all must be able to use these qualities in the artistic creation. Director Olofson explained that she didn't like any distinction made between the artistic and technical teams. 'Everyone needs to feel the rhythm of the artistic process', she argued, pointing to the work of the person driving the crane where the photographer and director are sometimes sitting with the camera when filming a moving object, for instance (Soila-Wadman, 2003a).

Improvisation is best performed in a group where the atmosphere is confident, trusting and appreciative; this in turn creates openness for something new to emerge, states Barrett. 'You want to have a team', says one director, 'which is on the same journey in all the turbulent situations.' Barrett writes about a phenomenon where one has the courage to let what is happening happen and does not try to

5.2 Cameraman Robert Nordström and director Olofson sitting on a crane during the shooting of Happy End, 1998

(Still photographer Joakim Strömholm)

control everything. This could be termed the *aesthetics of capitulation* (Soila-Wadman, 2003b). For this to happen in a film project, planning should take into consideration the possibility, even the likelihood, of change. The original plan should always include alternate strategies. And everyone should be aware that even the alternate plans might have to change. In a group, subtle, tacit knowledge is needed. Members should have open minds, sensitive to the emerging dynamics. The need is for aesthetics, not anaesthesia.

Death of heroic leadership

In the shooting phase of a film project, leadership can be viewed as para-doxical. On the one hand, there is a steep hierarchy, and on the other, a flat organization with relational communication processes. There is a need for a director who is a careful planner and capable decision-maker, as well as one who drives the process forward. A good director-leader is a playmaker engendering a field for creative flow. S/he is also a repair person with the ability to restore the flow of action, should it stop. Consequently, the role of the director-leader demands an ability to read a situation, and as Shotter (1995) points out, to also render a linguistic formulation for what is to be done.

With the appearance of command and control, leadership in a film project can easily be confused with traditional leadership. As mentioned earlier, film director Ahrne sees the director's tasks as being 'a commander, who manages the pitched battle that a shooting is like'. The director's right to the 'final cut' gives a formal position in the hierarchy from which to make the decisions in a project. When a new shooting phase of a film project is started, it is commonly assumed in a team that it is the director who has the responsibility for the overall action concerning the task: 'the film is the director's', as they say. That means that the director has to make perhaps hundreds of important, as well as trivial, decisions during the day. 'It is a cacophony', someone concludes. If the director fails in his/her decision-making responsibilities, the film-making process may go astray, producing unintended consequences. An outsider lacking experience in what goes on in a film shoot might there-fore mistake a leader for a hero who controls art from the top of his hierarchy.

Leadership in practice, however, is about shaping relations. On loca-tion the team's loyalty to the director's vision is apparent. Team members show a will to go through fire and water for it/him/her, but not as soldiers blindly following a command. The interactive negotiating process transpires in the whole team. Artistic expressions emerge as they perform their everyday tasks and they talk with each other. They listen, they tune in, they think, they watch and they feel. The negotiating process even takes place nonverbally through bodily movements, as the director and actors search for expressions, when the photographer and director try to find optimal camera angles, or when the art director with his assistants construct the desirable milieu. Planning and control become conditions for facilitating the organizing process; they are necessary but hardly sufficient. For the team to collaborate, the leader has to prepare the groundwork and condition the relational processes. This is accomplished by making correct decisions in order to keep the process going. When improvisation is needed, the whole team – not just the director – tackles the turbulence. As a director, according to Marianne Ahrne, 'you should be the artistic leader who catches the moods and creates a secure platform for the actors'.

What is this leadership about then? The Russian artist Ilja Kabakov gives the following advice to the art leader in situations where a universally accepted system of values is lacking:

> Your personality, your interests, your psychological reactions must cooperate with reactions in your ensemble. This interplay takes place on an almost biological, erotic level. And it will be eroticism which is the only socializing method, because all other methods have long ago collapsed. That is why the bodily characteristics play such a great role. (Cited in Guillet de Monthoux, 1998, p. 210)

Notes

1. No names are given because the team wishes to remain anonymous.
2. The concepts lead/manage and leader/manager are used here synonymously, with inspiration from Czarniawska-Joerges and Wolff (1991). They write that in practice the roles of leader and manager are difficult to separate. Additionally, they remind us not to forget the role of an entrepreneur. This is illustrative as it concerns management in Swedish film production with limited economic resources.
3. Different phases in leadership research are discussed by Yukl (2002) and Bryman (1996).
4. Documentary film on Bo Widerberg by film director Stefan Jarl.

References

Alvarez, J.L., C. Mazza, J. Strandgaard and S. Svejenova, (2002) Shielding idiosyncrasy from isomorphic pressures: The becoming of European film mavericks. Paper presented at EGOS 18th Colloquium, Barcelona, Spain.

Andersson, L.G. (1999) Decamerone: Europeisk konstfilm; auteurer och adaptationer. In L.G. Andersson and E. Hedling, *Film analys*, pp. 65–78. Lund: Studentlitteratur.

Barrett, F.J. (2000) Cultivating an aesthetic of unfolding: jazz improvisation as a self-organizing system. In S. Lindstead and H. Höpfl (eds), *The aesthetics of organization*, pp. 228–45. London: Sage.

Becker, H. (1982) *Art worlds*. Berkeley: University of California Press.

Bjerkman, A. (1992) *Projektmakare: en liten bok om att våga*. Floda: Xenon.

Björkegren, D. (1994) *Filmens företag*. Stockholm: Nerenius & Santerus AB.

Bordwell, D., and K. Thompson (1997) *Film art: an introduction*. New York: McGraw-Hill.

Brännberg, T. (1996) Eldsjälar och projektmakare. In I. Sahlin (ed.), *Projektets Paradoxer*, pp. 144–58. Lund: Studentlitteratur.

Bryman, A. (1996) Leadership in organizations. In S.R. Clegg, C. Hardy and W.R. Nord (eds), *Handbook of organization studies*, pp. 276–92. London: Sage.

Chia, R., and I.R. King (1998) The organizational structuring of novelty. *Organization*, 5 (4), pp. 461–78.

Czarniawska, B. (1997) *Narrating the organization*. London: University of Chicago Press.

Czarniawska-Joerges, B., and R. Wolff, (1991) Leaders, managers and entrepreneurs on and off the organizational stage. *Organization Studies*, 12 (4), pp. 529–46.

Dachler, H.P., and D.M. Hosking (1995) The primacy of relations in socially constructing organizational realities. In D.M. Hosking, H.P. Dachler and K.J. Gergen (eds), *Management and organization: relational alternatives to individualism*, pp. 1–28. Aldershot: Avebury.

De Fillippi, R.J., and M.B. Arthur (1998) Paradox in project-based enterprise: the case of film making. *California Management Review*, 40 (2), pp. 125–39.

Ekman, G. (2001) Constructing leadership in small talk. In S.-E. Sjöstrand, J. Sandberg and M. Tyrstrup (eds), *Invisible management*, pp. 224–39. London: Thomson Learning.

Gagliardi, P. (1996) Exploring the aesthetic side of organizational life. In C. Clegg, C. Hardy and W. Nord (eds), *Handbook of organization studies*, pp. 565–80. London: Sage.

Geertz, C. (1973) *The interpretation of cultures: selected essays*. New York: Basic Books.

Guillet de Monthoux, P. (1993) *Om det sublimas konstnärliga ledning*. Stockholm: Nerenius & Santerus.

Guillet de Monthoux, P. (1998) *Konstföretaget*. Göteborg: Bokförlaget Korpen.

Guillet de Monthoux, P. (2000) The art of management of aesthetic organizing. In S. Lindstead and H. Höpfl (eds), *The aesthetics of organization*, pp. 35–60. London: Sage.

Gustafsson, C. (1994) *Produktion av allvar*. Stockholm: Nerenius & Santerus.

Gustafsson, C., and M. Lindahl (2002) Improvisation and intuition – From a perspective of emergence theory. Paper presented at EURAM, II Annual Conference, Stockholm.

Hollows, J. (1995) Mass culture theory and political economy. In J. Hollows and M. Jancovich (eds), *Approaches to popular film*, pp. 15–36. Manchester University Press.

Jäckel, A. (ed.) (1998) *What convergence for which media?* Summary of papers presented to the First European Audiovisual Seminar. Bristol: University of the West of England.

Jones, C. (2001) Co-evolution of entrepreneurial careers, institutional rules and competitive dynamics in American film, 1895–1929. *Organization Studies*, 22 (6) pp. 911–44.

Koskinen, M. (2002) Auteuren – person eller konstruktion? In G. Gunér and R. Hamberger (eds), *Auteuren – återkomst eller farväl? Filmkonst* 77, pp. 13–26. Göteborg: Göteborg filmfestival.

Lapierre, L. (2001) Leadership and arts management. *International Journal of Arts Management*, 3 (3), pp. 4–12.

Lapsley, R., and M. Westlake (1988) *Film theory: an introduction.* Manchester University Press.

Law, J. (1994) *Organizing modernity.* Oxford: Blackwell.

Lindstead, S., and H. Höpfl (eds) (2000). *The aesthetics of organization.* London: Sage.

Ramirez, R. (1991) *The beauty of social organization.* Munich: Accedo.

Ropo, A., and J. Parviainen, (2001) Leadership and bodily knowledge in expert organizations: An epistemological rethinking. *Scandinavian Journal of Management*, 17 (1), pp. 1–18.

Shotter, J. (1995) The manager as a practical author: A rhetorical-responsive, social constructionist approach to social – organizational problems. In D.M. Hosking, H.P. Dachler and K.J. Gergen (eds), *Management and organization: relational alternatives to individualism*, pp. 125–47. Aldershot: Avebury.

Sjöstrand, S.-E., J. Sandberg and M. Tyrstrup (2001) *Invisible management.* London: Thomson Learning.

Soila-Wadman, M. (2003a) A film director's challenge: to manage – to manage? – A creative process in a film project. *Comportamento organizational e gestao*, 9 (1), pp. 19–36.

Soila-Wadman, M. (2003b) *Kapitulationens estetik. Organisering och ledarskap i filmprojekt.* Stockholm: Arvinius.

Stogdill, R.M. (1950) Leadership, membership and organization. *Psychological Bulletin*, 47, pp. 1–14.

Strati, A. (1996) Organization viewed through the lenses of aesthetics. *Organization* 3 (2), pp. 209–18.

Strati, A. (1999) *Organization and aesthetics.* London: Sage.

Strati, A. (2000) The aesthetic approach in organization studies. In Linstead and Höpfl.

Wolff, J. (1993) *The social production of art.* London: Macmillan.

Yukl, G. (2002) *Leadership in organizations.* New York: Prentice Hall.

Part II

Conditions for new leadership: business

6

Body business: projects for Weight Watchers

Emma Stenström

This is a story about a multinational company named Weight Watchers, a booming body business in the growing economic sector of the body industry. The story is more than just an industry success story, however. Since few alternatives to the Weight Watchers organization exist in Sweden, and since the company is closely connected to the public health sector, this weight-loss firm also plays an important role in shaping ideals and constructing the discourse of dieting.

Aesthetics and management – two forces internalized in the business itself as well as in its customers – are the focus of this story. Some argue that these forces are inseparable and together create the success of the company. These forces may also create success for the customer in a few rare cases. And while the low rate of customer success appears to have nothing to do with company success, it does set up an interesting paradox: the higher rate of failure for customers *seems* to lead to a higher rate of success for the business. Customers tend to come back and pay over and over again for the same service, the same experience, the same dream.

The Weight Watchers case illustrates how aesthetics works on different levels. The aesthetic ideal of the contemporary body – slim, fit and healthy – is an ideal continually produced and reproduced in society in general and in Weight Watchers in particular. Aesthetics also works on another level. Following the programme creates in itself an embodied experience. Anyone who has lost weight probably remembers the feeling of pleasure and pride, the feeling of *being* a body, instead of *having* a body. And since this programme works in the short run, this aesthetic feeling, this embodied experience, is created within the customers through deliberate management. This is managed aesthetics not only when it comes to the aesthetic ideal, which is obvious, but also when it comes to the aesthetic feeling, the embodied experience. The programme requires that one follow a rather rigid, almost Tayloristic or specialization-by-task approach. Participants constantly measure food and energy values in a sort of self-management. Through these activities, they seem to become liberated. They turn into successful sensing and sexual human beings – at least if one is to believe their testimonials.

This is also the story of how a fit and slender body is considered a beautiful body. And how a beautiful body is considered and constructed as capital in today's society. This is the story of Weight Watchers, but it could be the story of any body business where aesthetics and management have become incorporated in a double meaning.

The bodily turn

Weight Watchers belongs to the body business, a rather neglected field in business administration. Although the business is fast-growing in practice, little is known about how it functions. One explanation for the lack of knowledge might be that the body itself has seldom been explicitly expressed in business administration or in other human or social sciences either.

This oversight seems to be undergoing adjustment, however, just as it has in the fields of philosophy and sociology. These areas have witnessed what some call a 'bodily turn' (Welton, 1999; Casey, 2000) over the last decade. In other words, the body has emerged from the dark and come into focus as an organizing force in society, one impossible to dismiss if we are to understand contemporary life. Today's society, for example, can be characterized as a 'somatic society', a society 'within which major political and personal problems are both problematized in the body and expressed through it' (Turner, 1996, p. 1).

As the body moves into greater focus, how will it be perceived? Johannesson, drawing on Bakhtin, talks about the renaissance body as an 'open body', a body created and creating and always mirroring the world. This body is juxtaposed with the modern body, an autonomous body, rationalized and possible to control. This is a view of the body dominated by medicine and, to some extent, social policy (Johannesson, 1997). As she and many others argue, the emerging body has once again become an open body, a stage where nature and culture meet. According to Foucault, the body has become a platform for power and control, and Elias sees it as a focus for the process of civilization. The body has become a container for ideology and culture, a source for metaphors and a language in itself (Johannesson, 1997). Furthermore, as others have pointed out, the body collects a great deal of interest just because it spreads over so many borders. It is, for example, simultaneously physical and symbolic, a subject and an object, both nature and culture.

Though this may be a given, it is not obvious that we are embodied in management settings. Lennie makes the point that it is striking how many illustrations of heads and how few of bodies exist in textbooks on management and leadership. The body is, using Schilling's expression, 'an absent presence' (1993, p. 9) in mainstream management and organization theory. It has, for example, rarely been the centre of analysis. Instead management, leadership and work in general have been regarded as disembodied and disembodying practices (Lennie, 2000). Strati expresses it this way:

> As soon as a human person crosses the virtual or physical threshold of an organization, s/he is purged of corporeality, so that only her or his mind remains. Once a person has crossed this threshold, therefore, s/he is stripped of both clothing and body and consists of pure thought, which the organization equips with work instruments and thus reclothes. (1999, p. 3)

The notable exception in management and organization theory is gender studies. As is the case in feministic approaches in general, the body has seldom been taken for granted in studies of gender and organization. Rather, it has been problematized over and over again in relation to sexuality in organizations (Höök, 2001; Price and Shildrick, 1999).

In addition to gender studies, part of the explanation for the dismissal of the body in management and organization theory lies in the field of feminism. Management has been constructed by and large as a male practice in accordance with the construction of masculinity. Male leadership is the norm; female becomes the deviation. Since masculinity in the cultural, constructed sense is associated with the mind and femininity with the body, it comes as no surprise that the body has received little attention in management. The body is seen as something uncontrollable, something 'female'. Business management is all about gaining control, managing and being a 'man.' As Nietzsche postulated, the disregarding of the body is the outcome of a desire to make everything practical, comprehensible, controllable and exploitable.

On the other hand, body traces are clear and obvious in the work of Taylor, for example. His studies of the most rational movements of the human body at work come to mind almost immediately. Maslow and Herzberg are others who pay attention to bodies and bodily needs.

That said, it is still evident that the mind is superior in their work; for example, bodily needs take the lower steps in Maslow's hierarchy of needs and hygiene ones in Herzberg's theory of factors (Hancock and Tyler, 2000).

The body has been a vehicle for work and a site for rationalization for a long time. 'We labor on, in and with our bodies' (Turner, 1996, p. 185), and the body continues to be the premier medium through which work is carried out (Hancock and Tyler, 2000). It is difficult, for example, to think of a job or occupation without picturing somebody – a body – carrying it out. It also seems as if bodies have become increasingly more important as signifiers of certain organizations and organizational values, with body image becoming more important than ever (Hancock and Tyler, 2000).

Today's 'body industry' has grown into a multi-billion dollar industry and thus become a major sector of the economy (Schilling, 1993). Weight Watchers is part of this industry and can therefore be used as an example of how 'body business' is conducted in today's society.

A case of body business

In the early 1960s, Jean Nidetch, an American housewife living in the New York borough of Queens, invited some friends over to discuss how best to lose weight. Soon the meetings were held on a regular basis, and as more women joined the original group, the meetings had to be moved to a nearby church.

Today, over 1.5 million people attend approximately 44,000 Weight Watchers meetings led by over 15,400 leaders in 30 countries. In 40 years the company has become the world's leading provider of 'weight loss services', a term they themselves use to describe what they do. And although the programmes, services and products have changed over the years, the core of the business remains a weekly meeting, with weight loss promoted through education and group support. Nidetch's original business principle – the cost of a meeting should be equivalent to the pre-tax cost of a movie ticket – has also been preserved.

Nidetch remained the owner of the company until 1978, when she sold it to Heinz. Since Heinz had for many years produced frozen dinners in cooperation with Weight Watchers, the move was a logical one. In 1999, Heinz sold the company to Artal Luxembourg, the private European investment company that took Weight Watchers to the New York Stock Exchange in 2001. Heinz retained some interest, and today Heinz and Weight Watchers jointly own WW Foods.

The close connection between the food industry and Weight Watchers is an interesting one. Heinz produced everything from soups and ketchup to snacks. Until 2001, Artal was the owner of Keebler, the second largest manufacturer of cookies and crackers in the US, and the company continues to be a major player in the world's food business. In a recent report about China, for example, Artal is ranked number one when it comes to foreign interests in the food business.

Weight Watchers is a winning business concept. Over recent years, it has done well financially, and since its appearance on the Stock Exchange, its stock has risen approximately 75 %. In 2002, for example, earnings were a record high, with predictions of even higher earnings for the following fiscal year. In 2002, operating income went up 52 % to a record high $297 million, while revenues increased 30 %. Finally, product sales grew 39 % worldwide, accounting for 29 % of the revenue.

The first nine months of 2003 saw a continuation of the trend. Net revenues grew 17 %; operating income, 6.4 %. Worldwide attendance growth in company-owned operations was 10 %, while worldwide product sales increased 21 % over the previous year. Attendance did not grow quite as fast in the US as it did in the rest of the world, which President and CEO Linda Huett blames on the then-current hype about low-carb diets.

Although performing better than McDonald's, Weight Watchers is organized in a similar manner. It was founded about the same time and has pursued the same kind of franchising strategy in order to build a brand rapidly. Franchises usually pay 10 % of their meeting fees to Weight Watchers International.

The Swedish franchise was started by Lena Lindgren in 1972 and has stayed in the family ever since. Today Lena's daughter Helene manages the operation, and Helene's husband is the marketing director. Some sources claim the Swedish branch has the highest number of members per capita of all operations. The Swedish branch is unique because it has been allowed to operate under its Swedish name. It is not called Weight Watchers, as all the other branches are, but is labeled 'ViktVäktarna'. The brand is very strong, as it is in the US, and brand recognition in Sweden is said to be 96 %.

Approximately 175,000 Swedes become Weight Watchers each year; of these, about 95 % are women, despite several efforts to target men by adding special male meetings and male programmes. Members are expected to attend one of the weekly meetings at one of the 1350 groups held at over 350 locations. The majority come to open classes, but Weight Watchers also holds group classes for many organizations and companies. Customers include universities, cultural organizations, churches, companies like Ericsson and Ikea, municipalities, media, military organizations and, interestingly enough, the ruling Social Democratic Party in Sweden. Some 20 % of Members of Parliament have actually participated in a Weight Watchers programme.

In Sweden, Weight Watchers is also an institution recognized by the public health sector. Some doctors and hospitals have been known to give their patients discounts to Weight Watchers, justifying the programme as one that works...as long as the member follows it! The downside is that not many are able to do that in the long run. Fewer than 20 % of those who join Weight Watchers reach their goal of a Body Mass Index (BMI) of 20–25 %. In addition, it is impossible to accurately estimate how many of those who do reach the goal actually manage to keep the weight off over time. Studies reveal that only 2 % to 5 % of all dieters manage to keep the weight off over a five-year period, and one-third end up weighing more than they did when they started their weight-loss programme. Whether or not these numbers are accurate or even relevant to Weight Watchers, one thing is sure: the chances of succeeding are small.

Yet the company keeps growing and growing. Members, even if they have not succeeded before, return and re-enroll again and again. Weight Watchers itself describes this tendency: 'Members have historically demonstrated a strong re-enrollment pattern across many years.'

Project rhetoric

In the Weight Watchers organization, one is always called a member, never a customer. In the Swedish branch, for example, the rhetoric is that of a civil society rather than that of a commercial company. A number of people believe Weight Watchers belongs to the service sector and are surprised when they hear that a completely commercial American multinational company drives the operation.

Not only is one called a member, one is also treated like a member. Membership includes being part of a self-support group similar to AA or other help groups, and weekly meetings have a strong educational emphasis. Members may attend any meeting anywhere in the country or in the world, but without a valid reason they cannot miss more than six meetings without having to start all over again. The course, as it is called, is designed to cover 16 weeks; then, if a member reaches the goal, he or she is committed to at least an additional six weeks in order to develop eating strategies for maintenance of this goal weight. After finding the balance and maintaining the Weight Watchers' goal of a BMI somewhere between 20 and 25, then the individual becomes a Gold Member. This status carries the entitlement of free membership as long as weight is maintained and meetings are attended on a regular basis.

Over the years the programme at Weight Watchers has been modified and simplified. The current programme is a points programme, one which has eliminated weighing and measuring of ingredients. Depending on your weight, you are assigned a certain number of points per day to be used any way you wish. Nothing is forbidden per se. The programme is presented as having a strong scientific basis and as being a clinically proven approach to weight loss.

In the Points programme, all foods are assigned point values based on their fat and energy content. Some foods are low in points; some are almost without points. Anything high in fat is high in points. As long as you stay within your daily quota, weight loss is assured.

Compared to many other diets, ones which the dieter has to access through books and articles, the advantage of Weight Watchers is the weekly meeting with its support from both leader and group. According to Weight Watcher information, 'During the meetings, members build self-discipline, self-esteem, and self-confidence. This gives the member power to handle the events, temptations, and situations which cause overweight.'

Meetings all over the world follow the same ritual: pay the fee, weigh in, have a short one-on-one chat with a leader, attend a more formal lecture, join in group discussions and questions, and applaud those who have succeeded. This ritual, first devised by Jean Nidetch, has been maintained with only slight modifications throughout the years. Meeting themes are pre-selected, and leaders are trained to start conversations with members about how they have done over the past week.

In many countries leaders are paid on a commission basis. Every leader is a member who has succeeded on the programme. President and CEO Huett lost almost 12 kilos over five months in 1983 and then started her career with the company as a leader. Still faithful to the founding principles of the company, Huett says, 'What worked in Jean Nidetch's living room still works today. We all need to talk. It is talking, listening, and offering support that brings about success.'

Stories of success

Members who have been successful in their weight loss programme are invited to share their story with others at meetings, on the website, and through the Weight Watcher magazine. These obviously edited success stories follow the same general pattern. They start with a description of how the weight was gained, followed by an account of the member's point of realization or insight. This represents the first turning point in the person's life, when she or he starts following the programme, usually accompanied and encouraged by a friend or family member. In the beginning the person is usually skeptical, but when he or she starts losing – always with the help and support of the leader and the group – the attitude shifts. When goal is finally reached, the person's life changes completely.

While these success stories are called 'inspirational', they are also obviously great marketing tools for Weight Watchers. Most contain grateful testimonials: 'You cannot do it on your own. I've made it, thanks to Weight Watchers. To become a Weight Watcher is one of the best things I have done in my life. I know I will always be a Weight Watcher.'

Despite some cultural differences, the Weight Watchers pattern tends to be the same worldwide. In France, even those losing only a few kilos are celebrated as successes. The emphasis is generally on the food, on the possibility of eating everything, and on individual choice. In Australia, where the average member seems to be older, the rhetoric is much more health-oriented; in the US, participants seem to have a great deal more weight to lose. Further, marriage seems to be considered a great reward; a special magazine page is designated for those who marry after finishing the programme. One member even decided to retake wedding photos after having lost the weight.

Photos are also an important part of the success story. These pictures usually include 'before' and 'after' shots, and often the difference between these two photos falls in the areas of posture, clothing, makeup and hairstyle. The 'before' picture is a picture of the person sitting down and looking a bit sad, while the 'after' picture is the person standing up straight with a big smile. Sometimes the 'before' picture is in black and white, while the 'after' one is in color. Sometimes it looks like the first one was taken by an amateur and the second by a professional. Obviously, the participant chooses the 'before' to fit her/his perception of the worst, while the 'after' is selected as the best. The American website contains the following disclaimer under each success story: 'Results are not typical.'

Social fitness

Anyone who has lost weight seems to find it very rewarding, at least if one is to believe the stories. This is a typical quotation from one of these narrations. 'My colleagues think I am nicer and happier. My husband thinks I am better looking and sexier. My children think I am nicer and more patient.'

People around them notice them, sometimes for the first time: 'My life has totally changed. When I was fat, I had the feeling of being transparent. People did not pay any attention to me. Recently, a male colleague asked whether I was new in the company, although I have worked there for ten years. He had never seen me before!'

Members also gain self-confidence: 'I realize that the struggle will never end and that I will have to attend meetings and count my points as long as I want to maintain a healthy weight. It's a small price to pay for having regained my sense of self.'

Sometimes it seems as if it is not until they have reached their goal that they actually become sensual and sexual human beings: 'My body has now started to take shape and that is fun. I feel so very sexy. I have never had that feeling before.'

If one is to believe these success stories, then people generally feel a lot better after losing weight and conforming to the societal ideal. In this sense, losing weight is also an aesthetic, embodied experience. Other people like them better, so they like themselves better. They gain self-confidence and become healthier, happier and richer. They meet new partners or get new opportunities at work; even their closest family members seem to like them better after their weight loss. As one woman revealed, 'The turning point came when M. asked me to marry him.' Later, after she had lost weight and been photographed by a newspaper, the same M apparently said: 'How beautiful you are!' 'Then I felt really happy. My life had changed.' Another woman's story is similar. She tells of how her fiancé's interest grew when she became slim: 'He has never hidden the fact that he was not attracted to me until I had lost weight. Now he is my best watchdog.'

These stories show how the Weight Watcher organization, members and people around them all watch and reinforce the aesthetic ideals of society. They – *or we* – are all watchdogs of the aesthetic ideals. People who lose weight will feel better than before because they have themselves internalized the norms. They will probably command better treatment by others because of their gained confidence and because others share the same norms.

The influential position and large membership of Weight Watchers, especially in Swedish society where it almost has a monopoly on the weight-loss business, make the organization a key player when it comes to creating and recreating aesthetic ideals of the body. Using an institutional perspective towards art may be helpful. The aesthetic ideal of the body can be seen as an ideal created in ways similar to those used in an artistic creation. In other words, it is created in a world, a field, similar to what thinkers such as Bourdieu, Becker and many others have proposed when it comes to art. What is considered art and what is not considered art is determined by the interaction among several actors within a field.

On a micro-level, this could also be working within Weight Watchers. The ideal of a fit, slim body is reproduced over and over in written material and in the courses. It becomes unquestionable, a given, the goal everyone is striving for. It is an aesthetic ideal but also an aesthetic experience created through strong management from Weight Watchers and from the member her/himself. Without the aesthetic ideal and without the aesthetic embodied experience, there would probably be no 'body business', no Weight Watchers.

In the eyes of others

In the somatic society, 'body work' no longer means using your body at work, but rather working your body to have the right image (Schilling, 1993). This has become even more important in a society where experiences, entertainment and immaterial values have become key success factors. When the focus is on consumption rather than production, aesthetics becomes more important (Adkins and Lury, 2000). In culture industries, for example, employers – the casting directors – pay attention to employees (the actors on stage) in terms of looks and image, not only in terms of formal merits (Hancock and Tyler, 2000).

Part of the reason appearance and perception have become increasingly important is that we live in what some might call an aesthetic economy. Aesthetics, both in the more shallow sense of beauty, looks and appearance, and in the deeper sense of a perception through all senses, an embodied experience, is more important than ever. Pine and Gilmore (1999) call it the 'experience economy', where the creation of experiences is creating added value.

This aesthetic turn in society is likely to work in favour of companies like Weight Watchers. It makes it more important to have the 'right' look in order to succeed in the labour market. Part of having the 'right' look is of course having the 'right' weight, a weight that rarely surpasses the Weight Watchers' goal of BMI 25. Longhurst, in her study of managers' relationship to their bodies, shows how many managers long for a slim, fit body and how they directly link that to success for the firm and in work (2001).

Without a doubt, the body has become more central to a person's sense of self-identity in the secularized and individualized modern world. Many have noticed that the body has become a project for many people, something to work on, something to manage. Swedish sociologist Johansson (1997), who has studied fitness, uses the metaphor 'the body as piece of art' to describe how people in the gym relate to their bodies. The body is an 'aesthetic project', which needs to be managed.

Monaghan, referring to Bourdieu, says: 'it appears that in the sport and art of bodybuilding, commitment is dependent upon a "pictorial competence" learnt through habit and exercise' (2000, p. 285). He concludes on the following page: 'It is worth stressing that the body exists both as a sentient and a sensible being.' The sensuous experiences associated with training further contribute to the attraction of body work. Perhaps the pictorial competence is also a competence when it comes to dieting. If this is so, then the publication of photos and stories on the Weight Watchers website and in the Weight Watchers magazine becomes even more understandable.

Calling the body a piece of art or an aesthetic project is common not only in the world of fitness, however. Sociologist Jeudy (1998) calls this association typical for a society in which aesthetics have become idealized, and the body has more than ever become an object.

Women particularly seem to encounter this view of the body and be more or less obsessed with their bodies; this could explain the high number of female members in Weight Watchers (Brumberg, 1997). This is rarely addressed in public, however, and the ideals that are constructed seem to be left unproblematized: 'Thanks to him and Weight Watchers M. could realize an old dream – [his bride would] be thin and walk down the aisle in a princess-looking bride's dress, size 38.'

Brumberg (1997) has shown what a time- and money-consuming project this has turned into. According to her, the body became the central project for many American girls during the twentieth century. It was believed to be the ultimate expression of oneself, and the work on it became more and more intensive during the time, the 'century of svelte', as she calls it.

Today the aesthetic ideal is not just slimness. A contemporary body needs also to have a tight athletic look. According to Bordo (1993), this creates a paradoxical body, oscillating between minimalism and maximalism. Further, the aesthetic ideal today includes the 'aesthetics of health' (Markula, 2001). Spitzak, in Markula's article 'Firm but shapely, fit but sexy, strong but thin,' recognizes the need to be slim in today's society. If you are not fit and trim, you are a bad citizen, a bad employee, a bad wife, a bad mother or a bad whatever. You are bad for society, bad for yourself and bad for business.

Bodies as business

The body of today may be regarded as a piece of art, an aesthetic project, but it is not just art for art's sake. Rather, it is commercial art; a fit body has become capital in today's society (Bourdieu, 1984; Schilling, 1993). The success stories of Weight Watchers confirm it: 'There were several articles about her in a local newspaper and they even had a picture of her and her grandmother on the front page, there were radio interviews....'

In addition, Weight Watchers further capitalizes on this view of the body. Bourdieu (1984) talks about physical capital, a symbolic capital that can be converted into economic capital. Today this capital probably has a better exchange rate than ever before, since the body has not only become aestheticized, but also commodified. With commodification, a value such as health or beauty is turned into a product, a commodity that can be purchased. Featherstone (2001) explains it: 'In a consumer culture, the commodification of health, of body maintenance, develops into corresponding industries that are intimately connected to the whole political and economic system' (p. 67).

Weight Watchers can be regarded as a typical example of this: a profitable, multinational organization selling packaged programmes and products for weight loss and closely connected to a political need to have a healthier, more productive labor force. Featherstone (2001) also points out how this development becomes reinforced by state bureaucracies which need to reduce health costs: 'As the consumption of goods increases, the time required for care and maintenance increases, and the same instrumental rational orientation adopted towards goods is turned inwards onto the body' (p. 88).

Regarding the body as capital can also be seen as typical of modernity. Johannesson (1997) writes: 'It became modern, i.e. enlightened and rational, to view one's body as an individual capital....Interest was concentrated to the individual rather than the group/class and the social belonging. To keep the body fit, to show health and sanity became a new class-marker, a social marker – a way of marketing oneself' (pp. 252–3).

The body has indeed become a brand. It is regarded as a project with narcissistic ends such as personal health, happiness, social success and social acceptability. It is an individualized body, where the owner is the only responsible party.

Spitzak claims that women accept diets and their disciplining control of their bodies because there is always the promise of liberation (Markula, 2001). One Weight Watcher contends: 'To have control gives you a sense of freedom.' In order to reach liberation, one has to do the opposite and follow an almost extreme regime. Weight Watchers illustrates what Featherstone (2001) calls the new relationship between body and self: a calculating hedonism. Although the Weight Watchers programme is a lot more moderate and flexible than most other diets, one is still encouraged to write down and count absolutely everything one eats or drinks each day. There is a constant monitoring and calculating in order to end up consuming the right number of points per day and per week.

When Turner (1991) says that dieting can be understood as a government of the body, it is no exaggeration. Committing to any sort of a diet or becoming part of a Weight Watchers programme is probably one of the more extreme forms of government. Drawing on a Foucauldian view of the control of the body as well as a Weberian notion of the rationalization of industrial civilization, Turner argues that the discourse of dieting has a long history in Western medicine. It has, however, become more widespread than ever due to both the development of capitalism and the demography of Western society (Turner, 1991).

Viewing the body as a business has many implications. First, the body itself tends to become a kind of venture in need of management. Every time I step on the scale, for example, I receive notification of how the week has gone. Second, the language used is similar to business language. Business is used as a metaphor, food is called cheap or expensive, and evaluations are made on the basis of balance sheets and accounts. Karas' 2001 book *The business plan for the body* points out that the language of business management is easily applied to body management. Karas, who is a graduate of Wharton, applies business concepts to weight loss: creating a mission statement, analysing the market, crunching the numbers, allocating revenues, preserving capital and so on. All easily translate into a weight-loss plan like Weight Watchers. Finally, the body is viewed as capital that can be exchanged for economic capital. If one only loses weight, one will succeed in many areas ... including consuming: 'If she lost 30 pounds, he'd buy her diamond earrings.'

If the body is capital, it might also be inherited, not only in a biological sense but also in a social and cultural sense. An example of this is how many Weight Watchers members seem to have been inspired by their mothers, and how they in turn want to inspire their children. The Weight Watchers programme seems to be something that runs in the family, or as one expresses it, a 'family-tradition'. 'My mother became a member when I was 16, and I became a "co-member",' relates one person. Another one describes what her 12-year-old son tells her when she approaches the fridge: ' "Mummy, aren't you a Weight Watcher?" He remembers how awful I felt before; therefore, he is now my major supporter.' Family members are of course no exception when it comes to sharing the norms of society. One woman explained what happened the first time she met her mother after having lost weight: 'My mother started crying and told me that I had become beautiful.'

Aesthetics and management incorporated

The discourses of aesthetics and management/business may sometimes be regarded as oppositional. However, as the Weight Watchers case clearly shows, they can also be successfully combined and create a dynamic force. Somehow this combination of aesthetic ideals and self-management, of regarding the body as a piece of art and a business, seems to be characteristic of the body industry in general. Featherstone, for example, talks about how the contemporary discourse of the body, the consuming body, presupposes a combination of discipline and hedonism. The inner body (concerned with health) and the outer body (concerned with appearance) have become conjoined. What is demanded is a wide-awake, energetic, calculative, maximizing approach to life in order to reach the goals of youth, beauty, fitness, freedom and health (Featherstone, 1982, 2001).

Thinking and talking about Weight Watchers without thinking and talking about both aesthetics and management/business seem more or less impossible. Together they are the foundations of the whole business. They are, in a double meaning, incorporated in the business itself as well as in the customers.

The same might be said to create what Pine and Gilmore (1999) have called the 'experience economy'. Weight Watchers, or the body business in general, has entered the next stage of proposed development: the transformative economy. Certainly Weight Watchers does not fully succeed, but there is no doubt that their over-reaching goal is to transform people, to turn them into something they have not been before: slim, fit and healthy. By providing rules on how to live, Weight Watchers create the experience of what it feels like to be thin and fit. Those who succeed might be those who, built on experiences that are partly aesthetic – that is, experienced through the body – develop wisdom. They have learned how to live, but in order to succeed they must incorporate this wisdom in themselves; they must embody it, since no one can follow the programme and count points forever. This is, as we have seen, not easy.

Transformations are in many situations utopian. Goals can temporarily be achieved, and many people do lose weight with Weight Watchers. Most, unfortunately, tend to regain it again. What is created in the process, however, is the experience of having lost weight, and this experience rests in the memory. Interestingly enough, this memory might be one of the main reasons why so many members re-enroll in the programme over and over.

As a business idea, Weight Watchers is close to unbeatable. Through an almost Tayloristic approach, you create an aesthetical, embodied experience. You create the dream of transformation and it works, if only temporarily. Although it seldom works in the long run, this does not matter, as far as the business approach is concerned. Rather, success is found in the opposite. People come back and pay for the same service, experience, and dream again and again, and that is how the body business works.

Author's note: The study consists of several parts: a participatory study, interviews, and studies of success stories. In this paper, the material used comes from official releases, magazines and websites.

References

Adkins, L., and C. Lury (2000) Making bodies, making people, making work. In L. McKie and N. Watson (eds), *Organizing bodies: policies, institutions and work*, pp. 151–66. Basingstoke: Macmillan.

Bordo, S. (1993) *Unbearable weight. Feminism, Western culture, and the body*. Berkeley: University of California Press.

Bourdieu, P. (1984) *Distinction. A social critique of the judgement of taste*. London: Routledge.

Brumberg, J.J. (1997) *The body project. An intimate history of American girls*. New York: Vintage Books.

Casey, C. (2000) Sociology sensing the body: revitalizing a dissociative discourse. In J. Hassard, R. Holliday and H. Willmott (eds), *Body and organization*, pp. 52–70. London: Sage.

Featherstone, M. (ed.) (2000) *Body modification*. London: Sage.

Featherstone, M. (2001). The body in consumer culture. In J.R. Johnston (ed.), *The American body in context. An anthology*, pp. 18–33. Wilmington, DE: Scholarly Resources, Inc..

Featherstone, M., M. Hepworth and B. Turner (eds) (1991) *The body. Social process and cultural theory*. London: Sage.

Hancock, P., and M. Tyler (2000) Working bodies. In P. Hancock, B. Hughes, E. Jagger, K. Paterson, R. Russell, E. Tulle-Winton and M. Tyler (eds), *The body, culture and society*, pp. 84–100. Buckingham: Open University Press.

Höök, P. (2001) Management as uncontrollable sexuality. In S.-E. Sjöstrand, J. Sandberg and M. Tyrstrup, *Invisible management. The social construction of leadership*, pp. 149–66. London: Thomson Learning.

Jeudy, H.-P. (1998) *Le corps comme objet d'art*. Paris: Armand Colin.

Johannesson, K. (1997) *Kroppens tunna skal*. Stockholm: Norstedts.

Johansson, T. (1997) *Den skulpterade kroppen*. Stockholm: Carlssons.

Johnston, J.R. (ed.) (2001) *The American body in context. An anthology*. Wilmington, DE: Scholarly Resources, Inc.

Karas, J. (2001) *The business plan for the body*. New York: Three Rivers Press.

Lennie, I. (2000) Embodying management. In J. Hassard, R. Holliday and H. Willmott (eds), *Body and organization*, pp. 130–46. London: Sage.

Longhurst, R. (2001) *Bodies. Exploring fluid boundaries*. London: Routledge.

Markula, P. (2001) Firm but shapely, fit but sexy, strong but thin. The postmodern aerobicizing female bodies. In J.R. Johnston (ed.), *The American body in context. An anthology*, pp. 273–309. Wilmington, DE: Scholarly Resources, Inc.

Monaghan, L. (2000) Creating the perfect body: A variable project. In M. Featherstone (ed.), *Body modification*, pp. 267–90. London: Sage.

Pine, J., and J. Gilmore (1999) *The experience economy*. Cambridge, MA: Harvard University Press.

Price, J., and M. Shildrick (eds) (1999) *Feminist theory and the body*. New York: Routledge.

Schilling, C. (1993) *The body and social theory*. London: Sage.

Strati, A. (1999) *Organization and aesthetics*. London: Sage.

Turner, B. (1996) *The body and society*. 2nd ed. London: Sage.

Turner, B. (1991). The discourse of diet. In M. Featherstone, M. Hepworth and B. Turner (eds), *The body. Social process and cultural theory*, pp. 157–69. London: Sage.

Welton, D. (ed.) (1999) *Body and flesh: a philosophical reader*. Malden, MA: Blackwell.

7
Aesthetics at the heart of logic: on the role of beauty in computing innovation

Erik Piñeiro

Must rationality and aesthetics always be at loggerheads? Must the rational imperative suffocate aesthetic feeling? And must aesthetic feeling frustrate the rational imperative? This chapter considers these questions in an environment which at first sight looks lopsidedly unwelcoming to aesthetic concerns. The environment is computer programming, an environment where, even under strict logical and instrumental conditions, aesthetic concerns do flourish. Programmers do value the aesthetic aspects of their work.

This study does not solve the question of the relationship between rationality and aesthetics, but it may offer at least the following insight: even in the exact and demanding world of computer programming, there is a place for questions of an aesthetic nature. Regardless of the restrictions forced upon human activity, if there is as much as an ounce of creative work involved or permitted, aesthetic concerns will thrive.

The phenomenon of computer code aesthetics manifests itself in different ways – so many, in fact, that a single chapter does not have room to cover all of them. For this reason, this chapter focuses on only one of the manifestations of the aesthetic concerns of programmers: their complaints about what they see as unnecessary (and damaging) commercial constraints. The term 'commercial constraints' here refers to the restrictions put on them in the name of 'customer satisfaction', 'time to market', or 'cost savings', for example. Here the programmer is reacting against what might be referred to as economic rationality. And economic rationality might be synonymous with for-profit rationality, for-profit mentality or even short-term profit mentality, depending on whom you are listening to.[1]

This chapter focuses on the problem of programmers who dislike their managers for a specific reason. Not all programmers dislike their managers, of course, and those that do may have other reasons for disliking them than the one considered here, which has to do with the programmers' view of the managers' view of software design and programming.

Programming is a highly rational activity, and so it fits very well into the general opinion of what a rational endeavour is. Programs are logical structures, and computers can only execute direct commands. Therefore, there is absolutely no room for interpretations or vague sentences or explanations. Programming languages are logic, objective and clear. Programming 'nerds', abnormally dedicated programmers, are often depicted as socially impaired people (see, for instance, Turkle, 1997). Their associability is often argued for by explaining that they thrive in the world of perfect 'expectability'. While I do not particularly like the description of dedicated hackers as asocial people, it is true that computers are machines, and they always react in the same way, thereby making interaction with them very different than with humans. In short, programming is as rational as it gets. It is based on perfectly objective interactions with machines that have very detailed predetermined behaviour and do not allow for any sort of vagueness.

Programming is furthermore a very instrumental activity. Programs are written in order to achieve something; they are sets of commands that make the computer do something. This 'something' may turn out to be perfectly useless, but a program always has a mechanical meaning, so to speak. In both senses, the rational and the instrumental, code is the opposite of art. A computer does not understand any subjective subtleties, and a program always fills a function. It is written 'in order to'.

Programming would seem, then, to be a highly rational ambit of activity. Yet even in this world made up of the uncompromising logic of computing and the instrumental value of programs, there is a place for aesthetic feelings. There are beautiful programs and there are ugly programs, and there are many opinions about what it is that makes a program beautiful (Piñeiro, 2003). Consequently, there is also place for disliking managers who will not allow beautiful software to be created because it takes more time or because it cannot be continuously rearranged to fit the will of the user, for instance.

The fact that this aesthetic concern exists carries a number of implications. Most obviously it carries implications for the management of programmers, whose pride in their creations should not be underestimated. It also carries implications of a more general sense: if this concern exists here, shouldn't it exist in every other activity? More specifically, shouldn't it also be an important aspect of the corporation? Just what is the role of aesthetics in innovation? Let us start by looking at what programmers say about managers.

Slashdot

This chapter is based on conversations among programmers 'overheard' on the Internet. They were not speaking to me, and no one was interviewing them; they were simply exchanging opinions in an open forum which anyone (including researchers) can access. This is quite exciting really, having the chance to read what programmers have to say to each other without having to interrupt them...or having to be there at all.

This is a forum targeted towards 'nerds', but it is still a rather generalist one offering a great variety of discussion topics. The setting for this chapter is the *virtual* room where programmers discussed the issue of software aesthetics. The 200 programmers there made the conversation a very rich one; the discussion took all kinds of turns and touched upon many subjects.

The forum of programmers I overheard is called Slashdot (www. slashdot.org). It is probably *the* online forum for programmers, with over 5.9 million visitors and 120 million page views per month.[2] Its slogan, 'News for Nerds. Stuff that matters', is a good indication of the kind of people that frequent it: unapologetic programmers, a number of whom share both a passion for open-source projects, including – but by no means limited to – the operative system Linux, and a hatred of Microsoft.

7.1 Slashdot's homepage header

Much could be said about Slashdot, but if the reader is ready to accept its popularity with English-speaking programmers and the sincere earnestness of the expressed opinions, a short description of the mechanics of taking part in a discussion should suffice.

Moderators at Slashdot present about 15 to 20 different discussions each day for anyone's participation. Click on the corresponding link to access the messages that have already been sent (the virtual room where the discussion is taking place), and then on the other corresponding link to answer any of them. If you do this without registering, your message will appear as being sent by *Anonymous Coward*. On the other hand, registering and thereby becoming a member is a simple thing: fill in a no-fee form and choose an alias. From this moment on, you may log in to Slashdot, and your messages will be presented under your alias instead of the Anonymous Coward label. Becoming a member grants other extras as well: a log of your last messages and a sort of evaluation mark, called 'karma'. These extras do not affect this discussion, however.

Discussions are usually open for several days. In September 2001, Slashdot proposed a discussion carrying the title *Software Aesthetics*. The conversation became quite lively and ended up with 712 entries, although exactly how many individuals participated is hard to tell. Contributors can leave entries without registering (Anonymous Cowards), but the fact that the entry has a name on it does not insure that it is a separate individual because nothing prevents a participant from accessing the forum with different accounts and aliases. The figure of 200 participants, then, is only the result of a vague subjective impression. Nevertheless, the sort of commentaries about management and software uttered in the discussion are representative of a significant proportion of programmers. This is supported in interviews with programmers and by tales from the field. Oh, and one more thing: the discussion had already finished by the time I found it, so I accessed it at the site's archive, where one can read a past discussion but cannot contribute to it. The data were naturally occurring and dead; in other words, it was like a perfectly preserved frozen mammoth.

The choice of *Software aesthetics*[3] as a discussion topic was triggered by an article, as many of Slashdot's selections are. This time the article, entitled 'Software Stinks!' was written by programmer and consultant Charles Connell. As usual, Slashdot presented a summary of the article and a link to the whole thing. Slashdot's summary reads:

Most software design is lousy. Most software is so bad, in fact, that if it were a bridge, no one in his or her right mind would walk across it. If it were a house, we would be afraid to enter. The only reason we (software engineers) get away with this scam is that the general public cannot see inside of software systems. If software design were as visible as a bridge or house, we would be hiding our heads in shame. This article is a challenge to engineers, managers, executives, and software users (which is everyone) to raise our standards about software. We should expect the same level of quality and performance in software we demand in physical construction. Instead of trying to create software that works in a minimal sense, we should be creating software that has internal beauty. (Connell, 2001)[4]

Connell clearly is not impressed by the quality of today's software. Whether he actually has enough empirical evidence to be able to state that 'most software is lousy' is not the concern. For this discussion, the accuracy of his observation is not important, but the way programmers reacted to it is. Despite the broad variety of comments Connell received – and not everything was a compliment – no one actually contradicted him. All participants seemed to accept that software actually stinks, even those who felt insulted by Connell's suggestion that stinking software is the programmers' fault:

> **Re: Beauty for beauty's sake makes crappy software** by **Andrewkov** on 04.09, @04:20PM
>
> This article is demeaning to programmers. The reason quality is poor is due to unrealistic deadlines, the reason projects are over budget is due to poor planning. Most good programmers are capable of creating high quality, elegant code, but are not allowed to because of external pressures that are out of their control.

Programmers did not agree on the questions of what is ugly (or beautiful) software, why so much of it exists or whether bad software is such a bad thing. While the sum of 712 entries leaves ample space for diverse points of view, for the purpose of this chapter the complaints and, more specifically, the reasons given by programmers as to why there is so much ugly software out there are the focus.

Beautiful software

A discussion of what is beautiful software may help to get a handle on what is ugly software. Programmers use the adjective *beautiful* (or *elegant* or *clean*) in a very straightforward and common way: to denote admiration for the form and only the form. First, then, a beautiful program need not be good – as in *used for good causes* – or profitable, or popular or even useful.

When programmers say elegant software or program or application, they mean rather – and also usually say – *code*, that is, the lines of instructions in which the program is codified. In other words, they do not refer to the form of the program as it appears to the user

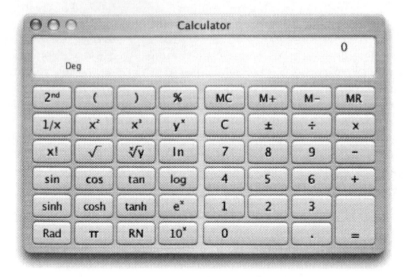

7.2 The program as it appears to the user

but as it appears to the programmer. The following is a very short example of how it appears to the programmer. The code of middle-sized programs contains a few tens of thousands of lines.

```
int m = 754974721, N, t[1 << 22], a, *p, i, e = 1 << 22, j, s, b, c, U;
f (d)
{
for (s = 1 << 23; s; s /= 2, d = d * 1LL * d % m)
  if (s < N)
    for (p = t; p < t + N; p += s)
        for (i = s, c = 1; i; i--)
        b = *p + p[s], p[s] = (m + *p - p[s]) *
        1LL * c % m, *p++ = b % m, c = c * 1LL * d % m;
    for (j = 0; i < N - 1;)
    {
    for (s = N / 2; !((j ^= s) & s); s /= 2);
    if (++i < j)
        a = t[i], t[i] = t[j], t[j] = a;
    }
}
main ()
{
```

```
*t = 2;
U = N = 1;
while (e /= 2)
  {
  N *= 2;
  U = U * 1LL * (m + 1) / 2 % m;
  f (362);
  for (p = t; p < t + N;)
      *p++ = (*p * 1LL ** p % m) * U % m;
  f (415027540);
  for (a = 0, p = t; p < t + N;)
      a += (6972593 & e ? 2 : 1) ** p, *p++ = a % 10, a /= 10;
  }
while (!*--p);
t[0]--;
while (p >= t)
  printf ("%d", *p--);⁵
```

The expression *beautiful program*, or *beautiful code*, is not even related to
what the program looks like once it is running (Figure 1) but what it
looks like when it is being constructed (Figure 2).

The layout of the code itself, often called *coding style*, is only a tiny part
of what programmers mean by beautiful code. Much more important
is the data structure codified in it. One needs to understand the corresponding programming language in order to see that construction, of
course, but it is perfectly possible to follow what Slashdotters say without
being able to read code.

According to the famous programmer and manager Frederick P. Brooks,
Jr., the man behind IBM's legendary OS/360 operating system, programming consists of 'the fashioning of the complex conceptual structures
that compose that abstract software entity, and ... the representation
of these abstract entities in programming languages within space and
speed constraints' (1995, p. 180). Programmers generally refer to these
two tasks as design and coding, respectively, and both require time
and attention. Any middle-sized application – to say nothing of large
ones – contains a huge number of data elements that must fit together.

How precise the fit has to be is not only a question of functionality
or economy. Every misfit is an error in the program, and an optimum
must be met between the cost of avoiding them and the cost of finding
them and fixing them once the program has been written. A precise fit
is also a question of pride and beauty, and without a doubt, a question

of skills, patience, time and stable technical specifications. The document containing the technical specifications – or simply, specifications – is supposed to be written, sealed and signed at the beginning of the programming project.

Ideally the customer explains what she needs, and the programmer takes careful notes, not missing a detail. Then the programmer transforms the customer's requirements into a consistent set of technical specifications which are then presented to the customer for final verification. The design phase follows, then the coding and the testing, and finally the installation. As far as the programmer is concerned, in a perfect world each one of these phases would be accorded its own time in the overall planning of the project.

This is the picture of paradise for many programmers: clear specifications and ample time to be able to construct beautiful code, code to be proud of, code that will display the wonders of its creator. Paradise, however, is only a promise, not a reality. What programmers find instead is that specifications are unclear, incorrect or missing entirely and that the customer, or the customer's contact, is uninterested or does not really know what he wants or does not know how to express it. Further, the programmer may be incapable of understanding what the customer means, or may dislike him, or may be incompetent, or may be having a bad day. The manager may change deadlines or simply not allow the time needed. She may consent to the modification of requirements *after* the design has been created or she may take off and her replacement may be utterly clueless. The dream of creating that beautiful program fades away as reality takes over.

While no one contradicted Connell's statement that there is a lot of 'butt-ugly' code, participants in fact proposed a number of explanations for it. Even if the message in the following comments does not change significantly, it is interesting to include a few examples in order to thicken the description and give a more vivid image of what discussions among programmers can look like. This is what they say when feeling frustrated at not being allowed to write elegant code.

Many of the complaints had to do with lack of time, and these were presented in various forms. Some messages were written in a neutral, objective tone:

When it's done. by **verbatim** on September 04, @04:44PM
   It comes down to time and person-power. I think the biggest failing (from personal experience ;)) of most software/system design comes from either a lack of time or a lack of planning for time. [...]

And some entries were dismissive of the people in charge:

Unrealistic Deadlines by J0ey4 on September 04, @04:04PM
  The main reason that most software design sucks is that the engineers are not given enough time to do the project right. The idea is that you just get it out to market and you can always patch it later. Try telling some guy with an MBA who's making all the decisions that it is better to take enough time to do a project properly. All he/she knows is that the "magic black box" will produce the same output whether the design is good enough.
  So the same scenario is repeated over and over:
  Engineer: "I can get this done in ten months"
  Manager: "Hmmm ….. we need to get it done in six."
  Engineer: "That's not enough time to design and implement a clean, extendable, reusable product!"
  Manager:(Confused by big words like 'extendable') "It'll work though right?"
  Engineer: "Well yeah, but…"
  Manager: "Just get it done in six months."
  As long as you have people who have no clue about software making deadline decisions, you're going to have to hack like hell for 60 hours a week just to get it out the door. It's sad but true. Granted this isn't ALWAYS the case but in my experience it is most of the time.

The lack of time is usually blamed on some sort of managerial greed. The figure of the manager here represents a short-sighted, for-profit attitude. The following quotes emphasize this recurring theme of profit-focused, ignorant managers against programmers who are not allowed to create their beautiful software. Sometimes, the hatred is extended to all commercial software, that is, software written under deadlines not chosen voluntarily by the programmer:

software is like building w/ toothpicks by MikeFM on September 04, @11:59PM
  I like to write beautiful code.. as I imagine most real programmers do.. us geeks that live, breath, and dream in code.. but in real life there usually is not enough time or resources given to manage to write really well planned out code. This is why Microsoft sucks and a popular motto is "When it's done!" among the truly geeky programming houses and why open source will eventually kill most commercial software.

Apart from lack of time, which obviously must have an impact on the care with which software can be designed and written, another problem haunts programmers: changing requirements (or specifications). Although programming involves the fitting together of a number of data elements, this fitting together can be done in a number of ways. Once the work starts, however, changes in the original plan can have disastrous consequences. Elements that originally fit well together have to be modified and do not work any longer. Then the programmer has to modify the surrounding bits, which may in turn misalign them so they also have to be modified. This is sometimes called patching up the code, and it can be done with some success – the program will more or less work – but it is generally considered ugly. What programmers need are clear, stable specifications allowing them to construct tightly fitting data structures; this is often not provided:

> **If bridges were programmed** ... by **An. (Coward)** on September 04, @04:37PM
> Project managers would see the balsa mock-up and tell the construction crews to just put the mock-up in place because it's good enough to use as is.
> Somebody would stop the project halfway through construction to insist that it be changed from a simple truss to a suspension bridge.
> Somebody else would stop the project to insist that it be changed from a suspension bridge to a tunnel, and furthermore, to demand delivery of a tunnel for simple truss prices.
> Massive traffic jams would occur as users stop at each end and call for help because they can't figure out how to drive across.
> Architects would be sent out to tow cars and fill potholes.

> **Re:complexity** by **sterno** on September 04, @07:34PM
> [...] I cannot recall at any point in my 4 year career as a software developer that any given project had concrete and immutable goals before beginning of development.
> On the best projects we'd have good documentation of requirements, etc, but EVERY time those requirements would change.

> **Specs Sucks!** by **Anonymous Coward** on Tuesday September 04, @04:12PM
> I'll start writing code as beautiful as a bridge when management stops changing the requirements throughout the programming process. How many bridges do you think would look good and be

stable if half way through the construction one person decided it needed three more lanes, another felt it should be double decked and yet another added the requirement that it be one way. Software sucks 90% of the time because the requirement specs suck. And no one ever looks at a bridge that is 70% complete and says "This looks good enough for now, let's start using it and work out the kinks as we go" like they do with software.

I agree most code look horrible and is a terrible mess, but that is a side effect of external forces, not because programmers need to be inspired to write clean beautiful code by some article.

At least these two participants got specifications, even if they sucked. FirstNoel was not that lucky:

Wow, You get a spec? by **FirstNoel** on September 05, @06:57AM
I'm lucky if I get a post-it note with a little chicken scratch on it.
Actually the only time I get a "spec-like" thing is when I get it from other programmers. It takes a lot to teach the average user how to write a spec. Most of them never quite get it.
I'd love to have real specs, ahhh let me dream....

The message is clear: specifications are not what they should be, and this is frustrating for programmers.

Whose fault is it that requirements are not written properly? Some participants blamed the users; they do not know how to write them – or even worse, they do not know what they want from the application:

Re:Your Job by **battjt** on September 05, @08:26AM
... Users are not designers nor programmers. They don't know what is possible with systems, nor how hard certain things are to do with systems.

Re:Beauty for beauty's sake makes crappy software by **Slide100** on September 04, @04:24PM
> Software has to: [Slide100 is replying to someone else. This bit was written by that someone else. The > sign points this out]
> 1. Meet user requirements
Unfortunately, in a great majority of cases, the user doesn't know what he/she needs.
I can't count the number of times I have installed a system in a hospital [communications systems], made it run exactly to spec, and

then have the staff say: "Why does it do that? We have absolutely no need for that! It should do this however." Generally, the specs are made by managers, not the people who actually use the program. This causes the spec to be what management perceives to be the need, not the actual need.

Granted, in a software situation, you are supposed to go through everything and find out what the user needs, but how often does this happen? In most cases, a programmer is given a spec and told to write the software to it.

Users are also blamed for an additional fatal blow to the dream of beautiful software. After all, they are the ones who buy the software. If they did not accept ugly software, then managers would have to make sure that the software produced is elegant, and all problems would be solved at once:

It's the buyers fault, not the programmer's fault. by **maitas** on September 05, @07:31AM

Crappy programmers are cheaper than good ones. People prefers to buy cheap software with lots of features, even if it doesn't work!! So right now the situation is that, or either you make crappy cheap software with lots of features fast and keep selling like crazy (Microsoft way), or you built expensive great code with only a fraction of the features (believe me, to add features to a given software takes lots of time) and no single person will buy it.

Don't kill the messenger!! Kill the software buyers!!

Wow, good one by **Sinical** on September 04, @04:03PM

I always try hard in code that I write to do the proper thing, but employers don't care about design, by and large: hell, most of them don't even care about maintainability – they want a working executable yesterday.

Sure, some developers are lazy, and some don't make the push for a clean design when they could probably get one. But until the public starts *demanding* reliable software, don't expect any of this to change.

Remember, all pressure has to come from the customer – the best designed, coded, debugged, and maintained software I see is the embedded code in missiles: it HAS to work, and well, or else. There are design documents, requirements documents, official documentation of bugs, simulations, etc., all to make sure that things will work correctly when they must. This means no six month product cycles, though – time is what is required for all good products, including software.

More law-abiding participants suggested instead that the blame for all the 'horrible mounds of [...] code' be laid on the lack of strict legislation. Connell compared software to civil engineering, much to the disadvantage of the former: 'We should expect the same level of quality and performance in software we demand in physical construction,' and a number of participants countered that bridges were of better quality than applications because of the legal consequences of misconstruction. Similar laws in the software world would make managers more keen on giving programmers the time they need to carefully write their code:

Re:Building codes by **DJerman** on September 04, @06:38PM
I suppose my rambling came around to the argument that if, like in civil engineering, there were

- professional licensing boards for Software Engineers
- certification of designs, plans, and built code by those engineers
- professional liability for the items they certify, and
- requirements for professional certification for commercial applications (building codes),

then we'd have more reliable software. Standards and regulations for what may and may not be certified ("sealed" in traditional parlance) can come later, but lack of accountability is the problem. Any method that legally requires accountability for quality and reliability in a class of software will force an improvement, and a corresponding rise in the cost of making that software (which is why it must be a legal requirement for all competitors, or it won't happen).

Not all problems come from the outside; some participants also blamed other programmers for the problem of stinking software. Most of the times the criticism was not directed at their lack of skills but at their lack of discipline: they seemed incapable of following a sound methodology:

Planning and review save time and money by **tim_maroney** on September 04, @04:11PM

... Software engineering is the only engineering discipline in which the practitioners are permitted to indulge themselves in work without planning or review, and that's the #1 reason that software sucks.

Re:software is incredibly complex ... by BWJones on September 04, @04:46PM

... Software too evolves, but well designed software is thought out and planned in advance with lots of end user input, subject matter expert input, and testing of code and interface to meet the users needs. In my experience with others code and commercial products, most software goes right into the writing phase with very little forethought or planning. "We'll get to that later" is the phrase I have heard again and again. The programmers that stay and get rewarded are the ones that can plan, work with subject matter experts, and listen and implement ideas and suggestions successfully.

These pieces of conversation suggest a number of possible reasons for the existence of so much stinking software. Participants complained about a number of things that made it impossible for them to write beautiful code. It seems safe to assume that the participants do want to write elegant software but that external circumstances prevent them from doing so.

Programmers' opinions about software aesthetics cover a rich variety of subjects, including a number of coding style issues, the readability of code, the convenience of aesthetic considerations, cleanness, efficiency, simplicity, tightness and a number of other characteristics about programming languages. Programmers commented about legendary hackers (programmers) and about neat tricks and horrible mounds of spaghetti code and so forth and so on. A proper description of this world would be impossible to fit into these few pages (but see Piñeiro, 2003), but abundant evidence points to the simple fact that software aesthetics is a significant concern of programmers and a rich source of discussion. Bottom line, the focus is the same: the consideration of the form of code, of the data structure it represents, and in a lesser measure, of its layout. Of course, this is not to deny that there are programmers who, even if they admit that code can be beautiful, may also believe that the issue has been blown up out of proportion. That, however, is another chapter in another anthology.

Why would programmers want to write beautiful code? The immediate answer is: programmers do not perceive code as only a virtual machine that does things but also as their creation. Their relationship to code is more that of creator to creation than of technician to machine. Their code then speaks of them: not only of their skills but also of their personal preferences in things like coding style, programming language and designing strategies.

This aesthetic concern is rather special for at least two reasons. First, programming languages are strictly logical; they do not allow the least deviation from the defined standards; and second, programming is an instrumental activity. Considered from this perspective, programming should not allow for much aesthetic possibility, but it does.

Innovation and beauty

Humans are capable of developing aesthetic concerns even within the logical strictness required by programming languages. People sensitive to this are called 'nerds'. This is not a very nice label, but nerds really don't seem to care. The existence of these concerns and the number of nerds says something about what 'strict logical' thinking is, and it also says something about the creative power of the human mind. What is inherent in these ideas is that 'strict logical' (that is, formally restricted) and 'creative' are not opposed. This is an interesting line of thought that Brooks examined earlier in his *The mythical man-month*, for instance. Many writers in the field of software development and in the management of software development have discussed it as well. This chapter, however, considers instead the connected question of how these aesthetic concerns relate to software innovation.

Much research from a number of different perspectives has been dedicated to the subject of technological innovation, or innovation *tout court*. Today's concern with economic growth spurred by innovation has generated much interest about innovation from academia, the state and private enterprise. Much of this research treats innovation as a process that is seriously carried out in a goal-oriented manner. In other cases, the concept of 'innovation' is simply the result of a mathematical analysis of numerical data and does not necessarily relate to any concrete activities. Above all, it is something that can be managed (cf. the 'Management of Innovation' tradition represented by Tidd *et al.*, 2001; and Trott, 2002). Such an approach has its advantages, but here we shall explore the possibility of innovation as the result of 'frivolous', non-instrumental, aesthetically driven thinking.

Due mainly to its relationship to economic growth, innovation is something very serious indeed. In fact, it is practically impossible to discuss innovation without discussing politics, given the role it is assigned in the future of regions, countries and even humankind. The commonly held idea that continuous growth is based on never-ending innovation can be found in the classic work of Schumpeter. Even if what this 'innovation' consists of is not absolutely clear, it seems fair to say that there are different kinds of innovation, including market, technological and organizational innovation (Sundbo and Fuglsang, 2002). Innovation thus understood is closely connected to the creation of employment and to the economic well-being of firms and nations. It is something good, and social, economic and political conditions must be managed so that innovation is encouraged. Any text on the subject can be read therefore as offering political/managerial advice; this one is not an exception.

Due to these wide connections, 'innovation' becomes a problematic term here. The question of deciding whether a new product, a new organizational model or a new production model is actually an innovation becomes a major complication in the use of the term. Innovation literature focuses on improvement and the positive aspects of development. Writers in the field differentiate between inventions that offer competitive advantage (innovations) and inventions which don't (just inventions, good ideas). In fact, innovation management is the art of transforming inventions (and good ideas) into innovations.

At any rate, innovation is a serious matter within managerial discourse. It is a proper subject and commands attention. It can engage a large network of actors and joins a long list of other serious aspects: profit, customer satisfaction, employee turnover, market share, efficiency, strategic management, and so on. These serious aspects, most visible at the practitioner level, are also the ones most often discussed at the research level. Extensive academic and popular literature about these subjects have resulted from this interest.

Code aesthetics, on the other hand, is a frivolous matter within managerial discourse. It isn't a proper subject, it isn't worth attention and it has little effect on the firm, at least in terms of the public discourse of the firm. This does not mean that the programmers' aesthetic concerns have no effect on the firm or that the concerns are not crucial to programmers themselves; it only means that the subject is not important at the firm's public level. The use of serious/frivolous is closely connected with legitimate/illegitimate and, as a result, with public/private. In addition, frivolity carries the connotation of causing damage, of stealing resources from other, more serious issues.

In his seminal book *Stone age economics* (1972), Sahlins presents his studies of primitive societies. He is struck by how members of these societies, which by our standards are very poor, do not seem to suffer from any *feeling* of scarcity. They act as if they had much more than they need. In contrast, we seem to live under the 'assumption of scarcity', the notion that, regardless of our resources, what we need always exceeds what we have. This idea, Sahlins argues, is one of the pillars of western economic thinking.

In this light, the difference between 'unimportant' and 'frivolous' becomes clear. Unimportant aspects are simply marginal; they don't require resources, they don't hamper productivity, they aren't damaging. Frivolous aspects, on the other hand, are those which are seen as unimportant *and at the same time* consume resources. Frivolous aspects of work are less easily ignored than the unimportant ones; they may even be actively suppressed. In everyday situations, however, the border between unimportant and frivolous is not always clear. At what point does something unimportant become expensive?

Code aesthetics remains a good example of a frivolous aspect of technological development, however. According to public discourse, the beauty of a program's code is of no interest whatsoever to the firm, but it requires the programmers' attention. McConnell (2003), author of *Rapid development*, lists 'Developer gold-plating' as one of the classic mistakes of software development. Fascinated by new technology, developers are sometimes anxious to try out new features of their language or environment or to create their own implementation of a slick feature they saw in another product, whether or not it's required in their product. The effort required to design, implement, test, document and support features that are not required lengthens the schedule (p. 47).

Writing aesthetically pleasing code almost always requires going further than what is absolutely necessary. Therefore it should be avoided and in no case encouraged. It is this attitude that provokes our Slashdotters. Programmers rebel against an attitude that deprives them of their right to write beautiful software. They want managers to give them realistic and stable conditions, such as deadlines and specifications. They want users to require high quality software and colleagues to program carefully. Only then will they obtain the conditions needed to create without turmoil.

The software industry is unique in the sense that a proper production phase does not exist. Once the software is written, tested and approved, it is either installed on the customer's system or burned on CD-ROMs and distributed. There is nothing like a production line where identical items are manufactured. In other words, programming means creating something new. Although parts of the program may be inherited from earlier projects, new code is always needed. Writing programs then is an unpredictable activity, for you never know in advance exactly how much time the software will require. In the most extreme cases, you may not even know whether it is viable. The industry believes there are huge economic gains to be made from a taylorization of programming, and so since the late 1960s many attempts have been made to eliminate this unpredictability. A milestone in this direction was taken as early as 1968 with the celebration of the first Software Engineering Conference in Germany (Aspray *et al.*, 1998). As a result of this and many other efforts, the software industry has seen some improvements in productivity but none of great significance (Brooks, 1995). Every programming project involves creation. Very seldom, if ever, is software written through simple repetition. Therefore, since creativity generally implies unpredictability, writing beautiful programs will likely be accomplished on its own timeline.

Programmers aren't complaining about not being allowed to create; what they complain about is not being able to do it undisturbed. They do not need playful office settings or Friday beers; what they need is peace. Programmers in our discussion blame managers, users and even other colleagues for disturbing their tranquility.

Levy (1984) relates the legend of the early hacker in an environment of work around the clock in absolute dedication to the task. There is no stress, for there are no managers changing the specifications, users lacking knowledge of the software or customers worrying about the cost. Hard work is certainly part of the programming mythology, but this effort does not oppose exploration and beauty. What does oppose beauty is the attitude of those who do not care about the nuances of code, who don't understand its intrinsic value. Once again, this is the attitude our Slashdotters rebel against.

In their own way, they rebel against the whole world. After all, the great majority of people see programming as an instrumental action; in other words, they only care about whether the program satisfies their needs and how much it costs. Programs are instruments of no intrinsic value; they are as worthy as the problems they solve. Whether or not the code is beautiful is irrelevant. Furthermore, whether or not programmers are allowed to create in peace is of no interest either, as long as one gets what one needs.

And would the beautiful software that our Slashdotters want to write *actually* provide a better solution for the users' problems or cost less? Some programmers claim it would, as the messages above make clear. Others, who also took part in the discussions but whose voice isn't represented here, didn't seem so sure. To be sure, in some cases there are gains to be made through careful, skillful programming, and in other cases there is no benefit. The important point is that some programmers dislike being forced to create stinking software. They rebel against that.

This rebellion has given rise to some interesting phenomena, including discussions like this one, but more significantly it has been one of the factors that fuel the Open Source movement. The concept behind the Open Source movement is: your computer can read the software you buy on CD-ROMs or through the Internet; that's why it works. But if you yourself tried to read it – by opening it with a text processor, for instance – you would see nothing but a meaningless string of strange characters:

```
K->gÊóoĺˆAŸ"ÿ\` Rx§± *ÃRÍŸz7∞*Í{}ÿ ∂ã»Q2(eS6¸ßúÄÜÙ?°ë˜°°¢°c¸
"?dT¸Td$Tdd‰*6¸É&B°L"ßã¸0˘?‰*®ÁÃÚê≤r†çá†-ãBxsZ...¿À*˜ø
#D(D@1—4è¸Æ?*rZ
>á| LkËÍˉflÉòèG~ ëÑë»cÌÎj? r»"fl?◇y¸M:l6'J...øm$úɪ"√ „`4øÌa
¥R¥?ÇÈˉö[É9?óŸÛGñ7f†Âˊúj:JùÉn'-fiÑë@«µL≥`ZÿA≫"ñaè]Ó
∂:c◇‡4YÉEt<, ¢ñ{4»adyù;<)†À,âfiÆ>}-Íᵀᴹ@ŸÛˉ˘s=˜;(ZKhòµ͵Ís7¨$<C©
VDx†À»Xç°óÃ2t¸Nïr4^ +7®Èïup†Êj|°ƒûÊ)ü}2ÅÖç°£€Kó}G„Bel
ˉÌ÷¸1B:&)¢h‹ƒsœ}≠ñm'ÖwÍÍ∑ ‡ 2òfi0fi\YCúÃáúÂΩÌpÌesø∞:'ÖÀ
Ö˘>?„I∑ ¢±ìʃQ'yéé·À;ñˆ¡õ?ø°8PY‹[‰€%ÃSîÔÊ-õÛͧ€Ê*tÍjŸ»àB
/^fi(¡¸CTeøÕ πÅ©flÑ≠RÑÌ¥'∂o*G€| M,V›å^... {{ß˘xæL} ¥QKTLâïO
```

Your text editor is trying to interpret a long string of ones and zeros as characters. It means nothing, and there is no way for you to understand how the software works. The programmers used a programming language to create their software. First they wrote the code in that language – where things make much more sense – and then they transformed it into machine code. That's where the ones and zeros come from. Going from those ones and zeros to the original code is practically impossible. When you buy a program, you buy the ones and zeros but not the original code, which is also called the source code. In this way, the authors prohibit your copying it or looking for security faults.

Some programmers like Richard Stallman found this disabling activity outrageous and started to write programs equivalent to those on the market. Stallman's programs, however, were free, and the source code was made available. This was the beginning of the Free Software Foundation, which over the years has developed quite some software. Rebellion against closed code was the Open Source Movement's initial driving force, and it still is an important factor in explaining its success. But there are other factors that have contributed and continue to contribute to it, among others the fact that programmers are in charge and that consequently the aesthetic values of code play a different role than in the commercial firm.

Today the Open Source Movement is a huge project, and virtually everyone knows about their flagship product, the Linux operating system. Fewer people know about other available programs, but there are word processors, e-mail managers, Internet servers and database engines. Add to these all the small programs written by some enthusiast at home and offered for free over the net. Their source code is not always available, but the driving force behind them is the same: a desire to write the programs you want the way you want.

In 2001, Harper Business published *Just for fun*, a book about the origins of Linux. The book is a long sort of biographical interview with Linus Torvalds. The same year Pekka Himanen came out with *The hacker ethics*, a book that can be read as an Open Source programmer's manifesto. In it Himanen quotes Eric Raymond saying:

> To do the Unix philosophy right, you have to be loyal to excellence. You have to believe that software is a craft worth all the intelligence and passion you can muster... Software design and implementation should be a joyous art, and a kind of high-level play. If this attitude seems preposterous or vaguely embarrassing to you, stop and think; ask yourself what you've forgotten. Why do you design software instead of doing something else to make money or pass the time? You must have thought software was worthy of your passions once ... To do the Unix philosophy right, you need to have (or recover) that attitude. You need to *care*. You need to *play*. You need to be willing to *explore*. (p. 6)

What is it that makes programming fun enough for Linus to start writing his operating system? What is it that makes hackers passionate about code? How is this driving force connected to aesthetic concerns in programming?

Anyone may enter an Open Source project. Take Linux, for instance. Its code is far too large for you to read it entirely, but perhaps you're particularly interested in, say, modem drivers, the programs that manage the flow of information through the modem. The current code is available on the Internet, and you just need to download it, study it and decide what part you want to work on. Say that you improve one of the drivers; for instance, you eliminate a bug. You then inform the 'project owner' that you've done this and send your code over. It is not yet certain that your modifications will be included in the official versions of Linux. It must first be controlled by the project owner. If it is judged good enough, it will be included.

One of the reasons Open Source projects are popular is that your code is actually studied by another programmer. Here you have a chance of proving your programming skills to someone who understands, someone who cares. Unlike the for-profit environment, code aesthetics here are not a frivolous matter. People recognize an elegant solution.

Open Source projects are meritocracies; your skills and your dedication define your position. You are not forced to work on any particular project, but people tend to participate on those run by competent programmers. Consequently, project owners are often acclaimed for their skills, which makes their decision to include your work in official releases even more satisfying. You may be proud of your work, for it is of high quality.

Compare this with the situation described by the messages above, situations where outsiders decide when your work is good enough and what the priorities are. Of course the worst situation is where profit more than beauty is what matters. Public discourse of the firm considers beautiful code frivolous, and steps are taken to avoid it. Certainly nothing is done to encourage it, as our Slashdotters complain.

The will to write code you can be proud of doesn't disappear just because it is not publicly supported, however; it finds alternative outlets. This is also true for other human activities, so programming is not a special case. At the private level, among colleagues, among those who understand and care, your work is an essential part of your identity. You want to make a good impression, but what makes you look good among peers doesn't necessarily make you look good at the public levels.

In the case of programmers, there are different public levels: the customers, managers, owners and users. All of them share the characteristic that they concern other people, non-programmers, and it is in this sense that I use 'public'. They are not members of the guild, so to speak, and can be defined as 'those who do not understand'. The word 'public' here also denotes the fact that these people form the 'general public' of the software industry.

The conditions that surround programming shape the kind of outlets available for writing impressive software. The fundamental trait of those conditions is the existence of the Internet. Not only do Slashdotters work on Internet terminals – and therefore they are constantly connected – but also the nature of their work fits very well with the medium. Code can easily be published and collaboration is made possible.

The Linux operating system contains several million lines of code, and the other Open Source systems are also giant projects. They require dedication, discipline, structure, skills and lots of time. They also require altruism, since there is no direct revenue to be expected from taking part in them. Economists (Kieseppä, 2002) have searched for different solutions to this economic paradox, suggesting for instance that programmers might expect better jobs if their name appears in the official releases. Some theories are based on peer recognition, and others on the pleasure of leading. All of them contain a measure of truth, but they ignore the likelihood that programmers, at least Open Source collaborators, simply enjoy solving problems. This desire to take on new difficulties and to try new solutions, perceived as both unnecessary and damaging at certain levels of the firm's discourse, must find alternative ways to manifest itself.

This desire is not exclusive to programmers. The very firm employing them may well have started as a fruit of someone's craving for new explorations. It may seem paradoxical that this craving is later judged both unnecessary and damaging, but it is perfectly reasonable. Different people are interested in different things, and one's explorations may be another's pointless risks.

Programmers are not the only ones ready to freely share the fruits of their work. The average programmer is neither more curious and more fascinated by exploration than the next lawyer. Still, Linux and other Open Source systems are remarkable feats, not only in their complexity but also in their innovativeness in the technical and the organizational realms.

These creations make you reconsider the power of the desire to construct things you can be proud of. It also makes you consider the strange nature of the mind, which not only can distinguish nuances in environments as strict as the logic of computer programming but also can become so attached to them that the desire to create them generates organizations as large and powerful as the Open Source movement. It makes you also reconsider the relationship between productivity, innovation and the future of corporations. Finally, it makes one reconsider the whole concept of patents and copyrights as the way to generate growth.

Notes

1. The reaction against commercial constraints can also be used as a manifestation of other kinds of phenomena, such as identity construction through narrative (Case and Piñeiro, 2004).

2. www.slashdot.org – on its page dedicated to advertising information.
3. This discussion is available online at http://slashdot.org/article.pl?sid= 01/09/04/1914242.
4. Connell makes an explicit comparison with structural engineering (bridges and houses), and several of the entries refer to this both ironically and earnestly.

References

Aspray, W., R., Keil-Slawik and D.L. Parnas (1998) *History of software engineering.* Available at http://www.kathrin.dagstuhl.de/9635/Report

Brooks, F.P. (1995) *The mythical man-month: Essays on software engineering.* Boston: Addison Wesley Longman.

Case, P., and E. Piñeiro (Forthcoming) Subversive aspirations and identity work in the narratives of a computer programming community, *Human Relations.*

Connell, C.H. (2001) Most software stinks! Retrieved from www.chc-3.com/pub/beautifulsoftware.htm.

Czarniawska-Joerges, B. (1995) Narration or science? Collapsing the division in organisation studies. *Organization* 2 (1).

Himanen, P. (2001) *The hacker ethic and the spirit of the information age.* 1st ed. New York: Random House.

Kieseppä, I.A. (2002) *Open source software and economics.* Retrieved from http://www.valt.helsinki.fi/blogs/kiema/oseconomics.pdf

Levy, S. (1984) *Hackers: heroes of the computer revolution.* 1st ed. Garden City, NY: Anchor Press.

McConnell, S. (2003) *Rapid development.* Microsoft Press.

Piñeiro, E. (2003) *The aesthetics of code.* Stockholm: Arvinius Förlag. Text available online at: http://urn.kb.se/resolve?urn=urn:nbn:se:kth:diva-3648 (2006-09-06)

Raymond, E.S. (2000) *The art of Unix programming.* Retrieved from www.faqs.org/docs/artu/

Sahlins, M. (1972) *Stone age economics.* New York: Aldine de Gruyter.

Slashdot (2001) Software aesthetics. Retrieved June 2004 from http://developers.slashdot.org/article.pl?sid=01/09/04/1914242

Sundbo, J., and L. Fuglsang (2002) *Innovation as strategic reflexivity.* London: Routledge.

Taylor, P.A. (1999) *Hackers.* London: Routledge.

Tidd, J., J. Bessant and K. Pavitt (2001) *Managing innovation: integrating technological, market, and organizational change.* New York: John Wiley & Sons.

Torvalds, L., and D. Diamond (2001) *Just for fun: the story of an accidental revolutionary.* New York: Harper Business.

Trott, Paul (2002) *Innovation management and new product development.* 2nd ed. London: FT Management.

Turkle, S. (1997) *Life on the screen: identity in the age of the internet.* New York: Simon and Schuster.

8
Aesthetics of financial judgements: on risk capitalists' confidence

Bertil González Guve

Philosophers like Gilbert Ryle and Ludwig Wittgenstein claim that neither conviction nor doubt is a matter of choice. Individuals cannot choose to be convinced if they are not. In this sense, then, judgement is a perception, something exercised in situations where the premises cannot tell a person what to do next, where a logical, deductive conclusion is simply not available. Further, when conviction does emerge, it is not concerned with parts but with the whole. When the sun eventually rises, it shines over the entire field.

Conviction has a significant role in management decision-making and this chapter explores how conviction plays that role. The empirical basis of the discussion is a case study of Industrifonden, the Swedish Industrial Development Fund, where an investment manager assesses a potential investment in a high-tech, high-risk project and then recommends to the board whether or not to invest in the project. The assessment process the investment manager uses to make up his mind and judge a potential investment is best understood in terms of the emergence of *conviction*. Evaluating the project is about taking the assessor from doubt to conviction – and doing it in a legitimate way.

Judgement at Industrifonden

Industrifonden was created with state capital in 1979 in order to fill gaps in the Swedish financial market for promotion of growth through innovations and industrial development projects that might otherwise be under-financed. The fund has equity of roughly 4 billion SEK (about 450 million euros) and typically invests in high-tech, high-risk industrial development projects. The fund does not 'support' companies or projects; it invests rather expensive capital in them. Investments are made either by becoming a stakeholder in the company or by lending capital at a high interest rate that ideally corresponds to the risk level of the project.

Before becoming a researcher I worked at Industrifonden for about three years, assessing potential investments in order to arrive at a recommendation about whether or not to invest. The recommendations I worked on, along with a project report, were presented to the president of the fund and the board of directors, who then made the actual decision to invest or not. The projects often concerned products yet to be developed for sale in markets yet to be created. Uncertainty characterized most – if not all – of the projects.

One day I was having a discussion with Vice President Wahren about how we carry out our assessments and arrive at our conclusions. During the course of our conversation, Wahren, my boss for several years and one of the most successful project assessors at the Fund, commented: 'Once you have made up your mind about a project, the work with trying to find the arguments starts.' Of course coming up with effective arguments requires figuring out how individuals make up their minds. In consideration of this challenge, this chapter touches on theoretical perspectives that are fruitful starting points in understanding the operation of the faculty of judgement.

Judgement in action

Along with my ambition to become good at assessing projects, my appetite for understanding how judgements are made also grew. Some features of the process of project judgement are easy to study. A Project Profile Chart, the list of project elements to be taken into account during the judgement process, serves as a guideline for the assessor. The chart contains categories like *financial status, profitability, management, owners, project characteristics, market, project economy* and *technology*. Each one of these is divided into subcategories for the assessor to grade from 1 to 5. For example, in the Project Profile Chart the category *management* is divided into *engagement in the project, overall competence in the company, sales organization, service organization* and *education*. In the report to the board of directors in charge of making the final decision, the projects are characterized in more or less the same way; the description is always couched in Project Profile Chart terminology.

In each project the argument used to qualify why the investment should or should not be made varies greatly. There is no manual for how the overall competence of management in the company should be graded; should it be a 3...or a 5? Neither is there a formula for determining whether a project graded with all 4s, for example, will be a good investment or not. Calculations of potential profit margins, project costs, market sizes and so on and so forth are a natural part of each project analysis, but rarely are there any 'facts' to input, just estimations and speculations, often subject to discussion.

The assessors, the president and members of the board never second-guessed their decision. None of them ever doubted their judgement once they came to a conclusion. This did not mean that they were mostly 'right', in the sense that the project would necessarily be a success either. On the contrary most of the projects ended up as losses. Although experience had taught my colleagues that the investment they were about to recommend or make could very well become an economic disaster, they still did not doubt their judgement.

Judgement in theory

Most of the time I could not predict the judgements or arguments that would surface in the projects. Even though I learned to anticipate which topics were up for discussion, I could not find a schedule or model for the judgements that were made.

So how are judgements actually arrived at? I was not particularly interested in a psychological analysis. Although it could probably provide models for how an individual's mind was influenced by thought patterns or personality characteristics, it was not the kind of *how* or *why* I was interested in. Furthermore, I could not conduct studies of that sort.

For me, what I could see and what I had experienced were more significant: what went on during meetings where projects were discussed, how consultants were hired, how projects were described, how participants listened and joined in the chat and how informal conversations during lunches and coffee breaks took place. On these occasions the project assessors often commented or made jokes about ongoing projects, earlier experiences, stories heard about other companies, and so on. Here I experienced what Claes Gustafsson (1994) refers to as the ongoing flow of chatting. Here I observed how Walter Fisher's (1989) 'storytelling man' lived what Barbara Czarniawska-Joerges (Czarniawska-Joerges and Guillet de Monthoux, 1994) called the organizational life as a long string of stories. As a result, as these writers and Alasdair MacIntyre (1984) explain, my theory building about organizational life would lie in my interpreting these stories.

From the narrative perspective, the judgement cannot be separated from the story or stories about what is being judged. To judge is to tell the story about the judgement. Where rationality draws upon a 'universally objective' deduction, judgement is far from the universal, instead being concerned with the particular. To judge is what we do when we make up our minds about something that concerns us. Although this does not explain how it happens, it does describe what it is we are talking about. Where rationality gains strength in its rule-following character (Beiner, 1983) – claiming by reference to 'objective' rules that the conclusion is the right one – judgement is easily and incorrectly relegated to the realm of the subjective. Hannah Arendt (1982) describes judgement – and this is crucial – as neither objective nor subjective, but inter-subjective, something we do as part of a social context, not by way of logical deduction but through our power of imagination. We judge by imagining ourselves in the place of others concerned with the judgement we are about to make. Arendt's (1982) point is that we judge by imagining ourselves where we actually are not.

Judging professionally

Compared to the everyday judgements we all make, the assessor's final recommendation is highly 'rational' in the sense it is motivated by economic models, calculations, analysis, facts, estimates and logical arguments. In economic market-ruled thinking, rationality is central and even one of the measures of the competence of the assessor.[1] Producing an interesting analysis then requires that we – the ones asking the questions – avoid the habitual mental cramp that usually forces itself upon us when we think about assessments and decisions. It is so easy to be seduced and trapped by the 'rational' when discussing economy, business or other areas traditionally known as 'serious'. Recalling what we were taught in the university and the official discourse of commercial and industrial life we remember that 'serious' matters are best dealt with rationally. Therefore, our open minds should see the assessment and the decisions made as something 'serious', in the sense of being rational and analytical. At the same time, however, we should also see the assessment process and the emerging decision as something messy, uncertain, incomplete, arbitrary perhaps, intuitive, existential, individual and spontaneous.

In traditional literature on decisions and assessment, the conclusion is arrived at by calculating and reasoning logically. The assessor is equipped with a universally valid method for carrying out rational and logical calculations and assessments. To ask *how* the assessment is made then is to ask this person to reconstruct this very rational process. In such a world, where both logic and method are universal, the assessment will be a logical consequence of the premises. In traditional logico-deductive analysis, an individual facing some kind of problem will analyse the situation in a logical and systematic manner until all relevant issues have been considered. Once she has done that – eureka! – she can make a decision.

Problem   →   Logico-deductive analysis   →   Eureka!

The analysis phase is the tricky part, since it leads to the solution. The decision itself is not the critical thing, since the individual, once the situation has been analysed logically, will naturally choose 'the best'.[2] This classical description of decision-making implies that the one facing the problem immediately starts analysing and will go on analysing until the solution is clear. As long as the calculations are done correctly, the assessment is directed by the premises and facts available. The work of assessing consists in getting the right input, after which the correct – and unavoidable – assessment will come to the assessor. It will spring from the calculations, the choice-automat, like a chocolate bar from the candy machine.

This description fits 'economic man' rather than the interviewees at Industrifonden. This tidy way of analysis is far from how the assessors I have met describe their work. When the field of study is the process leading to fabulously well-motivated assessments, as it is in this case, it is particularly important from the very beginning for the open mind not to don the straitjacket of 'universal validity'. Another opportunity for hobbling the thought process lies in the popular misunderstanding that every grammatically meaningful question has an equally grammatically meaningful and true answer. Pierre Guillet de Monthoux (1991) talks about the 'mad logician' who believes that every question *why* must have a logically compelling *therefore*. A severe case of this 'madness' is found in Simone de Beauvoir's (1972) character 'the Oblomov', for example. With a strong feeling of 'seriousness', he will be the adult defender of the absolute, factual, objective world, unsullied by human fingers. In his defence of the 'serious', he will deny his personal involvement and subjective engagement, thus basing his decisions and actions on pure objectivity.

The thought of a universally valid decision-making logic has always interested passionate thinkers. Bertrand Russell, who co-wrote *Principia matematica,* and Wittgenstein, author of *Tractatus logico-philosophicus,* are two well-known examples. They both later realized the (actual logical) impossibility of the project, however, and...well...simply changed their minds. In 1968, G.H. von Wright showed that the very grammar of decision-making logic, if such could exist, would require the answers to questions concerning the decision-making processes to be in the personal subjective grammatical form. *I* act according to *my* premises and *my* imaginings, which result in *me* doing something to realize *my* projects.

Judgement versus rationality

The idealization of the rational decision has to do with what Wittgenstein (1953/1992) criticizes as an idealization of exactness, which is closely related to his discussions about rule following or what Karl Popper (1990) calls our human tendency to determinism.

An analogy can be made between what our ideal of rational thinking sets up as goal and method for how to judge something on the one hand and the way philosophers have regarded the goal and method of philosophy on the other. It is an analogy between the ideal of the convincing, correct judgement and the philosophical aspiration to create a sort of discourse of the end, a final answer to a philosophical problem. Wittgenstein criticizes this ideal of exactness. Further, he does not take the discussion to the next level and improve it, which would be to follow the same aspiration of 'ending' the discussion. Instead he shows us – not like a mathematician or philosopher but rather like somebody showing us his apartment – that the ideal of exactness is a kind of structural lure of our language, a temptation, and following it is not only common, but normal.

Any individual making up his mind about an industrial development project must deal with what he cannot possibly foresee.[3] That is why we make estimations, a sort of 'fact' not taken from 'reality' but from our powers of imagination, powers used not when imagining fiction, but when imagining reality. It is easy to think that we 'base' our imagination – our suppositions and estimations – on our experience, and most of us would therefore probably give more validity to Wahren's judgement on a particular project than to mine. But – and here it starts to get interesting – what does it mean to 'base' our suppositions, our imagination, on our experience? When we make a judgement, do we 'base' it on our experience? If so, in what way?

'How can he *know* how he is to continue a pattern by himself— whatever instruction you give him?—Well, how do I know?—If that means "Have I reasons?" the answer is: my reasons will soon give out. And then I shall act, without reasons' (*Philosophical investigations*, §211) This is part of what I find so interesting and difficult to understand about this undramatic, ordinary and routine ability of ours to make judgements. The very idea of correctness, or rule-governed behaviour, seems to crumble here. If my action is not finally or fully grounded in reason or knowledge of definite rules, is it then not arbitrary? According to Wittgenstein we do not, cannot, 'base' our judgements on our experience in the sense of being able to deduce them from our experience. As Glendinning (1998) explains, we *must*, at some point 'leap, from instruction to action, from explanation to employment, without the aid of absolutely authoritative reasons or rules' (p. 101).

Wahren's reasons for judging a project to be 'good' will soon give out, and he will 'act, without reasons.' As Wahren himself put it, once he has 'made up his mind', he will work to find the arguments. But, we argue, surely Wahren has grounds for his judgements in his 13 years of experience as assessor at Industrifonden, as well as his previous 18 years in different areas of European industry. Using this type of argument in our objection we once more fall into the 'deterministic tendency' or the structural lure that lies in the ideal of exactness and our habitual misinterpretation of rule-following.

According to Wittgenstein, experience gives us no ground for our judgements or convictions. To be quite clear on this: even if our past judgements proved 'correct', our future judgements would have no logically deductive ground to stand on. Even if our expectations were fulfilled time and time again, our experience would still give us no ground for our game of judging (*On certainty*, §131). When we try to understand judgements, we will be tempted to look for order, universality and an even, regular contour but will instead find one torn to rags. Wahren continues to learn what it means to make judgements at Industrifonden through his experience, in following different projects, in chatting with colleagues and through the stories about the 'good examples' (Gottsegen, 1994).

In Wittgenstein's thinking, rules are not enough to establish a practice, however. Practice, in the form of examples, must 'speak for itself' (*On Certainty*, §139). The experience on which the practice is based can give no ground on which to base the 'right' judgement. No understanding exists beyond the example. Deduction from one example to the next particular situation is not possible. Practice cannot give us a ground out of which we can deduce the expression of the 'right' judgement in a specific situation.

But isn't it experience that teaches us to judge like *this*; that is to say, that it is correct to judge like this? But how does experience *teach* us, then? *We* may derive it from experience, but experience does not direct us to derive anything from experience. If it is the *ground* of our judging like this, and not just the cause, still we have no ground for seeing this in turn as a ground (*On certainty*, §130).

Experience may be the 'cause' of our judgements – in the sense a psychologist would explain our thoughts or feelings as being 'caused' by some previous experience – but it *cannot* be the 'ground' upon which we may logically deduce the correctness of our judgements. Wittgenstein continues: 'No, experience is not the ground for our game of judging. Nor is its outstanding success' (*On certainty*, §130). We reach our judgement through a leap, without ground even in our experience, and still we can – and the assessors at Industrifonden *must* – explain and motivate judgements in a conventionally rational way.

'Why is this a good project to invest in?' Gilbert Ryle (1949/1990) explains that we cannot choose what we decide through our will. We can neither – and the argument is analogical – choose what we are convinced about nor, as Wittgenstein (1975) showed, what we doubt. The lure lies in letting the arguments of Ryle or Wittgenstein be philosophically interesting while still protecting ourselves from them by not giving them meaning in our understanding of our daily lives or in our understanding of rationality as something rational and groundless at the same time.

Aesthetics of confidence

If rationality is groundless, if no argument is the first, if there is no ground holding up the rest, if the 'ground' itself is held up by the rest of our arguments, how are we to understand the arrival at a conclusion?

Rationality can be understood as a cultural phenomenon (Luria, 1976; Gustafsson, 1994) and its rule-following aspect (Vickers (1965/1995); Beiner, 1983) as based on the established practice, the action and not a sort of objectively derived logical deduction. But how do we understand the birth of our conclusion?

This phenomenon, order for free or *emergence*, has become quite a fad in many fields. Even dust-laden systems theory or cybernetics has experienced somewhat of a renaissance disguised in its new dress, complexity theory. Emergence, an evocative and sometimes perhaps provocative word, is commonly expressed in the form 'the whole is greater than the sum of its parts' (Kauffman 1995). Per Bak (1996), the author of a book with the slightly arrogant title *How nature works*, puts it in a similar though more cynical fashion: 'Because of our inability to directly calculate how complex phenomena at one level arise from the physical mechanisms working at a deeper level, scientists sometimes throw up their hands to these phenomena as "emergent." They just pop out of nowhere.'

Although perhaps strange or provocative, there is nothing mystical or transcendental involved in the emergence process. A brief detour into the realm of biology and chemistry reveals Stuart Kauffman's (1995) description of an emergence theory of life, a theory that he sees as complementary to Darwin's evolutionary theory. The basis for the emergence theory of life is the theory that sufficiently complex mixtures of chemicals can spontaneously crystallize into systems with the ability to catalyse the reactions by which the chemicals themselves are formed. The crystallized system would thus be a so-called autocatalytic set, a self-sustained network of chemical reactions with the ability to reproduce, a living metabolism. Consequently, 'life' in this sense is not to be found in the property of any single cell or molecule or anywhere in the details but is instead a collective property of the interacting molecules. Life emerges whole and has always remained whole. 'Life' as an emergent phenomenon does not exist until a system of molecules is autocatalytic and has the ability to reproduce; it is then whole and complete from the first moment.

This should, however, not be considered mystical. The situation is rather binary in the sense that a set of molecules either has or does not have the abilities of catalysing and reproducing from some simple food molecules. There is nothing in the whole that is not to be found in the parts, except the ability to reproduce and evolve. Accordingly, the whole is alive while the parts are just chemicals.

The parallel drawn to the world of economic assessment is that the economic assessment process works accordingly; its parts are mere tendencies, + or − pointing towards a 'yes' or a 'no', whereas the whole, greater than the sum of its parts, entails something more, something that is not to be found in any of its parts alone − conviction.

Leaping across the abyss

The leap, the transformation, may be described as the emergence of conviction, as the engine of our conclusive action, as something not arrived at by deducing something traceable to its premises. Finding conviction means finding something that was *not* there to find before, something that *emerges* from the web of syllogisms that constitutes our reasoning about the project, our tale about the project.

Our explanations and reasoning about our judgement – explaining how we arrive at this or that conclusion, describing why we recommend this or that course of action – will be ungrounded, but that does not mean that it won't be convincing. As Ryle and Wittgenstein have shown, there is no rule to explain how we are to follow a rule. The rule is not there and is not missing. It is simply not needed.

Thomas Kuhn (1996) argues in the postscript to his book that not even the researchers within natural science can deduce their findings. He argues against the currently common view that scientific knowledge is embedded in theory and rules and that problems are supplied to gain facility in their application. The reason he opposes this view is he believes it expresses a 'cognitive content of science [which] is wrong'. (Kuhn, 1996, p. 188) Even the arrival at one formula from another, Kuhn argues, may not be properly described as deduction or logical or mathematical manipulation. 'The case of free fall, $f = ma$, becomes... for a pair of harmonic oscillators... $m1(d2s1/dt2) + k1s1 = k2(s2 - s1 + d)$... the family resemblance of which to $f = ma$ is harder to discover.' (p. 189).

Kuhn does not speak of deduction, but of interrelatedness, of the ability to see one problem as another, to see resemblances and grasp analogies. By way of practice the scientist does not tread further on a logico-deductive path grounded in rules or laws but instead learns a way of viewing, an ability to see the 'family resemblance' of one phenomenon to another. When we judge the manager of a company we are about to invest in as competent, we do not deduce this judgement from our previous experience of competent managers. Instead we recognize a family resemblance. Our judgement is not so much a deduction as a way of seeing, and thus it is closely linked to aesthetics. If we were to continually question our judgement with the question *why*, our 'reasons would soon give out', and we would 'act without reasons'. This does not mean that we doubt. We simply act without grounded reason. We simply judge, without ground, through what we see and in that sense, aesthetically perceive.

We explain and motivate by way of logic and the use of syllogisms, theoretical, practical or dramatic, answering questions such as 'why?' (Burke, 1945/1969; Gustafsson, 1994). Our reasoning is like a web of syllogisms, a pattern in which no syllogism is the first nor last. 'As if giving grounds did not come to an end sometime. But the end is not an ungrounded presupposition: it is an ungrounded way of acting' (*On certainty*, §110).

No syllogism is 'ungrounded'. There is always another supporting it. No presupposition is the first, standing alone and ungrounded. Only action is ungrounded; our leap over the abyss is our judging.

Our web of judgements, reasoning and syllogisms explaining our reasons is our way of having 'made up our mind', as Wahren put it. Conviction – having made up our mind – rises, emerges, not as a syllogism, being part of our web, but as something we find in the whole of the web and not in its parts. Our web of syllogisms does not stand on our convictions as a ground. On the contrary, if our conviction emerges from the web, the syllogisms are the support of our convictions. 'I have arrived at the rock bottom of my convictions. And one might almost say that these foundation-walls are carried by the whole house' (Wittgenstein, *On certainty*, §248).

Conviction does not rise as a logically deductive conclusion. Neither does it emerge as something we can willingly choose or refuse. Neither does it surface as a linear consequence of a thread or web of syllogisms, for that will be rational and linear. Instead it appears as something greater than the aggregate sum of its parts. It emerges as something enabling us, propelling us to take the leap over the abyss, freeing us from the situation in which the 'right' course of action cannot be deduced from its premises, enabling us to judge.

Leaping across the abyss . . . while keeping your feet on the ground

Judging is not something we do alone, not even alone on a mountaintop. Neither are our convictions totally our own. As social beings in a social world the faculty of judgement is neither objective nor subjective, but inter-subjective. Our convictions analogically emerge from our social context. According to Ronald Beiner's (1983) interpretation of Kant, we cannot be convinced about something and simultaneously be convinced that nobody else shares our conviction. Our narration of judgements implies an audience and a belief in the possibility that we could convince. The *others* are present. When we, as Arendt (1982) explains, judge by imagining ourselves in the place of others, we are not performing something in order to improve our judgement. Instead it is something we do implicitly when we judge. The ground on which we keep our feet when we judge is to be found in the social context – in the inter-subjective.

In exploring the web of syllogisms by which we explain our judgements we will find no ground on which the rest may stand. The story of the old lady who explained to the physicist that the universe was held up by the back of a turtle clarifies this idea. When the physicist asked what was holding up the turtle, the lady explained that it too was held up by another turtle. The physicist then inquired what the second turtle was held up by, and the lady answered: 'Well, you see, there are turtles all the way down.' Our rationality must be ungrounded in the sense that no syllogism lacks another to support it. None of them will be standing on – be deducible from – a ground. As Wittgenstein (1969) states,

> Bit by bit there forms a system of what is believed, and in that system some things stand unshakably fast and some are more or less liable to shift. What stands fast does so, not because it is intrinsically obvious or convincing; it is rather held fast by what lies around it. (*On certainty*, §144)

The ground on which to keep our feet is not found through deduction, but through knowledge of the practice by which we judge and the legitimacy through which our judgements will be convincing to ourselves as well as others. Although engaged in a 'groundless' activity, the competent assessor keeps his/her feet solidly on the (social) ground.

Notes

1. See Giddens (1986).
2. The description is, of course, simplified, but hopefully reflects the point I am trying to make.
3. For example, in one of the projects the project leader suddenly left the company when his father died and decided to work for the family business instead. While the company searched for someone to replace him, some project activities, such as software development that they had been buying from a software consultant company for seven months, were on hold. After six months, when they wanted to renew the activities, the software consultants were busy with other clients. Software development had to be bought elsewhere. This in turn led to about another six months' delay since the new company practically had to start from the beginning.

References

Arendt, H. (1982) *Lectures on Kant's political philosophy*. University of Chicago Press.
Bak, P. (1996) *How nature works*. New York: Springer-Verlag.

Beiner, R. (1983) *Political judgment.* University of Chicago Press.

Burke, K. (1945/1969) *A grammar of motives.* Berkeley: University of California Press.

Czarniawska-Joerges, B., and Guillet de Monthoux, P. (1994) *Good novels, better management.* London: Harwood Academic Press.

de Beauvoir, S. (1972/1992) *För en tvetydighetens moral [Pour une morale de l'ambiguité].* Göteborg: Daidalos.

Fisher, W. (1989) *Human communication as narration: toward a philosophy of reason, value, and action.* Columbia, SC: University of South Carolina Press.

Giddens, A. (1986) *The constitution of society.* Berkeley: University of California Press.

Glendinning, S. (1998) *On being with others: Heidegger, Derrida, Wittgenstein.* London: Routledge.

Gottsegen, M. (1994) *The political thought of Hannah Arendt.* Albany: State University of New York Press.

Guillet de Monthoux, P. (1991) *Action and existence, art and anarchism for business administration.* Munich: Accedo Verlag.

Gustafsson, C. (1994) *Produktion av allvar. Om det ekonomiska förnuftets metafysik.* Stockholm: Nerenius & Santérus Förlag

Kauffman, S. (1995) *At home in the universe.* London: Penguin.

Kuhn, T. (1996) *The structure of scientific revolutions.* 3rd ed. University of Chicago Press.

Luria, A.R. (1976) *Cognitive development: its cultural and social foundations.* Cambridge, MA: Harvard University Press.

MacIntyre, A. (1984) *After virtue.* 2nd ed. Notre Dame, IN: University of Notre Dame Press.

Popper, K.R. (1990) *A world of propensities.* Bristol: Thoemmes Press.

Ryle, G. (1949/1990) *The concept of mind.* University of Chicago Press.

Vickers, G. (1965/1995). *The art of judgment.* Palo Alto: Sage Publications.

von Wright. G.H. (1968) *An essay in deontic logic.* Amsterdam: North Holland Publishing Company.

Wittgenstein, L. (1953/1973) *Philosophical investigations.* Oxford: Blackwell.

Wittgenstein, L. (1975) *On certainty.* Oxford: Blackwell.

9
Stengel's roller coasters: engineering thrills into projects

Helena Csarmann

Mean scream machines

You are waiting in line for a ride on the Olympia Looping, once a record-breaking ride of five loops in a row. It is almost your turn. You smell popcorn in the air and you hear people screaming and laughing. You anticipate the feeling you will get in your stomach as you defy gravity and jerk into space.

Imagine Euro Star, an inverted coaster, where the train runs under the track and your feet hang in the air. It is a creation on an 844-metre track with a top speed of 80.8 km/h, and it subjects its riders to 5.2 Gs of vertical acceleration. You climb into the wagon. As the train lurches off, you brace your arms against the sides of the car.

You are riding the Top Thrill Dragster. In 2004 it was the fastest and highest coaster in the world. You travel straight up the hill, going from 0 to 193 km/h in four seconds – no opportunity here to take in the view. You are rotated 270 degrees and dropped 128 m straight down to the finish line and the station.

The principle behind a roller coaster is simple. With the help of a mechanical lift or launch system, a car or train is hauled up to the top. Then by means of gravity the vehicle is returned along a closed track to the station where the brakes are applied.

Airplanes, trains and buses generally take passengers to new places, but people travelling by roller coaster do not really get anywhere; they exit at the same spot they enter. Many times other means of transportation return passengers to their starting place too, but there is a significant difference between the airplane, the train, the bus and amusement-park attractions. The difference is the adrenaline rush from the roller coaster ride. It begins with the tingle of expectation as you wait in line, prods your nervousness when it is finally your turn to take a seat, heightens when the train starts with a jerk, sharpens as your head thuds against the back of the seat, fortifies you as you grasp the safety bar, and falsely reassures you after your car has climbed to the highest spot and slows down. Then comes the sudden drop. Your blood rushes through your veins, and your stomach cannot quite tell where it belongs.

Speed is certainly part of what a roller coaster ride is all about, but it is also about alteration of that speed, acceleration and G force. People on earth travel through space at high speed every day without even thinking about it. It is simply transportation. The roller coaster is different. It is the changing speed that makes the experience; acceleration is the attribute that sells.

Even the term *change of speed* is not enough to describe what is being marketed. It is not just speed in two dimensions. A roller coaster ride includes different types of loops and inversions. Take the 'vertical loop', for example. While it is a simple loop, it collaborates with other configurations to produce an added value to its attraction. A case in point is the 'Immelman', which starts like the simple loop, but when the train nears the apex, it is inverted and returns in the direction it came from. The 'cobra roll'[1] includes two inverted half loops that face each other at 45°. The value added is a change of speed in *three* dimensions.

Olympia Looping, Euro Star and Top Thrill Dragster have one thing in common: they have all been on the drawing board of Stengel GmbH of Munich. No ordinary engineering firm, Stengel GmbH constructs thrills, and out of its office spring the most exciting roller coasters in the world.

Mr Stengel's business

Werner Stengel, founder of the firm, has been involved in amusement rides for more than 40 years. Now 68 and retired, he is often still seen at Stengel GmbH working on amusement-ride projects with ten other engineering experts. At the beginning the office calculated the static of attractions, but later they broadened their scope to the creation of whole concepts. Today most of their work is designing roller coasters, the major amusement attractions of the world.

Since his start in 1963, Stengel, nicknamed King of the Coasters,[2] has put every project number and name down in a blue exercise book. Recently he tabulated these projects for an exhibition and a book that was being written about him.[3] In the now-yellowed pages of the exercise book, he identified 453 coasters that had been built[4] before the end of

2002; now the number is 460. According to *Coaster Force*, 'the Web's only complete resource for learning about the amusement and theme park industry',[5] there were approximately 1727 coasters in the world in 2003. That means that a quarter of the world's roller coasters originated in the Stengel office. And every year 220 million people (Kranewitter, 2001) ride these coasters.

Ideas for exciting events

The choice of coaster design has to do with where the idea and the initiative for a new coaster come from, and these can come from a variety of sources. The management at an amusement park may want a new coaster because they have heard that a fresh design has arrived on the market and is getting fabulous reviews. Or perhaps the idea surfaces during discussions with a manufacturer or with Stengel GmbH who have an idea for a new prototype but need a park to test it in. Sometimes park management or the manufacturer specifically wants a particular design because of a park's special conditions.[6]

In addition to designing new attractions, Stengel also works on further development of existing coasters. Jetline, the roller coaster that went into use at the Swedish amusement park Gröna Lund in 1988, is one example. It was rebuilt for the season of 2000 and new elements[7] were added. According to Gröna Lund's park and ride manager Peter Osbeck, the reason for the rehab was not that the guests were bored but that the park wanted to make Jetline even more popular and thrilling. Stengel GmbH remade the rail, and the park heightened the lift hill and made the first drop go all the way to the ground level where a tunnel was added. The ride really zips through the new tunnel, belching smoke as it does. (The first time I went on a ride after the reconstruction, I fell for it. I believed that the smoke actually was coming from a burning hot dog stand beneath the tunnel entrance. Eventually I realized that the smoke was an element to enhance the experience, and it certainly enhanced mine.)

Another one of Stengel's challenges is The Wild Mouse, the new roller coaster at Gröna Lund. Built within Jetline's existing structure, it was presented for the park's 120th birthday and the season of 2003 (van Etksröm-Ahlby and Garvanovic, 2002, p. 15). The new track sits on Jetline's supports and actually entwines itself within its space. According to Stengel, this made the design one of the toughest around.

The design therefore might be more or less decided upon when Stengel GmbH begins on a new project. In some cases, like the projects for Gröna Lund, the conditions are multiple and the options for the design fewer, depending on where the initiative and the idea come from.

Engineering safe projects

The design of a roller coaster – like the design of every technologically advanced machine – has technical and economic restraints. The engineers have to fulfill certain conditions when designing a new coaster or developing an older one. Today electromagnetic motor-powered steel coasters are designed by means of computers. *Illumin*, an Internet magazine that tries to provide us with 'a review of everyday life and engineering', reports, 'roller coasters will continue to develop with the rest of the world. They will continue to go faster and higher with more tricks. With new materials being developed and safety programs being made, there will undoubtedly be even better roller coasters to get thrills from (or be sick over)'.[8] In the amusement ride industry, as in any other industry, there is a technological development that is important for the modelling of the ride. 'As a construction it [the roller coaster] belongs to engineering architecture and is to be compared to other technological modern high-rise buildings around 1900, as for example bridge constructions, but also the Eiffel Tower or the Ferris Wheel' (Blume, 2001, p. 46).

Like the design for a bridge or any other construction, the design for a coaster necessitates complex calculations and engineering competence. In his very first projects, Stengel used a table of logarithms to calculate the static of a coaster. Today the engineers use CAD, the Finite Element Method[9] and over 200 computer programs to calculate the mechanics. In a common 5000-hour project, 4000 equations have to be solved (Stein, 2001).

Unlike the design of a bridge, the design of a coaster taps into almost every branch of engineering (Baine, 2000). The library of the Stengel office, with its literature on bridge construction, strength analysis, chemistry, computing, electrical engineering, hydraulics, mechanical engineering, pneumatics and welding technology, testifies to this relationship.

Specific technological requirements have to be fulfilled to insure the safety of an attraction. Stengel, who is a member of the German standards institute as well as the European committee working on standards, developed construction guidelines for fairgrounds. He also took part in the research groups evaluating passenger limit values for roller coasters. In their design of coasters, Stengel's engineers have to abide by the safety standards specially developed for amusement park rides, a continually growing number of DIN A4-pages with standards to pay attention to.

The safety requirements for amusement attractions are more strict than those for many other constructions. According to Stengel, the trains of the German Bundesbahn that every year transport hundreds of millions of people have passenger cars with doors that can be opened when the train is at full speed. As a result, some travellers are killed each year because they open the wrong door by accident. According to regulation, the cars of a roller coaster must be locked and blocked in a way that riders cannot inadvertently release the safety bar during the ride. When the German-based Kuka wanted to break into the entertainment business with the 'Robocoaster' that was going to turn thousands of guests on their heads, the company first had to get through 'the most difficult safety certification process on the planet'.[10]

Besides issues of technology and standards, an important consideration is the business of an attraction and how to decide upon its price. Stengel GmbH built Germany's first steel coaster in 1964 at the cost of 320,000 DM. The price of the Catapulting Coaster in Soltau was 45 million DM (Bischoff, 2001). The cost of an attraction depends on whether it is custom-made or not. The exact price is decided upon during the negotiations with the purchaser. In most cases, Stengel GmbH has to price the project before the engineers start the actual design. Through practice gained in working on over 460 coasters already in operation, they know how much work is behind a certain design. Using that experience they estimate a price for the new project.

The price is not written in stone, however. Making a coaster earthquake-safe might mean an additional 120 hours work time, for example. In this case, Stengel GmbH still estimates the price using knowledge from previous projects but afterwards makes a revised calculation. The price of a design that is changed during production is hard to estimate. Sometimes the purchaser comes up with a completely new idea after the project is well under way; sometimes the engineers have already completed hours of work on or even finished the design. The purchaser might, for example, want an extra looping or a change in the placement of a certain element. Then the static and the drawings have to be remade, and the customer sometimes balks at paying for the extra effort that could hardly be calculated before the changes were known. According to Stengel, the total engineering of a roller coaster can be quite closely estimated, anyway. It is not important how many metres of track it has or how many metres high a construction is. The engineers know what kind of track, wagon and lift are used in the design, and this is what decides the price. This does not imply that Stengel GmbH has no limits in terms of the cost of a coaster, but money is just another restraint that limits the design.

Aesthetic restrictions must also be taken into account. The attraction and its most terrifying curves and drops have to be visible to park visitors so that their fear and curiosity will make them approach the coaster for a further look or even for a ride. In addition, the state authority has to accept a new attraction that alters the outer appearance of the park. Such an aesthetic circumstance might be a local height restriction based on how tall or flat the buildings surrounding the park are.

While the design of attractions has to fulfill certain conditions, it also has to be entertaining.[11] How does Stengel know what element of an attraction to choose in the design? What makes an attraction thrilling? One of the competences needed when constructing the experience of a roller coaster is knowledge about the thrill.

Measuring emotions

It is the designer who must come up with the thrill element, that certain something that will make the attraction successful and offer the guests the best experience.

> Today, the entertainment industry has more and better technical choices than ever before, and we tend to make those choices with less insight, less heart, and less idea of what it is we're communicating than ever before.... The technology may gather a crowd, but after you've gathered that crowd, you'd better have something more for them. Something that's really going to dazzle their eyes, stimulate their minds, and if you're lucky, touch their hearts.[12]

To be sure, this goes beyond the required knowledge of the technology, standards and economics involved.

Bennett (2000) claims that his book *Roller coaster* contains everything the roller coaster enthusiast wants to know about his favourite pastime. According to Bennett, the exhilaration of a ride is derived from G force and so-called airtime, the sensation of flying out of your seat during a ride. At 1 G, people experience their own body weight. At 2 G, people have the sensation of being two times heavier; at negative G – air time – they experience the sensation of being weightless and being lifted out of their seats. This airtime is experienced when the coaster descends or ascends a hill where the cars are made to follow a curvature that is slightly lower than the one they would follow if not held to the tracks.[13] The car leaves riders behind in the air while it drops out from underneath them. According to one, 'It was a whirlwind, lightheaded ride that was smooth and fast... an utterly painless experience that is astonishing for its variety of movement and out-of-body sensation. The vertical loop was the most timeless moment of the whole thing' (p. 99). Another describes it this way: 'The first drop launches the coaster like a rocket over shallow camel-hump dips on its way to the turn; the air time is phenomenal.... It's fast, breathless and gut wrenching all the way round' (p. 110). 'The drop that follows is pure air-time delight' (p. 109). 'Lofty summits, near-vertical drops and plenty of air time combine with other thrilling elements to produce the smoothest steel coaster ride of its type' and... 'the elusive "butterfly tickle" in the tummy lasts all the way to the ground' (p. 104). And finally, 'About half way we hit the first hill and negative G and air time, where you get the real sensation of weightlessness. My feet start coming out of my shoes' (p. 102).

Certainly it can be supposed that the change in G forces and the airtime give a certain feeling in the stomach, the feeling the Swedish amusement park Gröna Lund targeted when it displayed a stomach moving up and down in their 2002 advertising campaign. That something, the right feeling of an attraction, seems to mean different things to different customer groups, however. The smallest children do not appreciate the same attractions as the older ones (you and me), and the enthusiasts are fond of monsters like X, for example, 'the first dual direction, inverted, floorless, flying, flipping, vertical dropping, rotating roller coaster' (Sakowski, 2002).

An important design consideration is the acceleration experienced by the passengers. The roller coaster is a mechanism that through technology brings about experiences of motion. '[I]t is not about a uniform motion, but about an excessive combination of acceleration, force of gravity and instability that stimulates the ability of the senses to take in – comparable to an accident. It is a play with the power of speed and acceleration that every man fears' (Blume, 2001, p. 46).

The goal is to maximize the excitement of the ride without endangering the rider. How many G the rider can withstand depends on the magnitude, the duration and the onset of the G force and how quickly it is taken away, among other variables. The onset refers to the speed of the acceleration, which equates to how quickly the G force is applied to you. If the exposure of the acceleration is short, passengers can withstand immense force. In an automobile accident, for example, a person may be exposed to 80 or even 100 G in a frontal crash but still survive with the help of an airbag because the exposure lasts for just a millisecond. An alpine skier may be exposed to 20 G in the foot, 12 G at the knee, 6 G in the stomach and 2 G to the head. Even in your daily life, if you hop off a step, you are exposed to a gravitational pull of 8 G, depending on your jumping style. Without information about exposure time, then, the amount of G by itself does not say a lot about the danger involved.

In roller coasters, exposure to high G often lasts just fractions of a second, and it is possible to stand 7–8 G. Stengel knows that the borderline 6 G for one second is harmless for the average passenger. On Stengel's looping coasters, a billion passengers have ridden without being injured.

Equally significant is the exposure time to lower forces as well. At 3 G, 14 seconds' exposure may lead to a blackout, according to Stengel. G forces have many physiological effects; one is a redistribution of the blood supply. Therefore, even longer exposures to lower Gs represent a danger. Positive G forces can cause a pooling of blood in the feet and, as a result, the heart may not be able to circulate the blood effectively. If this happens, a person experiences a *grey out*, and when the forces increase, a *blackout*. Finally unconsciousness occurs. In case of negative G forces, the blood is forced to the brain, and the experience is then termed a *red out*. Tolerances vary by individual, and the time of exposure is significant in estimating physical strain. In the face of even short acceleration exposure, veins become unable to do their job and the cardiovascular system is stressed. Less blood is returning to the heart and cardiac output is compromised.

Acceleration is measured along three axes: vertical, lateral and fore and aft. Requirements for lateral G forces are very different from requirements for vertical G forces, so it is important to make clear which direction is referred to.[14] According to Stengel, the human body is better at handling straight drops than side-to-side motions. People can withstand accelerations of the order of 10 G in directions perpendicular to their bodies without any permanent adverse effects, but it is not possible to withstand 10 G of lateral acceleration.

Writing standards

To reduce lateral accelerations Stengel invented the construction principle of 'the heart-line spin', an invention he is proud of since it makes the attraction thrilling without making the rider feel ill.

Stengel and his colleagues managed that [to reduce lateral accelerations] by designing the entire coaster around what's known as the heart line—the path created by the center of the torso as the rider travels the length of the coaster. In a standard coaster, trains are forced to follow the steel backbone of the track wherever it goes, often yanking riders violently around twists and turns. In a heart-line coaster, by contrast, the tracks are molded around the rider's heart line in order to minimize side-to-side motion. So despite its incredible speed, the Millennium Force offers a very smooth ride, making it 'one of the safest means of public conveyance', Stengel says.[15]

Here is how it works. In only a few milliseconds after the coaster enters a curve, the rider is twisted into a new position. The rotation of the track is usually around the backbone or about the center of the track, and this results in a harsh turning of the body. In just this short space of time, the rider's head would be thrust one way, yet because of inertia it remains in its position. This is, according to Stengel, something that makes for an uncomfortable ride for the passenger.

Stengel's heart-line invention lets the head of the rider move a shorter distance than otherwise. If the point is that the head should be moved as little as possible, why not rotate around the head so that it has to move an even shorter distance, maybe not at all? To rotate around the heart line is a compromise. If the rotation is around the head, the legs are swung away more, which is not a problem since the G forces the legs are subjected to do no harm. Of greater concern is the effect on the car. It swings away more, and when it turns rapidly it is exposed to high acceleration, so the wheels hit the track hard. Besides, the location of rotation has to be a compromise because the passengers sitting next to each other are seldom the same height. Whatever line the body is rotated around will not affect both riders the same way. From this invention of the heart-line spin comes the element of the *heart roll*,[16] where the passenger rides straight around the middle and the rest is rotated around the centre line.

Designing scream machines is about functioning on a border. Somewhere between nausea and fun lies the boundary. On the wrong side is nausea; on the right side is pleasure. The ability to comprehend that correct feeling testifies to the competence of Stengel's designers, who truly understand their task is to design a good experience for different customer groups. This ability is of crucial importance to successful construction of a scream machine that gives the rider a kick and a certain feeling in the stomach – without nausea. The construction principle of Stengel's heart-line spin integrated in the design demonstrates an understanding of the appreciation of the right thrill.

Skills behind thrills

In addition to fulfilling technical and economic demands, a roller coaster must provide entertainment, be an experience, and insure the return of customers to the amusement park. Although the construction of a new roller coaster requires innovative design and competent follow-through, these two skills are not enough. Creating a new coaster involves using a rational, technological creative process to bring the emotional rewards of joy and pleasure to the riders. In the Stengel office the process links the rational with the reckless, the profound with the playful.

A design with well balanced G forces and airtime provides the right feeling in the stomach of a person riding a roller coaster. It is what gives you the sinking feeling when the car descends a drop and leaves you hanging in the air. Words like unique, rare and surprising are used to describe the experience in a coaster. 'The shock of the new' (de Cauter, 1993) is another way to label the moment of surprise that makes up the experience.

A roller coaster ends in the same spot as it begins, but in between are an endless number and variety of ups and downs. In the richness of variations lies the difficulty as well as the opportunity. Once again de Cauter's words emphasize that unpredictability is necessary to the success of the ride. If the rider is surprised, the roller coaster is successful. Stengel's skill is to find the successful surprising combination of elements among the variants. Explicit knowledge such as following standards and making careful calculations is absolutely necessary, but all the explicit knowledge in the world cannot make up for lack of consideration of that feeling in the stomach.

Stengel's ability to know about an attraction's thrill can be seen as intuitive or a gut feeling. Larsson (1892/1997) explains intuition as a rich synthesis of ideas. The eye cannot see every detail at the same time, but one's experiences and ideas are all available in the person's memory. The intuitive skill, according to Larsson, demands time for reflection to develop. Stengel, for example, has had time to develop his skill through his many years of experience in this highly specialized field of amusement rides. According to Larsson, ideas come from a person's earlier experiences and understanding. Stengel's expert designers, for example, blend their individual experience from different attractions all over the world to build their thrills.

Sjöstrand (1997), like Larsson (1892/1997), says intuition refers to experiences that the individual at a certain point in time is unable to articulate or communicate intersubjectively in any explicit linguistic form. Sjöstrand suggests that intuitive judgement plays an important part in turning strategic decisions and thinking into concrete organized practice. For the managers, as for the Stengel engineers, intuition is a vital ingredient and sometimes a key factor in realizing the action in the same way that calculation has its role in the context.

According to Sjöstrand, the intuition can also operate as a safeguard against strategic mistakes. In the Stengel office, 200 computer programs perform calculations on the constructions. Stengel claims that he can see the connections without the programs and that he therefore does not use them a great deal.[17] If he observes a load case, for example, he understands what the forces, torques and deformations must be like without having to calculate it. When he does use the programs, he is able to question the reality in the given answers. In this way his skill acts as a safeguard. Sjöstrand (1997) also refers to Michael Polanyi's related concept of 'tacit knowledge', a competence that is difficult to pass on to others, since there is no language to express the crucial knowledge or skill involved.

So how did Stengel learn about the right thrill? Did Stengel and his friends have a teacher from whom they learned this information or did they receive their skill through reading certain books? According to Stengel, one cannot study to become an amusement-ride designer. No coursework exists and no knowledge about this type of design appears in the literature. One has to grasp the connection in another way. One way is to be in the business for a long time and conduct research. Stengel has been in the business for over 40 years and during the years has collected data from many sources, including NASA. Another way to find out about the thrill is to test it. Stengel's record of rides in 200 different roller coasters is not an achievement the common man can brag about. Stengel and his colleagues compare their visits to different amusement parks and record their own reactions as well as the reactions of other coaster riders. They have learned about the gut feeling by being steeped in the business.

Breaking into the business is a complicated process. Two younger engineers are currently being trained in the Stengel office. At this point they have become familiar with the available computer programs, but they are not yet able to understand the thrill or question the answers given by the programs, according to Stengel, who demonstrates to the young engineers how he handles the construction task. Under Stengel's watchful eye, the two newcomers try, make mistakes, and try again. In the process they develop the right feeling and acquire their skill, according to Stengel. The tacit knowledge is passed on and absorbed through careful observation of the actions of the seasoned engineer.

In addition to intuition or tacit knowledge, another term for this skill is Gustafsson's (1994) 'Feeling of Zap'. This is the feeling that emerges from a concrete experience, is given time to develop, and then becomes the ability to discern a pattern. The fact that individuals are able to reason about and rationally analyse their acts does not necessarily mean that their acts in practice follow the same reasoning. Rationality is necessary, but it is not enough. The reasoning, according to Gustafsson, necessitates feelings. Connected to feelings, the reason leads to understanding and practice, and that is skill. The seasoned designers of Stengel GmbH have been riding different attractions for years. In individually different ways they have a concrete experience of the right feeling of an attraction. This gives them the ability to observe a pattern and predict the success or failure of a roller coaster ride. They finally see that something that makes the attraction successful and offers the passenger the best experience.

The design of a coaster is an organized timely process that takes engineering, business and thrill skill. The duration and intensity of the forces at work are calculated to offer that special something. Besides the analytical knowledge of technology and economics, non-analytical knowledge is also necessary in the design of this apparatus. Identifying the feeling of the right thrill of an attraction is fundamental to the production of a successful coaster.

This chapter identifies a management perspective sometimes repressed in the academic world, a certain competence coming from the hard areas as well as the soft areas of the emotions. The design of a successful roller coaster provides a first-class example of how an experience is built, an experience constructed on emotional as well as technological foundations.

Notes

1. This element is also known as 'batwing' or 'boomerang'.
2. Master of Horror, Godfather, Roller Coaster Pope, Master of the Loop and Inventor of Sweet Pain (*Der Spiegel*, 6/98) are some of his other nicknames.
3. Werner Stengel was asked to give permission for a book to be written about him for an exhibition in the city museum of Munich. The result was *Roller Coaster – Der Achterbahn-Designer Werner Stengel* by Schützmannsky (2001).

4. In addition to the 453 coasters which have actually been built, cost estimates for 257 more coasters have been done, and 211 sketches have been made of coasters not yet built.
5. http://www.coasterforce.com/index.php, 2003-04-09
6. For example: the sea forms the park boundary on the west and south sides of the Swedish amusement park Gröna Lund, and there is no spare land on the remaining east and north sides. For this reason the conditions for adding a new machine are special. The new machinery has to be squashed into a very small place.
7. An element is a section of track that can be added to a ride to increase its thrill factor.
8. http://www.usc.edu/dept/engineering/illumin/archives/fall2000/design/roller/index.htm, 2002-04-05
9. The finite element method is a method for solving partial differential equations (PDEs). The method is applicable to a wide range of physical and engineering problems, provided it can be expressed as a PDE.
10. http://www.funworldmagazine.com/2003/Mar03/Features/Robotic%20Revolution/RoboticRevolution.html, 2003-05-23
11. Stengel will not design an attraction that does not fulfill the economic and technological conditions, even if it is the most entertaining attraction ever seen.
12. http://www.brcweb.com/articles.html, 2003-06-02
13. http://www.coasterforce.com/Glossary, 2006-09-7
14. http://www.funworldmagazine.net/2003/Mar03/Features/G%20Forces/G%20Forces.html, 2003-05-23
15. http://www.discover.com/issues/jun-01/departments/Featphys/
16. Other names are 'Zero-G Roll' and 'Heartline Spin'.
17. Stengel GmbH always uses the programs to perform the calculations demanded by the customers.

References

Baine, C. (2000) *The fantastical engineer – A thrillseeker's guide to careers in theme park engineering*. Eugene, OR: Bonamy Publishing.

Bennett, D. (2000) *Roller coaster*. Secaucus, NJ: Chartwell Books.

Bischoff, J. (2001) Die Lust am freien Fall. *Lufthansa Magazin*, 5 (May), pp. 36–9.

Bittner, R. (2001) *Urbane Paradiese. Zur Kulturgeschichte modernen Vergnügens*. Frankfurt am Main: Campus Verlag.

Blume, T. (2001) Oder die Welt gerät Tempo, Tempo, vollständig aus den Fugen. In R. Bittner, *Urbane Paradiese. Zur Kulturgeschichte modernen Vergnügens*. Frankfurt am Main: Campus Verlag.

Blume, T. (2001) *Die Achterbahn – oder Die Welt Gerät Tempo, Tempo, Vollständig aus den Fugen*. Frankfurt am Main: Campus Verlag.

de Cauter, L. (1993) The panoramic ecstacy: on world exhibitions and the disintegration of experience. *Theory, Culture & Society*, 10, pp. 1–23.

Gustafsson, C. (1994) *Produktion av allvar*. Stockholm: Nerenius & Santérus.

Gustafsson, C. (2000) Känslan av ZAP. *Dialoger*, 53.

154   Aesthetic Leadership

Kranewitter, K. (2001) Das auf und ab der Werner Stengel. *München Süd*, 1 (18 April).

Larsson, H. (1892/1997) *Intuition – Några ord om diktning och vetenskap*. Stockholm: Dialoger.

Sakowski, E. (2002) Xtraordinary – Arrow hits the mark. *First Drop*, 58 pp. 22–7.

Schützmannsky, K. (2001) *Roller Coaster – Der Achterbahn-Designer Werner Stengel*. Heidelberg: Kehrer Verlag.

Scriba, J. (1998) Der Herr des Schreckens. *Der Spiegel*, 6, pp. 180–2.

Sjöstrand, S.-E. (1997) *The two faces of management*. London: Thomson International Business Press.

Stein, I. (2001) Im Rausch der Fliehkraft. *Mitteldeutsche Zeitung*, 31 (16 June).

van Ekström-Ahlby, D., and J. Garvanovic, (2002) Gröna Lund – It's more than a mouse. *First Drop*, 58, p. 15.

10
Engineering improvisation: the case of Wärtsilä

Marcus Lindahl

Creative engineering in industrial bureaucracy

Planning is always a challenge in turbulent environments, but executing those plans in an unstable context is even tougher – to say nothing of being unwise. Christensen and Kreiner (1991) call it a trade-off between reducing operational and contextual uncertainty. Whether the concern is traditional 'line' production or production through 'projects', a critical success factor in coping with troublesome circumstances is flexibility or improvisation. So much depends on the project manager's ability to maintain progress in the situation rather than stick to a plan that should not or cannot be followed without considerable extra cost.

Planning and improvisation should be recognized as necessary ingredients in project execution. The question is how to improvise in highly bureaucratic environments, how to make improvisation possible in sight of the prescribed plans of many different organizations. Improvisation must happen despite formal contractual agreements on scope and standard operating procedures imposed and maintained by headquarters. In addition, an equal challenge is determining how a bureaucratic system can be held intact despite many recurring improvisations.

The tension between a bureaucratic system and improvisation can be elaborated on by looking closely at two distinctive conditions for improvised actions. Improvisations usually occur when for some reason there is no plan of action. There may have been no such thing as a plan in the first place or whatever plan was envisioned may have become obsolete. In project improvisation, there was probably an initial plan. This means that a plan was probably used to organize, coordinate and control project actions. Equally important is the fact that it is probably still being used to organize, coordinate and control other actors or events *during* as well as *after* improvisation. This results in a situation with potential for tension created by management's need to coordinate the project through the 'normal' tools and techniques of project management. On the one hand, contractual agreements, detailed planning and earned value measurement-based follow-up are highly intrusive instruments designed to coordinate and control by domination of the subordinate. On the other hand, management must take advantage of the situation and act instantly with flexibility, agility and speed. In dramaturgical terms, management must pull off an 'Attic theatre', that is, management must merge the Apollonian mentality represented by standard project management tools and techniques with its Dionysian counterpart of fluxus, intoxication and improvisation (compare Nietzsche, 1867/1999).

Being flexible or being able to improvise has at least two components. One is the ability or skill to come up with alternative solutions like new products or new processes (cf. Moorman and Miner, 1998). The other component of being flexible or able to improvise has to do with the ability to initiate such activities in the existing organization. If the first component is a question of creating a solution, the other is a question of creating organizational and performance 'space' for such a solution (see also Lindahl, 2003). A continuous establishment of 'exceptions' mitigates this slightly paradoxical tension between the need for stability and the need for flexibility.

Engineering power plants

Engineers who work hard to manage large construction projects provide an effective case for elaboration on the peculiarity of exceptions. The case in point involves the construction of diesel power plants. The engineers manage the execution phase of these projects, and they are in charge of activities at the site. In this case, they supervise, coordinate and monitor the activities that are to turn a green area of a couple of hectares in Central America into an industrial compound including oil cisterns, buildings, roads, fuel-treatment facilities, cooling facilities, and of course engine and generator systems.

A project of this kind can by any standards be labeled complex. When components do not work properly or when already poured foundations prove to have less strength than intended, this complexity is of a technical nature. More often though, the complexity is of a managerial nature. Many types of equipment have to be put together. The location where the plants are being built is often wet, hot and relatively poor in terms of GNP/capita. Many different parties are involved, ranging from American customers and rigid local authorities to small subcontracting firms with sometimes questionable skills.

Last but not least, time is scarce, very scarce. From start to finish, from sales to delivery, the project must be carried out in just 10 to 14 months. During that period, the heap of equipment has to be transformed into an oil-combusting diesel power plant that produces a couple of hundred megawatts. Like any project worth a half a billion Swedish crowns and daily delay penalties in the range of 400,000 SEK, jobs are carefully planned, carefully monitored through advanced follow-up systems, and carefully controlled through a whole set of procedures and routines.

In 'real time', however, the unfolding of these projects seldom goes according to plan or procedure. A great deal of the project management's time is consumed by initiating quick changes in installation sequences, by shifting personnel from one area to another in seemingly random fashion, or by figuring out new means to persuade subcontractors to speed up, supervise, plan or monitor their work. Improvisation is abundant as well as crucial. By careful and skillful improvisation within a framework of relatively bureaucratic and intrusive routines, these engineers manage – surprisingly often – to finish the project on time, within budget and with a happy American customer to boot.

Looking at a site in India develops the argument further. Ibel, an ongoing power plant project, is located 100 kilometers south of Goa. The two site managers in charge were Tom and Janne, and they and their ten colleagues had the task of seeing that Wärtsilä, a Finnish manufacturing company building large diesel engines, delivered an operational diesel power plant with an output of 106 MW. It was to be built in only fifteen months, which is considered very fast in this type of business.

From project to event

Once in a while Tom and Janne had to go out and crack coconuts at the site. This was to awaken and inform Ganesh, the god with the elephant head. The priest rang a little bell, and Tom and Janne, with traditionally colored foreheads, had the honor of cracking the brown fruits against the concrete. It was important to have the approval of the god or the gods before beginning the construction process.

At three it was time for Puja in relation to the erection of the first chimney segment. One prays to Ganesh, and he is one of the most popular of all gods here. He is the leader of leaders, and there are some things that make him a good leader. A good leader always listens;

Ganesh has very big ears. A good leader must think and be intelligent; Ganesh has a very big head. A good leader must discover everything and know his environment. A good leader proceeds carefully; Ganesh is carried by a mouse that walks with small steps. A bit of hocus pocus is performed with coconuts, bananas, apples, and scents. Then one rings a bell to wake up the gods and tell them that we are about to start building. After that one paints a swastika on the chimney and decorates it with a flower. (Transcribed from field notes, 2000)

The Indian workforce regarded it as important for senior management to take part in the wakening of the gods at special occasions. Thus Tom and Janne as site managers were once in a while asked to take part in the ceremonies. If the ceremony was not conducted, it meant bad luck.

The question is whether or not Ganesh really woke up at the ringing of the bells, the scent and the fruit. According to the two site managers, the Ibel project was the worst project they had been involved in during their whole careers. This was not because of the exotic rituals or the almost tropical climate but because of all the complications that constantly surfaced during project execution. They had worked on many projects, and according to them, they were the two guys who were assigned when things were getting rough.

Soon, however, they had to wonder if they were actually the men for the job. The chance of finishing the project on time was poor, if not non-existent. Over 1,500 workers representing over 20 subcontracting firms made coordination very difficult. From day one, severe delays in most areas made the situation even worse. Delayed material, too little material, defective material, too little delayed defective material, delayed work, poor work and poor delayed work were all normal conditions. Very little in this project went according to plan.

Although this particular context may seem conspicuously exotic – gods have to be awakened with fruit, flowers and chants – the process of execution shares many similarities with other construction projects that have been studied. One common feature of particular interest is the status of the ongoing project in relation to the other projects that the company has performed or is performing. Project members commenting on their current project make strikingly similar responses. According to Tom and Janne, however, the Ibel project was the worst project they had ever managed. As they pointed out, running a fast-track project might work anywhere else in the world but not in India. They were frustrated that the sales department had agreed to the terms and above all that the management team had no say in which subcontractors were hired to do the work. They also noted, however, that this was exactly what was to be expected, and if anyone could pull it off, it was Tom and Janne. They saw themselves as the ones put in charge when things looked grim. As they told the junior site administrator:

> De som arbetar på andra projekt är djävla amatörer som glassar upp på någon flotte på någon djävla söderhavsö medan Janne och Tom är fångande att "småknulla upp ett kraftverk genom att snacka med Indier" som Tom uttryckte det. "Det kräver sin man". (T.S., June 4, 2000)
>
> Those working in other projects are fucking amateurs showing up on some raft on some Pacific island while Janne and Tom are caught to 'gently shag up a power plant by talking to Indians', as Tom put it. 'It takes a special man.' (Transcribed from field notes, 2000: the Swedish term 'småknulla' actually defies translation.)

A similar story can be told about a project in Central America. According to that project management team, the time schedule for the project was the tightest one ever, and the conditions for execution the toughest. Fortunately, the assembled project team members were handpicked on the basis of their excellent skill and experience. Studies of more than 14 power plant projects lead to the conclusion that almost every project seemed to be the one with the tightest schedule and the toughest conditions ever to be performed in company history. Another striking observation is how frequently the cliché 'all's fair in love and war', with the contextual add-on 'and in building power plants', is heard in the company's project management community.

Should one interpret this pattern of 'war stories' with von Wrightian or even Spenglerian pessimism? Assessing motivation and commitment provides some insight into these claims. By highlighting and exaggerating a task's difficulty, teams may knit together in the face of failure. By being proud of the skill and expertise of those in the group, teams encourage fortitude and the 'can do' mentality so vital to projects.

This phenomenon might also be viewed through a cultural lens. A Finnish company with a majority of Finns working in project management changes the battlefield but not the interpretation. In this light, the company mythology can be seen as reflection of the 'underdog mentality' and 'Sisu' celebrated in Finnish cultural treasures like 'Fänrik Ståls sägner' and in the commonly held 'memoirs' of war experiences told in the epic film 'Unknown Soldier', for instance.

Motivation and commitment are vital in project execution which cannot rest on the boring but persistent efficiency of the bureaucracy (Gustafsson, 1998). A complementary view can and should be taken as well. A consequence of these project descriptions is that each project is considered to be special, not belonging to the group of 'normal' projects that the company generally takes on. Through this description, every project becomes unique, not on a theoretical level that some project scholars love to promote but in a highly practical way. Since the project is unique compared to all other projects, general rules and procedures do not necessarily apply.

In 'Project management as boundary work', Sahlin-Andersson (2002) discusses the importance of managing the boundaries of the project. Formulating and reformulating the goal and the character of the project can influence the conditions for project execution. Sahlin-Andersson points to the early stages of what was to later become the so-called Stockholm Globe Arena and suggests that defining the project as 'extraordinary' played an important role in making it possible to execute the project the way it was.

By defining and understanding the project as 'extraordinary', those favouring the project emphasized that it was an exception. Hence, even though this particular case went against earlier policies, it did not mean that the policy was being questioned or was up for revision. Second, viewing the project as extraordinary meant that it was seen as unique, implying that no comparable objects or reference existed. This excused the lack of clear plans. The presentation of the project in quite spectacular, extraordinary and at times unexpected ways also partly buffered it from criticism (2002, p. 256).

The observations of Sahlin-Andersson seem to correspond to the rhetorical construction that the site management team is involved in.

This so-called exception, however, is not only rhetorical. A labelling of the project as 'extraordinary' takes place on several levels. In order to develop the argument further, it is necessary to consider some aspects of the context in which these projects are performed. Some recurring 'exceptional' situations are of particular interest.

These projects are executed through the substantial collaboration of several parties. As few as four and as many as twenty-plus subcontracting firms are usually hired to perform the actual construction work at the site. The site management team from Wärtsilä is responsible for overall coordination, control and technical expertise throughout the execution phase. According to contractual agreements and company policy, the subcontractors are paid in relation to progress. This means that payments are made when the subcontractor has achieved 20 per cent, 30 per cent, 40 per cent, and so forth of the agreed tasks. Top management has historically been concerned with cash-flow management and is insistent that the sites should not act as 'banks'. That is, they should not pay any bills before tasks are completed.

In practice this policy is generally ignored. When subcontractors file their bills, site management usually pays them immediately. In other instances, site management orders and pays for material that falls under the responsibility of other parties. In Ibel, for instance, site management paid all outstanding bills owed to a critical supplier by a subcontractor. Another subcontractor who in fact had done very little or close to nothing received 5/7 of contractual value in order to keep the workers at site. Other projects revealed this same sort of activity.

Another observable phenomenon is the frequent introduction of incentive systems, such as giving a bonus when a situation becomes critical. In Ibel the construction of a large water reservoir was particularly problematic. Site management had made several attempts to get the subcontractor to plan, coordinate and work more efficiently, but despite these efforts the result was disappointing. Finally Janne offered a bonus to the involved workers as well as a special bonus to three of the subcontractor's managers if the reservoir was finished according to the new, updated plan. The water reservoir was never delayed after this point.

Unique events for exceptional improvisations

These fragments show how site management may violate formal policy and agreements. When asked about accountability, managers usually explain there was no other way to get the project done on schedule. A common denominator is the labelling of these situations, as well as the actions taken, 'exceptional'.

Project execution seen through the frame of a Gantt chart of +2400 activities looks a great deal like an operation executed with almost military precision. To no one's surprise, however, this is not how projects develop in general. From a more ethnographic perspective a different image emerges. In this light the enterprise more resembles Lindblom's civil servants who, without much information or certainty, are forced to muddle their way from one decision or action to the next (Lindblom, 1959). Missing materials, delays and unforeseen events make the process of execution deviate from the planned course of action.

Executing a project in rural areas or in developing regions throughout the world carries with it significant uncertainty and turbulence. It is not uncommon for the original project schedule to gradually lose its ability to mirror what happens in the project, which also means that accurate follow-up becomes more difficult. Due to continuous disruptions caused by the unexpected, the planning horizon can suddenly shrink to a couple of weeks or during very problematic periods, to a couple of days. In order to maintain progress, management must take advantage of every situation that emerges. To a significant extent one has to improvise one's way through the whole project execution and come up with solutions continuously, not just in isolated magical moments.

Tom's and Janne's position in this situation is certainly problematic. The site managers, together with a handful of supervisors, are responsible for the execution of the construction activities where the plant is being built. However, the site team does not build anything. The ones who are actually performing the tasks at site are the 1500 workers representing the more than 20 different subcontractor firms. When it has to be used, improvisation can neither be said to happen within a clear group nor is it performed in relation to a commonly held goal. Neither is it a given then that the project will be viewed as one project. Rather, it can be seen as multiple interrelated projects. The goal for the management team – to deliver a power plant – can in the perspective of the subcontractors be formulated as a delivery of foundations and roads, of a house or of a given set of mechanical installations.

The single project therefore has the character of a matrix organization with its potential for conflicts. The subcontractors individually deliver different constructions. At the same time the site management team must see to it that an integrated system is handed over to the customer in fewer than 15 months. As a consequence of this, the different organizations may not even have the same view of the goal. While site management is responsible for a complete power plant, the subcontractor Alpha gets paid in relation to how many foundations they have been able to pour. Therefore, organizations will most likely have different views on what is the most efficient way of getting the work done. For site management it is not enough to see that the pouring is performed efficiently; overall progress must be satisfactory as well. As a consequence, a site manager is sometimes forced to compromise the efficiency of an individual activity, such as grouting, in order to maintain good overall progress.

When several organizations with potentially different interests are involved, improvisation quickly becomes a highly political issue from a site management perspective. Many interests and structures that presumably must be overcome stand between the management's desire to solve a problem in a different way than planned and the success of that improvisation.

In order for the improvisation to be successful, the site management team must sustain a long chain of action. This chain of action – since it is improvised – often cuts through previously established routines, rules and formal agreements. Despite different goals and/or interpretations of goals, all of the involved units emphasize the need for management to find a solution that technically works, and equally important, one that is acceptable to all the involved parties. The consequence of planning and follow-up is that at the same time the risk of aberrations decreases, the project becomes more sensitive to the aberrations that actually occur. The more site management uses its formal planning system to control the subcontractors, the more difficult it is to use the subcontractors for improvised actions.

Here is how it plays out. At the same time as site management has to rely heavily on the formal control system that uses planning and control as instruments to secure an efficient, foreseeable project execution, it has to find ways to persuade the subcontractors to abandon the formal rules and routines that have been imposed on them earlier by the same site management. The question is how management who has forced a subcontractor – often through threats and hard words – to plan and to stick to the plan, can then convince the subcontractor to temporarily give up the plan in order to do something in a completely different way. Not only that, site management must also be able to put the subcontractor back into the same formal system when the activities are on track.

The successful establishment of an exception or an exceptional state must be considered as central to the mitigation of this tension. Regardless of whether or not in reality the project is difficult or exceptional, this classification has its advantages. The label 'extraordinary' signals that existing rules and regulations may not necessarily be applicable in the specific case.

One 'exceptional' situation that stands out is the *crisis*. The crisis, or in more severe cases, the *disaster*, has many qualities that enable improvisation (see, for instance, Hutchins, 1991; Ciborra, 1999). One of the most important effects of the crisis is that the existing system of norms can be temporarily bracketed and replaced by another, and in an acute crisis a deepened form of collaboration occurs when different parties come together to face a common threat. Personal differences as well as many formal restrictions can at least temporarily be laid aside. The crisis thus provides an opening for unorthodox solutions and methods to be used to complete the project.

The crisis not only affects site management in terms of motivation, commitment and reinterpretation of formal regulations. Convincing the subcontractor that there is a project crisis and that the subcontractor's poor progress is responsible for the problematic situation gives site management more room for action. However, a crisis in the perception of site management may not translate to a crisis situation in the perception of the subcontractor. Site managers must emphasize the seriousness of the situation so that the other parties will be convinced that a crisis is indeed at hand, even though management might just want to gain time in order to improve conditions later in the project. In this case the crisis is constructed rather than genuine, and the objective is to make unorthodox solutions possible (compare Granlund, 2002). During times when the crisis label is questionable, planning fulfills an important function. Plans and follow-up have a strong legitimizing power since what is put into the plan and into the formal follow-up system can be seen as objective statements of the project's state. By participating in the planning and follow-up work, the parties therefore have a chance to influence the report on how 'well' or 'badly' the project is progressing. Negative progress statements sustain the feeling of urgency and crisis. The chances of persuading a subcontractor to increase to two shifts, to hire more workers or to accept sudden changes in installation sequences are thereby improved. Crisis may be the most comprehensive 'exceptional situation' in this context. The crisis does not necessarily produce permanent change. The change may only be temporary, which is of course significant in this case.

There are other forms of exceptional situations or states. Bonuses, for example, slightly alter the relationship between the parties. Instead of a purely formal relationship between two firms, the activity becomes personal. An agreement between individuals has been reached – such as the one between Janne and the subcontractor's supervisor Isaphan or between Janne and the worker Singh – which runs parallel or counter to the formal agreements between Wärtsilä and Alpha. Wärtsilä and Alpha still maintain their formal relationship, but Janne and Isaphan have made a deal, a deal that is personal and lies outside any formal agreement.

A similar pattern of exception can be noted in the 'altruistic' financing situation. In the case of 'altruistic' financing or procurement, the site management team manages to get the missing material and get the job done. At the same time it also helps a subcontractor in a very problematic situation. The next time site management is in a tight spot, the chances of getting a little extra help from the subcontractor are presumably better than before.

A last example of the state of exception is direct supervision. In theory the site management team is responsible for coordinating the whole execution process and for serving as technical consultants when necessary. Routine supervision and management of installation activities are normally tasks for the subcontractor's own management. When the process of installation is difficult due to its technical nature or when consecutive delays have made it necessary to improve progress significantly, a method frequently used is personal supervision. In practice this means that a supervisor takes charge of a group of men – two, five or 20 depending on what is to be done – and sees to it that the installations are done according to his expectations. During this period the Wärtsilä supervisor temporarily bypasses the subcontracting organization with regard to management. The subcontractor has momentarily become a firm that supplies only labour. Planning and control become an internal site team affair. As a consequence, responsibility on behalf of the subcontracting firm is temporarily inhibited. After the installation sequence, the 'borrowed' workforce is given back to the subcontracting firm, and the regular channels and procedures, such as planning and follow-up meetings can regulate work. This manoeuvre also produces a certain kind of exceptional state where normal rules and procedures do not apply. As in the other cases, however, it is an *exception* to the regular project management framework. It is thus, as Sahlin-Andersson points out, not valid as a reference in other situations.

Engineering exceptions inside bureaucracies

According to Carl Schmitt (1922), the *Ausnahmnezustand* or exceptional state is a great liberator both to those that desperately needs to get things done and to the organization that desperately relies on upholding order. Procedures and rules have evolved through praxis or through intentional engineering work. These procedures and rules are at work in the organization in general. They can be said to mirror the organization in its 'average' mode. They tell how things should be done in general, under normal conditions, under more or less ideal circumstances.

In practice, however, things are seldom normal. The 'average' mode becomes an aggregate of the organization operating in more stable-than-normal and more unstable-than-normal conditions. For some organizations the fluctuations around this 'normal' are small, and action according to procedures and rules can easily be approximated. In other organizations such as the ones described here, the fluctuations are of greater magnitude. It is here that the *Ausnahmezustand* plays an important role. The actors are liberated, at least temporarily, from the converging processes of regulation. As for the organization, its internal structure is shielded from unauthorized actions since these actions are carried out within a clearly circumscribed zone not actually belonging to the organization.

The *Ausnahmezustand* is an important mechanism in relation to management. Through its particular characteristics it enables, that is, it *legitimizes*, action, which according to the existing order or set of norms would not have been acceptable for one or more of the involved parties.

Making a short detour to the realm of mathematics, and especially the notion of transformations, clarifies these qualities. The mathematical transformation means that a certain expression is rewritten according to a new system of reference without changing its inherent meaning. This manipulation is very powerful since certain operations are significantly easier to perform in one system of reference than in another. When the specific operation has been performed – say the calculation of a function's derivate, for example – the expression can be written, that is transformed, back to its initial system of reference.

Thus management's intentions are frequently transformed into seemingly new expressions in the light of a unique, extraordinary situation. As in the mathematical case, this new system of intention, or reference, has more degrees of freedom than the present. One talks about the general 'objective' instead of sequences of installations, of the deal with Esteban rather than with Prinel Inc., about deals and promises instead of agreements and contracts. When the problem has been solved and the situation has calmed down, the rhetoric is re-transformed back to the formal plans, contractual agreements and number-crunching control.

If the action-enhancing power of the *Ausnahmezustand* has its origin in its ability to upset or inhibit structures that at a given moment constrain choices of actions, its temporal character amplifies its significance. An exception does not mean a final break up and departure, and it does not imply a beginning of a new order or era. The exception is just an exception. Explicitly or implicitly there exists an assumption of a limited duration in time and/or space. The exception does not necessarily apply to the whole organization and is only temporary. Within the exception lies an expectation that tomorrow or in 100 years, things will go back to 'normal', to the existing order. The departure from the existing norms and regimen is not an expression of revolution where the old regime is disassembled and replaced for good. Rather the 'old' is conserved until the world's state of affairs settles down and becomes stable once more.

Even if the *Ausnahmezustand* often implies seriousness in the actor's interpretation of a given situation, play is also observed. Most of the concerned parties would hardly agree that there is much 'play' or 'fun' involved in getting to terms with a couple of thousand gallons of crude oil leaking into a nearby swamp or seeing to it that an activity that is three months behind schedule will be finished in just five weeks. Still, the qualities of play and of the *Ausnahmezustand* are similar with respect to the relatively increased degrees of freedom, which is a consequence of leaving the ironclad logic of consistency and reason. James March (1971) writes:

> Playfulness is the deliberate, temporary relaxation of rules in order to explore the possibilities of other rules. When we are playful, we challenge the necessity of consistency. In effect, we announce – in advance – our rejection of the usual objections to behavior that does not fit the standard model of intelligence. Playfulness allows experimentation. At the same time, it acknowledges reason. It accepts an obligation that at some point either the playful behavior will be stopped or it will be integrated into the structure of intelligence in some way that makes sense. The suspension of the rules is temporary. (p. 77)

For organizations relying on standardized and routine procedures, the suspension of rules is of vital importance. The *Ausnahmezustand* decouples a set of action-related norms from preferred action itself in favour of some other set of action related norms (on coupling see Weick, 1976; and on coupling in relation to projects see Lundin and Söderholm, 1995). As a consequence, a larger set of action alternatives is possible to choose from and initiate. Projects are usually known as highly action-oriented in comparison with other organizational forms.

However, even with the action focus, these projects carry a significant amount of the baggage of bureaucracy. Standard project management tools and techniques would certainly have made Max Weber, Henry Ford and Charles Taylor proud. How then can the oxymoronic notion of 'expedient bureaucracy' be understood? For one thing, *Ausnahmezus-tand* is a vital mechanism in all human interaction, but it is clear that it is of central importance especially in a bureaucratic context. It not only stimulates action, but it enables the organization to save itself from calling its fundamental *raison-d'étre* into question. In these particular circumstances the organization can legitimately perform actions which it has prohibited through its design of 'standard operating procedures'. The organization – through the generation of *Ausnhamezustanden* – improves its general possibilities of acting through its increased degree of freedom of action. At the same time it manages to defend its core structure from a breakdown caused by ad hoc procedures. This defense is not absolute and this elicits a third and final observation relating to March's comment on play. Some actions taken during these special occasions are only expedient given the particular situation. Other actions, however, might prove to be expedient in a more general sense, and thereby they will gradually become institutionalized and integrated in the organization's 'normal' set of procedures. In this aspect the *Ausnahmezustand* has the quality of a controlled experimental and breeding chamber of the organization's incremental but organic procedural development.

Ausnahmezustanden are frequent enough in at least unstable and turbulent settings that they have an important and far-reaching impact on organizational action. The knowledge and ability to generate these conditions must be seen as a vital managerial skill within projects and anywhere else the heavy wheels of bureaucracy grind. As Schmitt (1922/1988) notes in *Political theology*, 'Sovereign is he who decides on the exception' ('Souverän ist, wer über den Ausnahmezustand entscheidet'.)

References

Christensen, S., and K. Kreiner (1991) *Projektledning – Att leda i en ofullkomlig värld.* Köpenhamn: Jurist-og Ekonomförbundets Förlag.

Ciborra, C. (1999) Notes on improvisation and time in organizations. *Accounting, Management and Information Technologies*, 9, pp. 77–94.

Granlund, M. (2002) Changing legitimate discourse: a case study. *Scandinavian Journal of Management*, 18, pp. 365–91.

Gustafsson, C. (1998) Det stora äventyret Om projektorganisationen s ledningsmässiga poänger. In P.-O. Berg and F. Poulfelt (eds), *Ledelselaeren i norden.* Fredrikshavn: Dafolo Förlag.

Hutchins, E. (1991) Organizing work by adaption. *Organization Science* special issue, 2, 1.

Lindahl, M. (2003) *Produktion till varje pris.* Stockholm: Arvinius Förlag.

Lindblom, C. (1959) The science of 'muddling through.' *Public Administration Review*, 19 (2), pp. 78–88.

Lundin, R., and A. Söderholm (1995) A theory of the temporary organization. *Scandinavian Journal of Management*, 11 (4), pp. 437–55.

March, J.G. (1971) The technology of foolishness, *Civilokonomen* (May) pp. 7–12.

Moorman, C., and A. Miner (1998) The convergence between planning and execution: improvisation in new product development. *Journal of Marketing*, 62, pp. 1–20.

Nietzsche, F. (1867/1999) *The birth of tragedy*. Cambridge University Press.

Sahlin-Andersson, K. (2002) Project management as boundary work. In K. Sahlin-Andersson and A. Soderholm (eds), *Beyond project management*. Copenhagen: Business School Press.

Schmitt, C. (1922/1988) *Political theology*. Cambridge, MA: MIT Press.

Weick, K. (1976) Educational organizations as loosely coupled systems. *Administrative Science Quarterly*, 21, pp. 1–19.

Part III

Conditions for new leadership: art and business

11

Dissonances, awareness and aesthetization: theatre in a home care organization

Stefan Meisiek

Slowly the spartan hall fills with people. About a hundred chairs arranged in eight rows and separated by a centre aisle are waiting for the audience. The chairs face a movable stage containing a bed, an armchair and two tables. On a canvas behind the furniture are living room images: old paintings and statues on a floral tapestry. The people entering the auditorium are mostly women between the ages of 20 and 60. They all work in a home care organization in a mid-sized municipality. They are nurses, secretaries, cooks, drivers and other staff members. They take their places, some attempting to sit next to their favourite colleagues, and talk to each other in low tones. When everyone is seated, a female manager and a man dressed in black come to the stage. After asking for attention, the manager explains to the audience what is about to happen. They are about to watch and – if they wish to – participate in an organization theatre performance. This, they are told, is thought to help make changes in areas troubling the home care organization. After the manager has finished and left the stage, the man in black introduces himself as a 'joker'. That is the title, he explains, for a consultant who mediates between audience and stage. Next he describes what the day's organization theatre will be about.

At first glance it may seem unusual that an art form might initiate change in an organization. Even though theatre has a long and rich history, since it is defined as a part of the humanities it seldom has contact with organizations beyond the relationship of patronage. In light of this, some questions come to mind when one considers the scene of home care personnel watching and participating in a theatrical performance. How will the nurses, secretaries, cooks, drivers and other employees receive a theatrical performance about their daily work? Why was organization theatre chosen to foster change in the home care organization? Will there be any impact on the home care organization, and if there is, what will the impact be? Will it be in line with what the managers intended when they commissioned the play? This chapter explores these questions. After providing the reader with background information about organization theatre and its applications in private and public organizations, the text describes what was happening in the home care organization before and during the performance and details what happened following it. Through this case study, the chapter illuminates the way organizational members interact with the performance and how they do or do not transfer the experience into their work life. By means of relevant theories, the chapter explains how audience dissonance may lead to awareness and, further, to a fruitful sensemaking process.

Organization theatre

Everyday life is a theatre of sorts. This idea grows out of Shakespeare's observation that 'All the world's a stage, / And all the men and women merely players:/ They have their exits and their entrances;/ And one man in his time plays many parts.... ' A few centuries later, Kenneth Burke (1945) described the way everyday life is theatre in a literal sense, and Erving Goffman (1959) used theatre as a helpful metaphor for the presentation of self in everyday life. Purposeful human actions in organizations make no exception to these theories. Organizations even seem to be stages with specific properties.

The providers of organization theatre take the perspective of life-as-theatre literally and employ the techniques of theatre to stage plays for the benefit of employee audiences. Organization theatre then offers a perspective on organizations and theatre that plays with the notions of Burke and Goffman. Countering theatre with theatre, it is the conscious use of theatrical techniques in organizations at a specific point in time (Meisiek, 2002).

In organization theatre, nearly everyone involved knows that it is *just* theatre. A stage is built, employees are the audience and, in most cases, trained actors play the roles. Theatrical techniques can be combined in almost infinite ways to create new forms, and this makes it difficult to provide a technical definition. Schreyögg (1999a) provides a rough overview when classifying organization theatere performances as 'turnkey' productions, which are in similar form staged before multiple organizations and as 'tailor-made' plays, which are especially produced for one organization. The play may contain improvisations that involve active audience participation, or the play may be altogether improvised on the basis of ideas from the audience. In any case, managers order the play, define the content and usually attend a dress rehearsal or a demonstration before it is staged in front of employees.

Organization theatre differs profoundly from performances at Christmas parties or company conventions, which seem to aim at entertainment and amusement – sometimes at the bosses' expense (Rosen, 1988). The professional providers of organization theatre rather see themselves as consultants to the company. Their work is supposed to serve organizational purposes, as defined by human resource management or strategic management, for example (Meisiek, 2003).

Reception theory

Theatre is an old art form, and since the advent of the academic humanist tradition, many universities have employed theatre theorists who, among other things, develop and teach reception theory as it relates to public and private theatres. It could be assumed from this that the existent body of literature already contains the solution to the questions motivating this chapter. That assumption, however, has some problems.

A limitation of the research on audiences in public and private theatres is that it necessarily stops when the audience leaves the theatre and blends into society once again (Schoenmakers, 1992). By contrast, in organization theatre the audience is made up of the distinct population of an organization, department or group. Organization theatre thus encounters an audience that possesses intimate knowledge of the various aspects of daily work routines and knows the ongoing political manoeuvering inside the organization. Instead of dispersing into an anonymous society, the members of the audience continue to work together.

Bennett (1990) noticed that the cultural background of the audience influences their reception of a play, and it also limits the way theatrical productions can be set up. For example, Broadway shows draw almost exclusively white, middle- to upper-class, well-educated audiences who have certain expectations about how a play should be put on. Only off-Broadway plays such as the ones performed by 'El Teatro Campesino' can hope to draw different audiences with specific problems that can be addressed on stage, in this case Chicanos and their immigrant status in the United States (Bennett, 1990). Accordingly, audience research has focused in a descriptive manner on such diverse aspects as the spectators' geographical origin, occupational background, age, motivation for attending the play, taste (low-brow vs high brow) and reception of the play in terms of venue, stage direction, diversity of the public, participation or the subject of the play (Schoenmakers, 1992). Attending an organization theatre performance is often not voluntary for the employees, however, and so the audience is defined in advance. And while other considerations are not completely irrelevant for organization theatre, they do fall short of the intended effects of theatrical performances in organizations, which are thought to serve specific purposes.

In organization theatre, the audience is well defined and the play is specially designed to address their day-to-day problems. Organization theatre therefore plays to audiences with shared beliefs and values grounded in organizational culture. These audiences are fairly homogeneous because they share a common background in their profession; they have often received similar training, followed similar career paths and possess a distinctive work identity. This homogeneity, however, is not perceived as a disadvantage; it is a desired trait in organization theatre. It facilitates connecting the theatre experience with the routine work life of the employee.

The organization theatre performance is certainly followed by social interaction among audience members on an everyday basis. The employees who have viewed the play can be expected to talk to each other about the quality and the content of the performance, and they may influence each other in terms of how the play is accepted or rejected after the fact. It can be assumed that the employees will engage in a sensemaking process (Weick, 1995). They may connect the play to what they know about their organization, and they may wonder why it was shown to them. They might also use descriptions of the various scenes to illustrate their daily communication about work issues. Existing reception theory covers these aftereffects insufficiently because it was not developed for this kind of setting and audience.

Further, in reception theory the communicative action in a theatre is often assumed to be one way: from the stage to the audience. In terms of communication, audiences are generally confined to expressing their approval or disapproval through applause or a standing ovation after the play (Schoenmakers, 1992). Members of the audience experience the play as a collective, however, and the reactions of other audience members certainly influence individual reactions and reception of the play. As the present case study of a performance in an organization will show, organization theatre does not necessarily favour one-way communication. Rather, the performances concern everyday work life, and the audiences are thought to be more fruitfully engaged when the barrier between stage and audience is permeable.

And while one size does not fit all, reception theory does provide several orientation marks for research in organization theatre. Boal (1995), whose theories concern active audiences, and Schoenmakers (1996), who is concerned with the aftereffects of theatre, will serve us in this chapter.

The home care organization

The home care organization in this case study is one part of the services provided in a municipality of about 250,000 citizens. This branch of services has approximately 3000 employees, almost all of whom are women between the ages of 20 and 60. Home care activity is divided into seven equal-size districts.

The atmosphere in the home care organization prior to the theatrical performances was loaded. The municipality was experiencing sinking tax revenues and, as a consequence, a restructuring was envisioned and implemented for community services. This meant the home care organization would experience downsizing, funding cuts and reorganization. Districts and areas of responsibility were shuffled and several members of the home care service were afraid of losing their jobs. For personnel, funding cuts translated into less flexibility, especially regarding working hours and difficult clients. Overall, a feeling of insecurity prevailed and home care workers had the impression that nobody listened to their concerns.

Faced with this negative atmosphere, two managers at the municipal level had the idea of using organization theatre to start a general discussion about restructuring efforts and the difficulties faced by the home care workers in their daily work routines. The managers thought that every employee of the home care organization should see the play so that nobody would feel left behind. They sought the support of a local politician and successfully sold the idea to him; then they contacted Dacapo Teatret, an organization theatre company.

The municipality had used theatrical performances from Dacapo for other branches of its services before, but this was the first time for the home care sector. Over a one-year period, Decapo gave about 30 identical performances with about 100 employees in each audience. The rationale behind buying many identical performances instead of having one large performance was to sample an audience from all districts for each performance. Their colleagues who did not attend the play at the same time could keep the organization going and take care of the elderly and disabled. Also, the small audience sizes were supposed to enable an interactive theatre performance.

Such multiple-performance cases are rare, however. More common are one-day or one-weekend arrangements. This case offered a unique opportunity to study the effects of organization theatre.

Dacapo's organization theatre

Dacapo started as a change management project in the early 1990s when two consultants experimented with theatre as a way of encouraging reflection and stimulating discussions. Since then Dacapo has grown into a small business corporation with about 25 employees. Such an industry-based beginning explains the composition of Dacapo's work force. While many received various forms of theatre training, several others had concentrated on the coaching and consultant aspects of the activity only. In contrast, many organization theatre providers started as traditional theatre companies and later 'discovered' organizations as a profitable field of work.

Dacapo's list of references includes medium to large corporations, non-profit organizations and government organizations. For a long time, its main business came from turnkey productions using theatrical techniques derived from Boal's forum theatre (1979; 1995). Lately, however, Dacapo has specialized more in playback theatre, a purely improvisational theater form.

'I bear it with a smile', the play used for the home care organization, had already been performed several times in hospitals, at a health care fair and in other health industry-related organizations. Dacapo merely adapted it to the demands of the home care services. The first performances were put on in April, another set of performances was presented in the autumn and a final set of performances took place around February of the following year.

The specific choice of a theatrical performance based on the techniques of Boal's forum theatre indicates what the two managers of the home care organization hoped to achieve by investing in organization theatre. Boal sees theatre as a mechanism for developing action motivation. He builds on the theories of Artaud (1938/1985) and Grotowski (1984) which imply that theatre can actually be used to produce an emotional dissonance in the audience. Such dissonance generates an impulse for action that carries over into everyday life. Later Boal refined and elaborated this approach, declaring that emotional dissonance among audience members leads to the motivation for actions previously disregarded or considered to be impossible.

Boal himself draws heavily on *Pedagogy of the oppressed* by Freire (2000), which has its roots in emancipation and revolutionary movements in Brazil. Freire argues that the main principle of enlightenment and pedagogic work is the *conscientização*, roughly translated as 'making somebody aware of something.' To him, *conscientização* means the process of learning necessary in order to understand social, political and economic paradoxes. The *conscientização* motivates the individual to take action against disadvantageous conditions. This means that the *conscientização* also involves changing the real situation and is not limited to a cognitive process; it is a unity of reflection and action. Freire assumes that the oppressed recognize the forces of oppression, but they do not always acknowledge them. They have adapted to a situation, and they have an image of themselves in this situation. What is lacking is a new image showing how to foster change. Freire describes this as a boundary situation. Individuals cannot cross the boundaries intellectually to see which possibilities for action exist on the other side. He is convinced that new modes of action are developed when the boundary for the individual no longer runs between 'being' and 'non-being', but between 'being' and 'being more'.

Boal (1979) underlines these principles when he allows the audience to test actions on stage. He subsumes his techniques under the title of the *Theatre of the oppressed*, which contains newspaper theatre, statue theatre, invisible theatre and forum theatre. Boal developed theatrical techniques for the political education of farmers in Brazil with the intention of motivating audiences to improve their own situations independently. The purpose of his work was to combat illiteracy and to enlighten the underprivileged segments of the population. During exile in France, Boal adapted his theatre theories and techniques to the conditions of Western society where people have internalized the mechanisms of limitation even though they are not subject to external coercion. Boal describes theatre as a way of enriching action patterns, which fosters motivation for new action in real life.

The members of the audience in the theatre of the oppressed are asked to design actions for themselves. The actors present a fiction with the expectation that it will be destroyed by the audience in the cause of creating a better fiction. In this context Boal regards it as involvement if the members of the audience start preparing for action internally, even if they do not develop it further on the stage.

The techniques of forum theatre, invisible theatre, and statue theatre have made their way into organization theatre, but on the way they have necessarily lost a bit of their ideological ballast. In the present case the employees were not asked to question the whole organization as such but only to focus on the issues at hand under the conditions set by management. The absolute freedom of thought and action envisioned by Boal was compromised when forum theatre became a technique in organization theatre. This limitation, which may explain the success of organization theatre, led Timothy Clark and I. Mangham (2004b) to call it 'Boal lite'. Nevertheless, it seems that the managers in the municipality intended to present their employees with a play that allowed them to seek new ground under the conditions of the reorganization. The managers sacrificed a degree of control in order to let the employees play with the situation at hand.

In 'I bear it with a smile,' this meant that the managers wanted the employees to discard the content of the play in order to gain action motivation. The basic process is one of rejection and not of acceptance. Rejection is seen as making space for reconceiving the situation at hand. In this way, the employees also regain the feeling of being heard. It meant giving them an indirect opportunity to adapt to the restructuring and reorganization that had taken place.

Boal (1995) explains that emotional dissonance in the audience should lead not to resignation but to activation. He regards the stage as an aesthetic space that unites plasticity, dichotomy and 'tele-microscopy'. By plasticity he means that with the help of fantasy everything is possible in the aesthetic space. Time, objects and actions are all variable. Unlike the situations of everyday life, the aesthetic space is not binding and there is always the possibility of leaving it. The dichotomy in the aesthetic space is the division between fiction and reality. Boal explains that the individual members of the audience can become part of the fiction by entering the aesthetic space where they find themselves surrounded by a fiction that they can influence. The fiction thus exists alongside the reality of participating in a theatrical performance. This enables the members of the audience to perform self-observations. The aesthetic space is tele-microscopic, so that it becomes possible to turn one's attention to past events. On the stage, events acquire a dimension different from that of everyday life. Like a tele-microscope, the aesthetic space lets actions and objects appear closer to the participants. The basic features of the forum theatre, which drove the play 'I bear it with a smile' in the home care organization, will help in understanding what happened during and after the play.

The performance

The stage set is the living room of Ejnar Madsen, an old widower who is a home care client. The frail Madsen and Inger, an experienced home care worker, enter the scene. This is the beginning of the play. In the hour that follows, a story unfolds about the everyday hassles in the home care organization. Inger gets into conflict with Pernille, a young home care assistant, who in her recently finished education has learned new ways to treat a client. Their conflict results in a dissatisfied client, who in the end loses his trust in the home care organization.

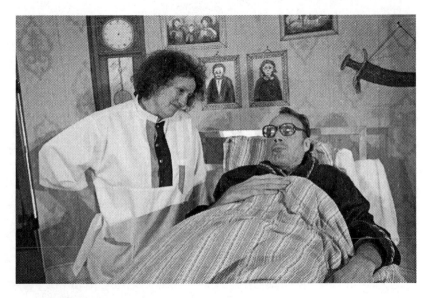

11.1 Still from the play 'I bear it with a smile'

In the second half of the play, the audience is introduced to bureaucratic procedures in the home care organization, the district leader Flemming, the middle manager Lisbeth and the security representative Hans.

At this point instead of going over the play scene by scene, concentrating on the tele-microscopic foci of the play becomes more helpful. These foci can be presented alongside the different interpersonal relationships that characterize the play: home care worker/client, home care worker/home care worker; home care worker/manager, and finally

11.2 Still from the play 'I bear it with a smile'

manager/manager. The relationships are introduced to the audience in the order of the organizational hierarchy. This covers home care personnel in direct contact with the client as well as the managers. In contrast to classic forum theatre, the play does not identify specific roles as oppressed and oppressor. The play 'I bear it with a smile' thus refrains from identifying someone as source of the problem. The performance rather focuses on the interdependencies between the employees of the organization that create or contain negative routines. Thus, it could be argued, it distances itself from the theoretical background of Boal and becomes a 'Boal lite' performance (Clark and Mangham, 2004b).

Relationships

Home care worker/client

The relationship between the home care worker and the client is characterized by demands of efficiency set against the restrictions of time that sometimes prohibit *adequate* service, according to the nursing staff. How to define the word *adequate* is the issue: how far can home care workers go out of their way to help the client? How close should the relationship to the client be? This is linked to the question of how to establish a good relationship with the client and how to avoid health risks both for the home care worker and the client. As clients get older, they may lose some of their abilities and the home care worker is then confronted with the question of how much can be asked of a client in terms of changes in the home care.

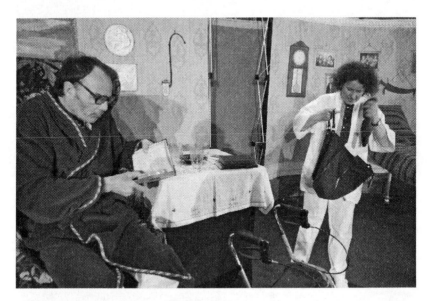

11.3   Still from the play 'I bear it with a smile'

Home care worker/home care worker

The questions regarding the right way to interact with the client also colour the interactions between the home care workers. In the theatrical performance the focus is on helping each other without interfering or questioning each other's competencies. Especially salient is the conflict of new versus old ideas on how to do the job. This relates to the problem of what to expect from each other, how to help each other and how to communicate effectively with each other to keep the client satisfied and to offer good service.

Home care worker/manager

The disposition of work time emerges as the main problem in the relationship between the home care workers and managers. Managers may not show enough consideration for the concerns of the employees in that they delegate tasks too lightheartedly and do not offer enough support for the home care workers. Another problem is that home care workers have difficulty asking the managers for help because of their

11.4 Still from the play 'I bear it with a smile'

11.5 Still from the play 'I bear it with a smile'

inaccessibility. Due to the interpersonal distance between the home care worker and the manager, home care workers have trouble understanding and handling complaints from management, especially in terms of services provided. They also feel that it is difficult to address their needs to the managers.

Manager/manager

The final relationship – the one between district and middle managers – takes much less time in the play than the three preceding relationships. Managers' problems are portrayed as giving priority to the right issues, effective problem-solving and communicating criticism effectively. It becomes apparent that the middle managers feel caught between the demands of their superiors and the reactions of the home care workers.

11.6 Still from the play 'I bear it with a smile'

After the 'structured' play ends, the 'joker' steps to the stage and encourages the audience to share ideas, to propose solutions or to come to the stage and assume one of the roles. In all of the plays researched, the home care personnel held a discussion with the consultant and the actors, and several scenes were played again, reflecting the various ideas of the audience; however, only a few employees dared to go on stage and interact with the actors directly. Nevertheless, the audience always showed interest in the performance and seemed to enjoy the opportunity to voice concerns, to play with the different roles and to try different approaches. They enjoyed the three properties of Boal-inspired theatre: plasticity (several alternatives were played), dichotomy (the fiction was rejected) and 'tele-microscopy' (focus on the four inter-personal relationships). It seems the play spoke to the beliefs, values and practices of the audience members. Following Boal's reception theory, the audience members would have been motivated to change their everyday work-life now. But such a conclusion may be premature. Although Boal provides insights into the principles that drive forum theatre and helped us to explore the background and the performance of 'I bear it with a smile,' it is Henri Schoenmakers' ideas on reception theory that may help us to understand what is happening in the specific case of organization theatre after the performance.

Schoenmakers (1996) takes empirical observations and psychology as starting points for his ideas and observes that instead of being calm and balanced, audiences are often quite excited and stimulated when they leave the theatre. Therefore Schoenmakers doubts that the effect of a theatrical performance is limited to the duration of the play and seeks another explanation for the effects of theatre on the emotions of the audience. He suggests that the study of audience reception should start from Frijda's (1986) theory of emotions. This theory contends that experienced emotions lead to a search for regulation as individuals seek to re-obtain a sense of an inner equilibrium. Using coping behaviours, individuals make sense of the emotional dissonance. They ask why and in what context a certain emotion was experienced. When a plausible answer is found, the coping behaviour abates and the emotional exper-ience becomes integrated in the beliefs and values of the individuals. These ideas tie up with Weick's (1995), who assumes that disrupted routines lead to emotion and thus to sense-making until the disruption is resolved. In organization theatre, however, the feeling of disruption is visibly created on stage.

Schoenmakers also explored the way audiences rate their affective experience of a play. His focus was on negative affect, which obviously lies at the heart of Boal's forum theatre. He found a correlation between the intensity of negative emotions experienced during the play and a preference for particular scenes. This means the more a spectator is emotionally involved, the more he or she likes the play.

From these findings Schoenmakers concludes that the perception of negative emotions in everyday life is different from the perception of such feelings during a theatrical performance. Negative emotions such as grief, fear and anger, for example, are usually avoided in everyday life. In the theatre, on the other hand, the audience enjoys these feelings. Theatre appeals to beliefs, values, norms and interests shared by the members of the audience and yields affective experiences that resemble those of everyday life. During and after every affective experience a process of regulation occurs. Individuals attempt to regain their equilibrium not only through somatic regulation but also by making sense of the events.

In everyday work life, this process of regulation does not always happen in a way that satisfies the employee because he or she is much too involved in the event to be clear about its aspects. In the theatre, however, employees are able to regulate their emotions and to make further sense of them because the employees are conscious that the origin of the emotions is a fiction. In this way, the employees maintain the necessary distance from the emotion. The regulation process does not mean that audience members are released completely from negative emotions, however. These are still present, but the process of regulation makes them lose the negative values attached to them in everyday life.

Schoenmakers refers to the notion of the joy stemming from the experience of intense emotions in theatre as the 'functionality hypothesis'. He explains that two conditions need to be fulfilled for any subsequent regulation. First, the audience must be aware of the theatrical frame; they have to know with certainty that the emotions are being elicited in the context of a theatrical presentation. For the audience, these emotions are the product of an artifact. Second, the emotions must be perceived as reasonable; they fulfill a function and have a value for the audience. Of course not all members of the audience will agree about which emotions make sense in this way, and this explains why the responses can vary.

Finally, Schoenmakers differentiates between aestheticized and aesthetic emotions. This distinction is necessary to separate the effects of the fiction and the effects of the work of art. If members of the audience experience negative emotions because they dislike the level of sophistication of the play or the kind of performance, this is a matter of taste. They do not like that particular artifact. These aesthetic emotions have little in common with the everyday emotions that are invoked by the fiction. Aesthetization refers only to emotions aroused by the fictitious world of theatre. When speaking about the audience's rejection of the fiction, as Boal envisions, this rejection is only useful if it is based on aesthetization. Dissonance and awareness, aroused by the forum theatre, would lead to a sense-making process after the play. The great activity in the interactive part of Dacapo's theatre performance may indicate aesthetization. Such an effect of organization theatre would become salient in the aftereffects of the play. The empirical data that we collected on the 'I bear it with a smile' case allow us to explore this proposition.

The aftereffects

When asked about the effects the theatre performances had in the home care organization, the managers quoted results from an annual employee satisfaction questionnaire. According to questionnaire responses, over the year that the performances were put on in the organization, employee satisfaction had risen. The managers attributed this attitude change to their theatre initiative; they are thoroughly convinced that it was a worthwhile investment. Other influential factors, such as the absence of further downsizing and funding cuts during the same year, may impact this analysis.

The managers did relatively little to follow up on thoughts and ideas that the play could have elicited in the audience members. They made no concentrated effort to discuss the play in a group setting. Home care workers returned to their work responsibilities the day after the play and went routinely about their duties. The only follow-up was the printing of a deck of cards given to all employees; each card showed a scene from the play, the lines spoken during the scene, some indication of the problems portrayed in that scene, and a word of encouragement about discussing the issue. The district managers interviewed maintained that while the card decks served as a reminder of the play, they never got used systematically.

This would not be an issue if the effects of organization theatre were limited to the performance itself. Schoenmakers indicates, however, that audience members carry their impressions out of the theatre, and Schreyögg (1999b) points out the necessity of taking care of the thoughts and feelings elicited by the play. To a certain extent, it can be expected that the involvement of the spectators in the interactive part takes care of this. This seems to be Boal's assumption. However, the question remains: what happened when the audience members/employees returned to their everyday work lives?

Some descriptive statistics from the questionnaire may help in clarifying the post-performance reception of the play. Of the 1500 employees who received the questionnaire one week after the performance, 446 replied, a 30 per cent response rate. On a 1-to-9-point scale, the audience members enjoyed the play greatly (M = 7.91, SD = 1.43), while on average, audience members thought that it applied a bit less directly to their work situation (M = 6.48, SD = 2.2). A few audience members rejected the play due to its form; they made the aesthetic judgement that they did not like the theatre that was presented to them, or that they did not like theatre in general. Meanwhile, the great majority of the audience members liked the play and were open to discarding it due to its content. (Discarding it meant discussing it or talking about it.) The general reception of the play seems to present favourable conditions for aesthetization.

When asked how much they could use the ideas and solutions worked out in the interactive part of the play, 84 per cent said that they had not had the chance to use it in their daily life. Another 12 per cent insisted they had used something once, and 4 per cent indicated that they had used an idea or solution from the play several times. This could indicate that the level of abstraction was too high, and though engaging, the play was not a showcase for what happens in the routine work life of the individual home care worker. Further, there is only a small direct carry-over effect from theatre to everyday work life, even if the audience members are active participants. However, Boal (1995) and Dacapo do not expect audience members to transfer solutions tried during the performance one-to-one into everyday life. Rather, dissonance and awareness are supposed to motivate them to act. Asked if the performance had made them aware of problems at their workplace, 52 per cent answered affirmatively. Further, when asked if their attitude toward persisting work conditions had changed, 31 per cent indicated such a change.

Some other numbers reveal post-performance reception as well. In the week following the performance they saw, 58 per cent of the home care personnel talked several times with colleagues about the play. While 37 per cent indicated that they had talked at least once with colleagues about the performance, only 5 per cent reported they had never talked with a colleague about the play. This high degree of verbal sharing of the theatre experience indicates that the emotional dissonance created by the play – the aesthetization – was carried over into everyday work life. Employees were making sense of the play in collaboration with their colleagues *after* the performance.

This finding corresponds to another observation: 77 per cent of the respondents indicated they had talked primarily with colleagues that had seen the play *with* them, while 64 per cent primarily talked with people who had seen the play *before* them, and only 22 per cent had talked to people who hadn't seen the play yet. (Since the home care workers could talk to several people about the play, the numbers do not add up to 100 per cent.) In search of an understanding counterpart, most people talked to colleagues who had seen the same performance, or they talked with colleagues who had seen the play before them and thus knew what it was about. The play is mostly made sense of – and in the process discarded – with the help of colleagues who shared the experience. Discarding the play leads to a workforce-centred understanding, which indicates its relevance for the beliefs and values in the home care organization.

An additional interesting point surfaced from the questionnaire. Almost all respondents (95 per cent) indicated that they had not talked about the performance with a client, even though clients had a crucial part in the play itself. The workplace issues seemed to be discussed on an internal level only. It is likely a sign that the play was relevant to the home care organization's situation.

These descriptive results give the impression that the performances stimulated a vivid dialogue among organizational members in their work life situations following the performance. The ongoing performances seemed to have kept this dialogue alive throughout the one-year period of time. In contrast to shows performed only once, these performances continued to raise subjects again and again as more and more home care workers from a district saw the play. The descriptive statistics regarding the aftereffects give illustrative evidence of the audience's experiencing aesthetization.

The discardable conversation piece

How then do theatrical performances affect the audience, and how does this effect influence the organization as a whole? It has been proposed elsewhere that audience members go through a process of second-order observation where they perceive themselves through the performed interpretation of the actors (Schreyögg, 1999b), that they experience a cathartic alleviation that leads to relief, creativity or action motivation as a consequence of an emotional activation (Meisiek, 2004), and/or that they witness an imaginative truth that strengthens values and beliefs through a celebration of the organization on stage (Clark and Mangham, 2004a).

The present case study of organization theatre has certainly revisited certain aspects of these propositions. In addition, however, the case highlights a critical aspect of organization theatre as well. A play can be regarded as a 'discardable'. In this 'inventing through discarding', the members of the audience are not supposed to be able to use the solutions shown on stage or elaborated in the interactive play in their everyday work life. While most change-management initiatives seem to work with affirmation – employees are supposed to understand the value of a new solution and accept it willingly – organization theatre seems to thrive on rejection – the solutions presented are to be acknowledged as insufficient and to be replaced in an improvisational way in the everyday work life. This 'new' way is by no means clearly defined by the managers prior to the performance nor is it determined through the interaction on the day of the performance. Rather it develops further in the conversations around the play in the time following the theatrical performance.

Bearing this in mind, we return to the motivating questions for this chapter: Why was the play commissioned? How was it received? What were the effects of the play and were these in the interest of the managers? It became obvious that the play was commissioned to give employees the feeling of being heard, to spark a discussion about the situation in the organization and to allow them to play with a pre-defined situation that resembles their everyday work life. The fulfillment of these goals received their expression, the managers assumed, in the rise of employee satisfaction. Distinct changes in practice were desired but were by no means a prerequisite.

The play was well received among the home care workers. Only a few disliked it due to its appearance; in other words, they rejected it due to its aesthetic form. The reception can be separated into three distinct parts. First, the employees observe the play as it unfolds on the stage. This represents a form of one-way communication, and the employees can only react in the classic way of approval, applause. This part is thought to provoke the audience and to speak to their beliefs and values and illustrate their practices. Second, the interactive play follows. The ideas that the play gives way to are now taken up in discussions, in re-enactment and by giving the audience a place on the stage. Third, the employees are nevertheless still aware of their experience when they leave the theatre, and in the days that follow the play they converse about the experience. They may use the vocabulary or the scenes of the play to exemplify, to illustrate or to satirize their own daily experiences and routines.

The organization theatre performance reached the goals envisioned by the managers: it started discussions. If this also improved the general job satisfaction, as indicated by the annual job satisfaction measurement in the home care organization, cannot be established causally at this point. However, other aftereffects can be marked. The proposition that audience dissonance may lead to awareness (Boal, 1995) and later to sense-making in the form of aesthetization (Schoenmakers, 1996) gained support through the case study of 'I bear it with a smile.' The three different parts of the proposition may be captured by describing the theatrical performance as a conversation piece (Barry and Palmer, 2001). In the case study, the conversation piece is the play as it is presented on stage again and again over the one-year period. Around this conversation piece social action starts to spin, driven by the interests of the differently involved employees. This happens initially in the interactive part of the play and continues in the mundane talk that follows. The conversation piece therefore mediates social change, while it itself is at the same time discardable. Changes in employees' beliefs and values may be occurring, and these changes may be directly or indirectly linked to the theatrical performance. The complex nature of the development of such changes does not allow the establishment of a clear causal relationship, but the empirical material collected during the study points in the direction of such a link.

The case of organization theatre highlights the role that traditional humanities subjects like drama can play in promoting understanding of the social construction of reality in organizations. Art forms like theatre may lead to critical reflection and make employees conscious (Freire, 2000: *conscientização*) in ways that conventional change-management approaches do not. The humanities and business studies may have more to say to each other than first appearances would suggest.

The difference between theatre as art and organization theatre may be characterized as follows: theatre as a pure art form searches for specific expressions of the universal, while organization theatre searches for specific expressions for organizational problems – a rather modest aim in comparison. It may relate to the court theatres in the eighteenth and nineteenth centuries, which were embedded in the specific organization of the royal courts of Europe. Schiller, for example, saw the task of the court theatre not in entertainment and amusement, but in being a medium to enlighten the audiences and to address ethical problems that were prominent in the state. As an admirer of Kant, he wanted to see theatre used as a way to give audiences the courage to use their own reason (*sapere aude*). Nevertheless, he accepted that for the time being, the content of the performances was dictated by the needs of the courts and thus not completely free.

Note: This chapter would not have been possible without the support, advice and help of the late Michael Dawids of the Creative Alliance and Learning Lab Denmark. The case study is part of a larger research project conducted at Learning Lab Denmark. Collected data include interviews with two managers at the municipal level, five managers at the district level and four representatives of Dacapo Teatret. In addition, eleven theatrical performances and audience reception of them were videotaped and analysed. Finally, a questionnaire made up of qualitative and quantitative elements was sent to audience members about a week after they had participated in the organization theatre event.

References

Artaud, A. (1938/1985) *Le théâtre et son double*. Paris: Gallimard.
Barry, D., and E. Palmer, (2001) *Serious questions about serious play: problems and prospects in the study of mediated innovation*. Proceedings of the ANZAM (Australian and New Zealand Academy of Management) Conference, Auckland, New Zealand, 5–7 December 2001.
Bennett, S. (1990) *Theatre audiences: a theory of production and reception*. London: Sage.
Boal, A. (1979) *Theatre of the oppressed*. London: Pluto Press.
Boal, A. (1995) *The rainbow of desire. The Boal method of theater and therapy*. London: Routledge.
Burke, K. (1945) *A grammar of motives*. Berkeley: University of California Press.
Clark, T., and I. Mangham, (2004a) From dramaturgy to theater as technology: the case of corporate theater. *Journal of Management Studies*, 41 (1).
Clark, T., and I. Mangham, (2004b) Stripping to the undercoat: organization theater and forum theater. *Organization Studies*, 25 (5).
Freire, P. (2000) *Pedagogy of the oppressed*. 30th anniversary ed. New York: Continuum.
Frijda, N.H. (1986) *The emotions*. Cambridge University Press.
Goffman, E. (1959) *The presentation of self in everyday life*. Garden City, NY: Doubleday.
Grotowski, J. (1984) *Towards a poor theatre*. London: Methuen.
Meisiek, S. (2002) Situation drama in change management: types and effects of a new managerial tool. *International Journal of Arts Management*, 4, pp. 48–55.
Meisiek, S. (2003) From theater theory to business practice: theories of action of an organization theater company. In S. Meisiek, Beyond the emotional work event: Social sharing of emotion in organizations. Dissertation. EFI: Stockholm, pp. 1–32.
Meisiek, S. (2004) Which catharsis do they mean? Aristotle, Moreno, Boal and Organization Theater. *Organization Studies*, 25 (5).

Rosen, M. (1988) You asked for it: Christmas at the boss's expense. *Journal of Management Studies*, 25, pp. 463–80.

Schoenmakers, H. (ed.) (1992) *Performance theory, reception and audience research*. Amsterdam: Intitute voor Theaterwetenschap.

Schoenmakers, H. (1996) Catharsis as aesthetisation. *ASSAPH*, 12, pp. 85–93.

Schreyögg, G. (1999a) Definitionen und Typen des bedarfsorientierten Theatereinsatzes in Unternehmen. In G. Schreyögg and R. Dabitz (eds), *Unternehmenstheater*, pp. 3–22. Wiesbaden: Gabler.

Schreyögg, G. (1999b) Beobachtungen zweiter Ordnung: Unternehmenstheater als dublizierte Wirklichkeit. In G. Schreyögg and R. Dabitz (eds), *Unternehmenstheater*, pp. 84–94. Wiesbaden: Gabler.

Weick, K.E. (1995) *Sensemaking in organizations*. Thousand Oaks, CA: Sage.

12

Eros and Apollo: the curator as pas-de-deux leader

Katja Lindqvist

Cases of curatorship

The making of an exhibition is a process of metamorphosis, where visions and ideas are translated into material form and artefacts for knowledge and sensual experiences. Exhibition production is also an event where the wills of various participating actors confront each other and the potentiality of the enterprise. Restraining influences surface each moment in the process of realization (Fogh Kirkeby, 2004). How should or could exhibition production as metamorphosis, as translation from mental to material, be managed? Who in an exhibition production team should decide these matters? What drives are inherent in the realization of an exhibition?

This chapter addresses these questions through examples of exhibition enterprise *mis*management and through the suggestion of a metaphor for the contending forces and wills of exhibition enterprises as a pas-de-deux between Eros and Apollo.

Expo.01 – Visions and structure: fractions of exhibition *mis*management

Pipilotti of Rist, world-renowned conceptual artist, became *directeur artistique* of the Swiss national exhibition project Expo.01 in 1997.[1] Expo.01 was to emerge at four venues built for the purpose in the Western Three-Lake area of Switzerland in May 2001 and stand until October of the same year. It was to host approximately 50 exhibitions and provide additional spaces and events as well. With the help of a creative team at the *direction artistique* of the Expo office, Rist was to develop the exhibition concepts for the numerous exhibitions of the Expo. As *directeur artistique* she was also part of the managerial group of the Expo office. The rest of the group included the heads of the finance, technical and marketing departments in addition to the president. The Expo office was a temporary organization in the form of a limited company with the sole aim of developing, realizing and finally demounting the national exhibition.

The choice of Pipilotti Rist for the position of *directeur artistique* was welcomed by many involved in the arts sector in Switzerland:

> Getting Pipilotti to do the job was a perfect idea, probably the brightest idea general director Jacqueline Fendt ever had. Pipilotti is enormously popular with young people, and she's very famous. Pipilotti could really awaken enthusiasm in people who hadn't been interested in the Expo at all, people who would never think of going to a Landesausstellung any time in their life, people who generally considered the event outdated and stodgy. Through her personality, Pipilotti managed to interest a wide circle of disinterested people inside Switzerland, and she was very useful for this thing at that moment.[2]

The realization of the exhibitions from a temporary project office proved to be much more difficult than any of Rist's previous art projects. The members of the Expo office had very different ideas about the project they were contributing to. Rist's job was keeper of the exhibitions, the aesthetic core of the whole enterprise, and she felt her position was not understood by the other managers, who did not recognize or accept the central role of the exhibition concepts for the whole enterprise. They grew impatient when the exhibition ideas that were the starting point for their own work did not materialize as quickly as they wanted them to. A member of the *direction artistique* expressed it this way:

> Under a young artist like Pipilotti Rist, we had a hard time proving ourselves. Other departments in the organization thought that artists have no idea of how an Expo should be run because it's this huge technocratic organization, which is growing day by day. Pipilotti was not being taken seriously. At the weekly board meeting with the other directors, she was absolutely taken for a ride.

The personal characteristics that made Pipilotti Rist a good artist/manager made her less respected in the eyes of the other directors concerned with finance and the more technical phases of the realization of the Expo project. According to Rist, the other managers were the cause of the internal problems of the organization.

What was lacking was the ability to get a functioning structure to work on a basic level. They never realized that a cultural event in its realization is just as brutal, hierarchical and tough as the construction of a jumbo jet. The managing group should have been given content-related directions, and the organization should have been structured according to the needs of the enterprise. Above all, a professional board of trustees should have been in place, a group that would have executed control. The directeur artistique must also be on an equal footing with the general director. That is what Heller [her successor] struggles for right now.

The department directors seemed to share the opinion that the work of each department was supposed to be conducted in isolation; only certain points required a presentation of outcomes or were related to the work of the other departments. This seemed justified by the fact that the work undertaken in the different departments was so diverse. This was called simultaneous engineering. In the everyday work, however, employees faced uncertainties because their work was in fact related to and dependent on work being undertaken at other departments:

> Our opinion was always that the direction artistique couldn't work if the other departments didn't do their work or if we couldn't work together. This is because if the sponsorship department doesn't do their work, we don't have any money for the exhibitions, and if the platforms aren't getting built, we can't put our exhibitions anywhere. If the marketing doesn't work, there's no good information about the Expo for the public and press; it all depends on interconnection, working together.

The difference between Rist's management and that of the other managers of the Expo office was manifested through divergent actions, communication, appearance and work assignments.

> When Pipilotti said that she thought it all went in the wrong direction, she was told to organize her department before starting to tell other departments what to do.... They weren't really against her, but sometimes they tried to teach her or help her. But I think that the basic trust wasn't there, so it couldn't work out in the long run. I think it's no coincidence that no one from that time is working here anymore. I guess it's rather common in big projects like this. There's been a total change of management as well. And maybe it's

got to do with phases. A large project changes, and demands change. I think Pipilotti and Jacqueline were great but I have to say that I'm quite happy it has turned out the way it has. I think Martin was the first to put the project down realistically.

Rist accused the other managers of mismanaging the Expo and pursuing their own individual goals instead of having a unified vision of the national exhibition:

> Each member [of the managerial group] had her or his own idea of the Expo. The president wanted—I think—a sort of theme park. The director of finance wanted a fair with stands and prospectuses. The president of the strategic committee envisioned an Expo with important themes. The technical director wanted to propagate a number of large building projects and a raft to command.... And the marketing director, I guess, just wanted a golden ribbon to cut.

The lack of respect and communication in the Expo office – along with difficulties in raising sponsorship income – led to severe difficulties on various levels in the organization. Gravest were the financial and organizational problems that fostered distrust in the media and in political allies. This situation provided little common ground on which to develop a well-functioning exhibition realization vehicle.

According to Rist, the directors appointed for the Expo had no experience with such large enterprises where creative processes play a vital part. Therefore they were not able to make decisions or take action when accumulating incidents in the day-to-day work required either decisions or action. As a result of this inability to take action, the pressure on the directors increased. According to Rist, the politicians recruited for the project got their positions as political rewards, not because of their expertise in managing a complex enterprise on a day-to-day basis. The combination of inexperienced politicians and only technically educated managers for the Expo was in her eyes the reason for its internal management failures.

> When I pointed out the idling to my Expo colleagues, I was reprimanded. They categorized me as a hysterical artist. Once when I made the director of finance conscious of the problems with Fendt, he said to me, 'It doesn't matter if the figurehead doesn't accomplish anything. If we only build the ship beneath her properly, it will all

work out.'. . . I had already told Fendt in November 1997 that she had to install a functioning managerial team.

Rist's criticism of the lack of common vision and engagement was later endorsed by organizational consultants commissioned to analyse the financial and organizational structures of the Expo and its project organization. At the same time, however, the press criticized Rist for her conceived inability to deliver reliable exhibition concepts that were marketable to potential sponsors.

There was a basic lack of trust between the managers and differing views on how to realize such a large project as 50 exhibitions comprising a national exhibition.[3] Paradoxically, Pipilotti Rist as artist/manager seemed more focused on developing a vision from which to perform different kinds of tasks while the other directors saw the artistic as just one element to incorporate in the overall jigsaw puzzle that constituted the Expo. If the directors of the non-aesthetic departments had had an understanding of the character of aesthetic work processes, as well as of the huge machinery that was dependent on the performance of the *direction artistique*, the different sides might have come together without the costs in time and resources that plagued this enterprise.

In December 1998, in the midst of the project, Rist left her position. Martin Heller, previously director of a museum in Zurich, replaced Rist and remained *directeur artistique* until the Expo was completed. When Heller stepped in, the overall concept of the Expo had already been developed and elaborated.

Remembering the periods of Rist and Heller, a member of the *direction artistique* makes some comparisons:

> I think it is very, very difficult to make dreams come true, to make the visions, which she definitely had, come true. And she had to quit because everything else, the meetings, the sessions, the administrative work, was so overbearing, and she wasn't free any longer to develop her ideas. She was blocked from several sides. She was like a bird whose wings are cut. So actually I think she could not have continued. In a way, we all suffered when she left, but in a way it was a good decision in the end. And this is as I see it now.
>
> I think it was normal or natural, this evolution. It started with artistic ideas, with beautiful visions and dreams. Eventually, when Pipilotti, who is a lovely person, was unable to fulfill administrative demands, the management tasks that were just too heavy on her – and on everyone else I have to admit – she finally quit. And with Martin

Heller, former director of a museum, came a man with experience. Of course he understands the visions, he understands the artistic side completely, but he also knows how to manage and how to make things function, and that is the difference between the two of them. And after Pipilotti, we definitely needed a manager.

Heller, the experienced museum director, managed to combine aesthetic sensibility with the discipline needed for a structured realization of the complexity of an exhibition. He was also able, or given the trust, to communicate in a way that the other managers of the Expo and the creative professionals at the *direction artistique* understood.

Eight months after Rist's resignation Jacqueline Fendt, the president of the Expo, was dismissed. This was a decision of the managers of the Expo office, and the stated reason was a lack of confidence in her management of the Expo. *Expo.01* suffered from an increasing economic crisis during its realization. Eventually an external consultancy group offered the project office organizational and economic analysis and advice. After massive restructuring and a decrease in the total number of exhibitions, *Expo.02* was finally realized in 2002.

Vita rockar

At the Museum of Work in Norrköping, Sweden, the research and exhibition project 'Vita rockar', or White Coats, was initiated in 1996. It resulted in a travelling exhibition in early 1998. The travelling exhibition contained texts, sculptures and photographs that an ethnologist, a sculptor and a photographer produced as documentation of the daily work at a hospital department and at a health care centre. At the Museum of Work, where the exhibition was first shown, an additional part related to current issues in health care.

In this project the producer, who was fully responsible for the development and aesthetic quality of the exhibition, commissioned the sculptor – in addition to his task of making sculptures for the exhibition – to develop a design of the screens for the travelling exhibition. He then had a little less to take care of himself. The sculptor had previously designed a successful screen module for another travelling exhibition produced by the museum.

The suggestion for the design of the screens for 'Vita rockar' that the sculptor presented was very similar to the screen module he had previously designed. It featured a very long and narrow space for the photographs. The photographer's pictures, however, were based on traditional camera image proportions, which are much more square.

When presented with the screen design, suddenly the photographer saw her images shredded to pieces by the screen design of the sculptor.

> It was as if I lost my grip on it. I just got confused. I got locked into this idea of the sculptor that my pictures would be oblong and very cut down, and in that situation there no longer seemed any possibility I might find my own form and my way of shooting. It felt more as if I was just wallpaper for the sculptures. My pictures would be squeezed into that doorway hole. And... then I started to think in terms of 6x6 format, ... because that's better if you're supposed to make such enlarged copies to match a doorway.

The photographer, feeling subordinate to the suggested screen module design, lost both her engagement and quality of performance due to the sculptor's inability to recognize her images as demanding a specific space and shape. The producer eventually realized their stylistic differences and designed another screen module where the photographs were allowed the space they needed.

The sculptor was not able to grasp the whole of the exhibition in a way that accommodated all the different forms in the exhibition concept. Only the producer had this overall view, and he expressly worked with as flexible elements as possible for the exhibition in order to give each text, sculpture and photograph maximum focus. Here again, the restraints of overly strict frames within which the creative content was to be fitted caused a participating creative professional to lose her artistic strength. The task of the producer or curator is to minimize such aesthetic losses – the losses that may lessen the quality of the end result – while at the same time acknowledging restrictions in available resources. In this case the restraining role was held by an artist and not a technically trained manager as in the Expo case. The incident points to the importance of a holistic perspective in respect of aesthetic enterprises and to the importance of commitment and trust among all contributors to the whole of the enterprise.

Divers memories

Developed by British artist Chris Dorsett, Divers Memories is a series of independent art exhibitions in folklore museums in the United Kingdom and other countries. Dorsett realized the exhibitions as an art project and acted as both curator and contributing artist. The last Divers Memories exhibition was realized in Hong Kong in 1998.

Through a former student, Dorsett was introduced to a Hong Kong curator interested in realizing an art exhibition at a venue he was establishing on the border between Hong Kong and mainland China. The Hong Kong curator was familiar with the arts administrative organizations on the island and managed to secure funding for the project. Dorsett and the Chinese curator agreed to work on an exhibition with contemporary Hong Kong and British artists in an interesting social context, but when it was time to realize it, it became evident that the Hong Kong curator and Dorsett had different views on the role of the curator and the participating artists. The Chinese curator did not consider Dorsett's participation in the exhibition as artist appropriate since Dorsett was curator, and the curator was only to conceive and produce the exhibition, not participate in the event as an artist. This would blur the role and assignment of the curator.

Dorsett tried to work the same way in the Hong Kong project as he had before, developing the exhibition from a continuous discussion with the participating artists:

> He seemed to want the type of curating I wasn't interested in. However, I could see that I wouldn't be able to persuade him to operate differently. I would have preferred a much more organic approach, something that would develop from the ground up and be allowed to grow. My projects are not about curatorial authority. Of course, Divers Memories has to be organized, someone has to take responsibility and push things along, but up until [the Hong Kong project] I had always done this from the position of a go-between, a person who moves backward and forward from the participating artists to the curators at the host museum. In this way I've been able to enjoy influencing the evolution of each exhibition without being a lead player. I know that I have been able to make creative things happen from this apparently subsidiary position.

> [The Hong Kong curator's] idea was that I would decide all the things that would happen. By this point he didn't want to come up with any ideas of his own for the exhibition, he was just going to do the administration. He wanted me to have all the ideas. Again, that's not exactly how I work – and I wasn't keen on it – but I eventually worked out how to proceed after talking to the artists. When I know what the artists are going to do, I have some sense of the general direction I should work toward.

Apparently, the exhibition concept that Dorsett had developed and successfully realized in a number of versions was difficult to share with someone he did not know and who had quite a different point of departure for realizing an exhibition.

Divers Memories was an exhibition project developed and managed by an individual artist as an art project. With the entrance of a second curator on the same level, the form of execution and the role of artist and curator were challenged. This led to friction in the management of the project, especially as the differences in understanding what an exhibition could and should be like were only discovered as work realizing the project progressed. Cooperation is at risk when views on areas of authority, roles and modes of working are not articulated or when the partners are not willing to negotiate them. Artistic management is holistic and experimental, whereas a more administrative logic of management is based on departmentalization and division of labour. In this case, the difference between the explorative interpretation of the curatorial role clashed with a more divisive understanding of the relationship between curator and other participants in an exhibition enterprise.

In visible light

Art student Russell Roberts came up with the idea for a photography exhibition on taxonomy and classification during a student internship in the photography department of the Victoria & Albert Museum in London in the early 1990s. In 1997 this exhibition concept was realized as In Visible Light at Modern Art Oxford, formerly the Museum of Modern Art (MOMA),[4] and other venues. Roberts had not curated any exhibition before and discovered that he and the staff of the Kunsthalle had varying ideas of how to make an exhibition.

Apart from differences in perception of the time frames for work with the exhibition, additional problems evolved over the phrasing of the exhibition. Roberts wanted a flowing or discursive form in the display of the photographs in the exhibition; the educational staff of the museum wanted clarity and simplicity in interpretation for the audience, who were considered incapable of digesting an exhibition without headings and grouping of pictures. Roberts explains:

I had to work with MOMA's education department with the text panels. There were a lot of negotiations and dialogue about this exhibition because some of the staff found it quite difficult to understand certain ideas within the exhibition. Obviously they found it unclear. As I hadn't done that kind of work before, I suddenly found that I couldn't describe the project with the kind of language they required. These descriptions of the exhibition had to be in their terms. It was a bit of a jolt. I became quite protective of the integrity of the project and the ideas that for me originally had fuelled it.

The education department wanted something that would give the visitor a handle, a brief introduction and overview. The categories were needed in order for people to make sense of the material. I would have preferred a much more intimate way of describing the photographs, to have had information on extended labels for each photograph so that when you entered the exhibition, there would have been a whole wall of display cases with material, and there would have been no comfort, because you wouldn't know the framework. There would have been an uncertainty in the viewing experience. Then if the visitor became curious about a certain image, he or she could read the extended label adjacent to it. But there are the needs of the institution in terms of education and customer care. So we had to have categories to give a context to the photographs.

In the end, the feedback I got from various visitors who had different points of entry to and knowledge about the material on show was that the categories disappeared after some time spent in the exhibition. Eventually, people would become more interested in overlaps between the categories. So I think there is possibly an argument that you needed the categories there in order to realize how arbitrary they were. But I would have loved to see it much more fluid.

The educational staff of the museum was worried about the ambiguity of the exhibition as intended by the curator, for they were concerned with making the content of the exhibition accessible to a general public. On the other hand, the curator himself admitted that some visitors would probably have had difficulties grasping the original exhibition. For public art venues and museums, communication is based on clarity. The public art institution vicariously makes a judgement on the level of understanding of the visitor beforehand and adjusts the phrasing of the exhibition according to what is deemed accessible by the targeted public. For an artistic curator, such as Roberts in this case, or Dorsett or Rist in the previous cases, ambiguity and incompleteness are important elements of the exhibition experience for the visitor. Thus, a more artistic or creative approach to exhibitions leaves more for the visitor to complete in the understanding of what is at hand.

The dance of Eros and Apollo

These cases all present situations where drives and priorities diverge or clash in exhibition projects. On the one hand are the limitlessness, fluidity and openness of creativity and creative thought, and on the other, definite thought and the restriction and structure necessary for the coordination of resources.[5] Associative generative thinking and rule breaking are core elements of playful, creative activities, whether in aesthetic, artistic or business activities (Plato, *Laws*, vii; Huizinga, 1939/1950; de Bono, 1970; Sahlin, 2001). The creative element rewrites current perceptions of established modus operandi. Creativity as a force thus has an unpredictable dimension, and it may therefore be perceived as challenging or inspiring, depending on one's attitude towards predictability and planning. The polarity inherent in aesthetic and creative production calls for integrated and situational management that takes both these dimensions into account.[6]

As culture and aesthetic products do today, the stories of the gods of Olympus offered explanations of human and natural conditions and drives in a narrative and impersonated form in Greek antiquity. In Greek mythology the force of creativity can be found in the figure of Eros; the need for distinction and moderation in Apollo.

The act of creation is a striving for immortality by mortal humans. Eros is the desire and drive towards this immortality and breeds art, children, monuments, violence and death, among other things (Nilsson, 1919; Sartre, 1943/1956; Lefebvre, 1974/1991). Eros is our life instinct (Marcuse, 1955); it embodies not self-interest or gain or reasonable calculation but the desire to create being from non-being (Plato, *Symposium*). Neither is Eros a simple desire for satisfaction of the flesh, but a passion for the whole of an idea or a person (May, 1969). In other words, Eros is the striving for that which is outside the self and embodies the strength and courage to perform and the inspiration of the soul. If this desire is not managed, however, Eros is a force that can bring destruction as well.

Creative desire, Eros, is not the mania and palpitation of Dionysus, the god of wilderness and rage, of restless wandering and palpitation.[7] Eros should not be perceived as *agape* either. Agape, charity, is a Christian notion, and thus from another universe (Nygren, 1930; Osborne, 1994).[8]

In exhibition projects and other aesthetic or creative enterprises, Eros is the creative force, giving a concept or an individual element a distinct gestalt. Eros is expressed in the vision of the initiator, curator or artist and propels the work with its realization. The unbound character of the Erotic force may cause such visions to be perceived as appearing out of the blue, unrealistic or incomprehensible by a mind bent on feasibility and structure. Apollo, on the other hand, is the god of reason, temperance, clarity and harmony, foresight, and masculinity.[9]

In contrast to Eros, Apollo enforces restriction. He reminds us that we are mortal and urges us to remember our limitations and not to develop hubris. This is the meaning of the line 'Know thyself', the inscription at the Temple of Apollo in Delphi. Apollo demands purity from Man but also offers a sense of security through the predictability of the prophecies offered by his oracles (Nietzsche, 1872; Nilsson, 1919; Otto, 1933/1965; Sørensen, 1989).[10] Apollo is expressed in a logic of economy and feasibility in tradition and best practice. In exhibition projects Apollo guides work with finding resources, using resources efficiently and accounting. Creative professionals may perceive this sober Apollonian zeal with its push for structure and transparency as suffocating creativity.

Aesthetic enterprises are like parties where Eros is the honorary guest and Apollo the host. Apollo is needed for the party to happen, for everything to be taken care of. He simultaneously serves and supervises. Eros secures the spirit of the party, and Apollo secures its actual happening. As is evident in the cases presented, both creative and structuring elements are central to exhibition projects, as projects are a combination. Each side needs to acknowledge the importance of the other for the project not to come to grief. Equally fatal to exhibition projects are creative suffocation and economic ignorance or recklessness. Eros and Apollo have to engage in a mutual dance for the project to materialize.

Watch Eros and Apollo dancing. Squeezing each other, holding arms and shoulders. Moving back and forth, back and around, around and forth again. Not slackening their grip except for change of posture. The faces of the two characters – close to each other – are red from the strain and the pressure. The steps sometimes form the choreography of a wrestle with blows dealt. Their dance seems original, since we cannot make out any familiar steps to form a dance from their evolving moves. The succession of steps and motions unfolds in ways not known to them or us. We are voyeurs of a simultaneously intimate and public performance, designed as it is performed.

Leadership of clarity and creativity

Why does Eros have to face Apollo? Couldn't he dance by himself and let his strength manifest itself unfettered? The success or realization of an exhibition project is dependent on the joint performance of Eros *and* Apollo. If Apollo leads Eros out in too tight a grip in their mutual dance, the eloquence of Eros is smothered. If Eros on the other hand is held too slackly by Apollo or if they cannot engage in a mutual dance, he engages in his private dance, and the joint performance is ended. Apollo is not there to leash Eros, however. Instead, the two need to hold each other for the dance to be a performance proper and the enterprise to be successful.

Imagination is not fettered to the here and now. Realization is. Having to incorporate both imagination and realization, the task of management is to offer the best conditions possible for the realization of a project, cherishing imagination as its core. Apollo could not manage a creative enterprise by himself because creativity implies a release of control, at least temporarily. Apollo is eager to win and considers everyone a rival, but his superiority is sterile. Engaging with Eros means abating control, since to enjoy the fruits of love we must surrender to it.[11] That is why Apollo may resent a dance with Eros.

The two forces of creativity and clarity, here metaphorically rendered through the characters of Eros and Apollo, should be understood as ideal types of drives or logics towards exhibition realization. They can be combined in one person or be departmentalized within an institution. Thus Eros and Apollo should not be understood simply as synonymous with the roles of the artist and administrator respectively. An individual actor may in one person embody a combination of Eros and Apollo or have more of one or the other as a dominating trait.

Returning to the cases opening this chapter, we can now understand the *mis*management occurring as an inability to balance the creative and the structuring forces of an exhibition enterprise. The *Expo.01* case illustrates a situation where mutual distrust between creative and administrative staff threatens the realization of a large exhibition project. The case displays two different approaches to development of a single exhibition event: the creative process approach embodied by the first artist *directeur artistique* and the technical, financial and marketing approach by the other managers of the Expo organization. Interestingly enough, each side accused the other of mismanagement. Artist Rist had successfully realized a number of large art projects of her own, and the other managers were experienced in their field as well. What they had not done was work on a joint venture of the kind they were now engaged in. Most of the managers and staff changed before the exhibition enterprise could be brought to realization. The initial visionaries of the Expo had to be replaced with pragmatic realists for the national exhibition to materialize.

Management of exhibition enterprises requires a sensitivity to the desire and visions that form the core of aesthetic processes, the ability to translate the visions into physical shape for the necessary realization and the skill to structure resources for the maximum benefit of the aesthetic vision. A carte blanche is lethal for creativity, says the in-house producer of exhibitions at the Museum of Work, who was engaged in the Vita rockar project. Nevertheless, just *any* restrictions will not do. The individual styles of the artists involved have to be acknowledged, and the curator must cultivate the exhibition both in terms of creation and structure.

Two perceptions of the role of the curator clashed in the case of the Divers Memories exhibition in Hong Kong. The artist perceived the curatorial role as one in which flux is acceptable. For him artistic expression and administration were both covered by the curator role. The Hong Kong curator saw the same role as that of an administrator making decisions on overall objectives and selection of artists. In other words, the same role was defined by one of the parties in terms of a manager who delegates according to predefined aims, and by the other as a mediator in the process itself. The inability of one curator to allow for a different curator role for the other caused friction in the realization of the project.

In the In Visible Light case, the guest curator who wanted to do an experimental and ambiguous exhibition design met a demand for clarity and structure from the educational staff of the Kunsthalle. This cooperation succeeded due to the ability of both sides to harbour or accept the vision or need of the counterpart within their own overall vision. The urge to realize the envisioned exhibition weighed heavier than the will to realize their ideal exhibition concept.

The balancing act of creation and structure in exhibitions is a skill not taught in management schools or art schools. Such a skill grows out of personal style. It grows from the urge to bring structure to a vision and demands both sensibility to cultivation processes, as well as tending and trimming of what is growing. Experience of previous exhibition projects does not necessarily make a better curator or aesthetic manager. It is rather based on courage to engage in the dance of Eros and Apollo and willingness to bring it to conclusion. Curiosity about the potentiality of the enterprise is a good start for a pas-de-deux leader.

Notes

1. Later the realization of the Expo was postponed due to economic and organizational problems and renamed *Expo.02*. The exhibition venues were open from May to October 2002 and were visited by 4 million people (repeat visits excluded).
2. All quotes are from Lindqvist (2003).
3. For an overview and evaluation of the exhibitions and project, cf. Lüchinger (2002).
4. In 1992 renamed Modern Art Oxford. The venue has never functioned as a museum, even though that was the intention at the establishment of the venue in the 1960s.
5. Becker (1982) uses the notions *core* and *support* art activities. Cf. also Caves (2000).
6. This is a major concern for both governments and professional art managers (Cf. Creative Europe, 2002).
7. Dionysus represents more a restless break with established order, a flight *from* rather than a desire *to* (Detienne, 1986).
8. By *agape* (charity) is meant the Christian God's love of humanity. In Greek antique understanding, love is placed in Man. Also Thanatos, death, has been suggested as a rival of Eros, but this pairing pertains more to psychoanalytical descriptions of basic human instincts in the course of the life process (Marcuse, 1955).
9. Apollo is also the god of music, which was considered a form of expression based on rules and principles (Kristeller, 1951).
10. For the benefit of Mankind, Dionysus and Apollo share the temple at Delphi, since cold reason and clarity do not always suffice for human life, some prophetic *mania* is also needed to become sensibly human. The human soul consists both of sense and distraction (Plato, *Phaedrus*; Söderström, 1960; Sørensen, 1989).
11. Cf. the notion of surrender in collective creation as described in Barrett, (2000).

References

Barrett, F.J. (2000) Cultivating an aesthetic of unfolding: jazz improvisation as a self-organising system. In S. Linstead and H. Höpfl (eds), *The aesthetics of organization*. London: Sage.

Becker, H. (1982) *Art worlds*. Berkeley: University of California Press.

Caves, R. (2000) *Creative industries. Contracts between art and commerce*. Cambridge, MA: Harvard University Press.

Creative Europe (2002) *On governance and management of artistic creativity in Europe*. European Research Institute for Comparative Cultural Policy and the Arts (ERICarts), Bonn.

de Bono, E. (1970) *Lateral thinking. A textbook of creativity.* London: Ward Lock Education.

Detienne, M. (1986) *Dionysos at large.* Cambridge, MA: Harvard University Press.

Fogh Kirkeby, O. (2004) *Det nye lederskab.* Copenhagen: Børsens Forlag.

Huizinga, J. (1939/1950) *Homo ludens. A study of the play element in culture.* Boston: Beacon Press.

Kristeller, P. (1951) The modern system of the arts. *Journal of the History of Ideas,* 12, pp. 496–527.

Lefebvre, H. (1974/1991) *The production of space.* Trans. D. Nicholson-Smith. Oxford: Basil Blackwell.

Lindqvist, K. (2003) *Exhibition enterprising. Six cases of realisation from idea to institution.* Stockholm: Stockholm University School of Business.

Lüchinger, R. (2002) *Expo.02: Überforderte Schweiz? Die Landesausstellung zwischen Wirtschaft, Politik und Kultur.* Zurich: Bilanz.

Marcuse, H. (1955) *Eros and civilization.* Boston: Beacon Press.

May, R. (1969) *Love and will.* New York: Norton.

Mossetto, G. (1993) *Aesthetics and economics.* Dordrecht: Kluwer.

Nietzsche, F. (1872) *Die Geburt der Tragödie aus dem Geiste der Musik.* Leipzig: E.W. Fritzsch.

Nilsson, M.P. (1919) *Olympen.* Stockholm: Hugo Gebers.

Nygren, A. (1930) *Den kristna kärlekstanken genom tiderna. Eros och agape.* Part 1. Stockholm: Svenska kyrkans diakonistyrelses bokförlag.

Osborne, C. (1994) *Eros unveiled. Plato and the god of love.* Oxford: Clarendon Press.

Otto, W.F. (1933/1965) *Dionysus. Myth and cult.* Bloomington: Indiana University Press.

Sahlin, N.-E. (2001) *Kreativitetens filosofi.* Nora: Nya Doxa.

Sartre, J.-P. (1943/1956) *Being and nothingness. An essay on phenomenological ontology.* New York: Philosophical Library.

Söderström, G. (1960) *Grekisk-romersk kult och mytologi. Med anknytning till den svenska diktningen.* Stockholm: Norstedts/Svenska bokförlaget.

Sørensen, V. (1989) *Apollons uppror. De odödligas historia.* Stockholm: Atlantis.

13
Culinary judgement, aesthetic refinement and badmouthing as innovation management: the business sense of Antonin Carême

Alf Rehn

> Hunger ist Hunger, aber Hunger, der sich durch gekochtes, mit Gabel und Messer gegeßnes Fleisch befriedigt, ist ein andrer Hunger, als der rohes Fleisch mit Hilfe von Hand, Nagel und Zahn verschlingt. Nicht nur der Gegenstand der Konsumtion, sondern auch die Weise der Konsumtion wird daher durch die Produktion produziert, nicht nur objektiv, sondern auch subjektiv. Die Produktion schafft also den Konsumenten.
>
> (Marx, 1857)

What's in a sauce? A mere dressing for food made out of spiced and thickened liquid, it doesn't strike one as a probable focal point for economic arguments or heated aesthetic debates. More generally, the sauce represents the kind of ephemeral follies that seem destined to be studied in either anthropology or cultural studies, not in the efficiency-minded field of business studies. After all, we don't really need sauces, for as old folk wisdom would have it, hunger is a mighty fine sauce in itself. Relishes are instead the kind of thing business studies of the bean-counting variety have a problem comprehending. And even in those cases where business studies might comprehend the sauce as a phenomenon for marketing or an 'experience', it really doesn't see the sauce as very central in itself. Sauces, for business studies, are incidental phenomena.

Nevertheless, sauces do exist, and a lot of people have passionate beliefs about them. The field of culinary arts is awash with well-argued and aggressively held positions on the role and nature of sauces and their creators. In fact, sauces are on a long list of fiercely debated topics in the culinary arena; nearly every ingredient and technique is subject to this scrutiny. From a culinary perspective, then, food – including sauces – is not to be trifled with. It alone outfits a test kitchen for judgement and criticism, innovation and dogma, and, naturally, a gustatory aesthetic. For economics, such notions are incidental, but from a business perspective they form the basis for a very particular type of value production. Culinary critique or judgement, and the sauces inspiring these convictions, form a field where many kinds of value are created, and among them is economic value. This very real economic dimension of sauces is usually treated as a sauce itself, and thereby an incidental thing.

This chapter argues that by looking at how food turns refined (and thereby expensive/valuable), we might well discover something important about value production generally. Food as a business phenomenon has normally been classified within the rather limited categories of nourishment and commodities. Although these aspects are important, they hide the important fact that the mere utility of food represents the minutest part of the food economy, at least in regions not afflicted by starvation. Since food is a primary phenomenon both in the economy and in the upkeep of the human body, cultural values do enter in at a fundamental stage. If we look at what kind of food is needed to actually sustain human life, we are struck by the triviality of it all.

As Mennell (1996, p. 48) and Goody (1982, pp. 97–153) show, food eaten by the lower classes has traditionally been simple and not particularly flavourful, and the whole idea of a hearty rural cuisine seems to be a relatively late invention. The food of the working class until recently consisted of bland stews and soups, boiled concoctions of whatever was at hand. Variety was limited to infrequent feasts and, based on the little information we have, variations in taste must have been almost nonexistent in the day-to-day diet. Often the same stew was eaten at every meal of the day. In some regions, porridge or frumenty was a staple, and this further narrowed variation. This type of food is definitively sufficient for human beings, and people seen as a set of biological entities need little more. In fact, even this bland and relatively tasteless fare is more than we need; humans can sustain themselves on even less. There is no real need for food to taste good or to be enjoyable. Although some foods, especially spoiled foods or particularly strong-tasting plants, may need preparation in order to assist in swallowing, a more logical alternative would be to just not eat such foods. This is true even in the most popularly held functional explanation for the development of cuisine: it helped people eat rotten meat. Rotten meat is toxic, and the rational solution would be to not eat it at all. Further, as studies of hunter-gatherers have shown so eloquently (see Gowdy, 1998), original man seems to have lived a well-supported life with little or no need to seek sustenance in spoiled food, except in the most extreme circumstances.

For these and a number of other explanations, the argument that cuisine develops for practical reasons is highly suspect, and as Mennell points out: 'The overwhelming evidence is that people come positively to like foods which developing social standards define as desirable' (p. 53). In other words, what we understand as food is in part created through the cultural process called cuisine, not the other way around. To a certain extent, this argument is similar to the claims made within the developing field of cultural economy (see Callon, 1998; du Gay and Pryke, 2002) but with some important differences. These claims focus on how one can use cultural studies to analyse the economy or the ways in which economic issues have cultural elements. The contention in this discussion is that this often still leaves 'the economy' as an insufficiently problematized notion. Many such studies implicitly assume that there is a functional base to the economy that has later been affected by 'culture', something that comes through in the fact, for example, that such studies rarely address the studies on original economies that have been presented in economic anthropology.

As Godelier observed in 1965, studies of a thing like the 'economy' by necessity entail either incorporating extraneous elements or excluding necessary ones. Another way to say this is that culture and economy do not (as often assumed in 'cultural economy') co-constitute each other and that instead culture is the necessary foundation of economy. All, not just some, of the foundational notions of the economy – function, use, utility, need, necessity, choice, exchange – are unthinkable outside of a culture and are thus created through one.

Consequently, it may not be possible to disentangle the cultural and the 'functional' aspects of any commodity; this is particularly so when we discuss the value of foods. Here, as in art, the emergence and process of judgement and critique are continuously creating, destroying and recreating value. An early example is the way early hominids took to eating roasted meat, something we may take for granted but which must have entailed a massive reorientation in the sociogenesis of man (cf. Levi-Strauss, 1970; Elias, 1991). Although we are accustomed to eating treated meat, the sensation for early man may have been fear and repulsion and would in any case have needed a whole new understanding of food and eating. We simply do not know, and the assumption that we can take a functionalist perspective on the birth of cooking is reductionist. The meaning of food constitutes a core value, and the tracking of such meaning must be undertaken in a sensitive manner. Take the case of sauce béarnaise, a classic sauce in French haute cuisine. A rich and succulent sauce favoured by Auguste Escoffier, it is basically 'a mayonnaise with butter' (Escoffier, 1903/1989, p. 33) and at one point signaled fine cooking. Although Fannie Farmer's *The Boston Cooking School Cookbook* (1918) dismisses it as a sauce for relatively simple dishes such as baked stuffed smelts and as a fine addition to poached eggs, béarnaise had greater respect in the French kitchen. Later, at least in Scandinavian countries, steak with sauce béarnaise became an iconic standard; it stood for something one might order in a restaurant priding itself on tradition. In certain narratives, readers still find the dish used to conjure up an air of travelling salesmen dining at hotels past their prime. The sauce then detoured to the menus of roadside cafés as the kind of inexpensive but symbolically luxurious dish a truck driver away from home might order.

In the world of haute cuisine, béarnaise sauce became a casualty of the nouvelle cuisine movement started by Fernand Point. Interestingly, although the movement hated heavy sauces, Point himself did not hate béarnaise, a fact often forgotten in writing about haute cuisine. Point acknowledges an appreciation of the sauce himself: 'What is a béarnaise sauce? An egg yolk, some shallots, some tarragon. But believe me, it requires years of practice for the result to be perfect! Take your eyes off it for an instant and it will be unusable' (1974, p. 53).

Supporters of the young nouvelle cuisine designated béarnaise sauce as the enemy. Although not named specifically, it is obvious that it belongs to the sauces Henri Gault and Christian Millau decry when they state how 'the new chefs recognize the pretension, the inanity, the mediocrity of rich and heavy sauces' (cited in Kurlansky, 2002, p. 29). It languished, as many other sauces did, and appeared only on the menus of traditional restaurants. In the 1980s it had a small revival as a 'retro-sauce', and both modern and traditionally minded new chefs on the contemporary food scene experimented with bringing it back as a recollection or as a postmodern deconstructed nod to the past. In this way final judgement on the béarnaise has been everlastingly postponed. It has simmered from classic finery to stale news and changed status from despicable reactionary to become 'retro' and postmodern irony. This one humble sauce has been subject to a number of changing tides in the culinary sphere.

The economic value of this 'mayonnaise with butter' has also never been pinned down. If one looks at its ingredients, one would say it is worth very little. It requires very few tools to prepare and can be made quite quickly, at least if compared to a 'leading' sauce such as an espagnole, which requires first making a roux. As Chef Point acknowledges, you do need to have quite a lot of know-how to make it perfectly, which gives it some specific value. Still, most of its worth seems to come from the way it is positioned in the gustatory universe and the culinary critique. Depending on whether the times and places cherish or berate classical cooking, sauce béarnaise can be valued or devalued. Whether it tastes good or not so good may seem like a highly individual decision, but the symbolic values afforded to it have the power to change taste preferences, as Mennell observes. The value of food, often seen as based on its potential to sate and nourish, becomes evaluated by what 'developing social standards define as desirable'. Seen from this perspective, culinary judgement not only works within the economic sphere, it in part co-creates it.

The following case highlights this operation and also demonstrates a process I call the culinary logic of late capitalism. Considering how a major chef, Antonin Carême, uses culinary judgement and notions of refinement to create a business out of cooking informs an understanding of how cultural practices form a base for the economy rather than functioning as its superstructure. Further definitive statements about the way such practices develop are risky. Preconceived notions of economic development and history may blind us to the way judgement and aesthetics have existed as central aspects in economy and business for long periods of time, possibly since the very beginning of formalized exchange. Likewise, taking words imbued with positive sentiments to mean that there is a simple, functional process behind specific development is naïve. Words such as judgement, taste and refinement tend to change our focus so that the less elegant and even distasteful processes are glossed over in the name of aesthetics. Such developments nevertheless exist even in the refined area of cuisine and, much like sauces, they do have analytical interest.

Every professional in every field is supposed to exhibit and work from good and balanced judgement. The art of judging fairly and well is routinely championed as a central leadership skill and as the hallmark of a professional. Good judgement is thought to lead to good results, and vice versa. The idea that bad judgement could result in anything else but unmitigated disaster is seldom discussed. However, this may not always be true. Pornographer Larry Flynt, creator of *Hustler* magazine, is not particularly known for his sound judgement (see Flynt, 1997). His decision to run a cover photo-montage of a naked woman being run through a meat-grinder does not fall into the category of what we normally mean by 'good judgement'. However, from the perspective of a pornographer, shock tactics may well boost sales and enhance one's notoriety. If you are of this persuasion, the outcome might well vindicate the decision; it could be a good economic call.

Judgement, then, can mean a number of things, depending on what is being discussed. Sometimes the words are the context, as when we select words in order to enhance the nobility of decision-makers. Good judgement is presented as a fait accompli quite unhindered by the fact that even the best judgement cannot guarantee a result since a judgement call by logical necessity indicates questionable and uncertain outcomes. Several concerns come to mind: what about those cases, such as the caricatured Flynt case, when bad judgement turns good? Or to be more precise, when good judgement might equate to lying, cheating and/or stealing? Or posed in another way, how does a judgement turn into a judgement?

This is a story about a man who, depending on how you feel inclined to judge him, was either a genius and innovator or a blowhard and liar. Or maybe all of them. He was an accomplished artist who thought that sugar works were the acme of the architectural arts who became rich by writing about his art and who died doing manual labour. This is a story about Antonin Carême (1783–1833), who was by all accounts a man apart.

The story does not originate with him, though. Instead, inasmuch as this tale has a beginning, it starts with François Pierre de la Varenne (1615?–1678), the father of French classical cooking. It is of course impossible to attribute the development of a cultural field to a specific individual or the development of judgement to a specific year or even span of years. Medieval tomes detail, in some detail, what does and does not constitute 'good taste' in food. Even the *Satyricon* does so in its own inimitable way. Certainly Varenne was not the first famous cook. Several chefs from the eras of Ancient Greece and Imperial Rome precede him, and information about advanced cooking and cooks in China and India from the same time or earlier exist as well (cf. Symons, 2000). In modern Europe, the famed Taillevent predates Varenne by about 300 years. Both culinary judgement and famous chefs have been around for a long time. Despite his chronological place in culinary history, Varenne is important because he produced the standard work against which cuisine is measured.

The assumption is that judgement is not something static, not just a faculty through which the raw information of the world is processed. Often such non-formal methods of decision-making – intuition, improvisation, judgement, and taste – are presented as something one either has or does not have, or in some cases as something that all have and

13.1 Antonin Carême (1783–1833)

which can be developed within a person. The ways in which judgement exists as a shared 'notion in motion' between individuals has received less interest, and we could criticize the use of such notions for often lacking a power dimension. As Bourdieu (1984) has discussed, the notion of distinction is not something that exists in a vacuum but exists as a dynamic in a cultural field. Still, Bourdieu has been attacked for presenting taste as something that may develop on some meta-plane but which cannot in any meaningful way be affected by individuals, for example.

The focus here lies instead on the way in which judgement can be a productive power, though not exactly in a Foucauldian way. François Pierre de la Varenne became part of the culinary pantheon by publishing *La Cuisinier françois* in 1651. While the book is merely a cookbook, it is also a remarkable feat of modernization. It presents French cuisine as it had developed up until then, but it also makes fine cooking something that extends beyond the somewhat cramped confines of the noble kitchen. Its language is easily understood, and many of the dishes are actually manageable without an army of assistants. As Willan (2000, p. 59) notes, it is a seminal book in that it ushers in haute cuisine, thus distancing itself from the massive banquets of medieval cooking. By discussing things like the preparation of vegetables and the basics of cooking, it is in a way the renaissance of French cuisine. It also conspicuously shies away from the massive and ostentatious displays so popular in earlier years and actually introduces a kind of simplicity to the art.

We know little about Varenne, as he died almost completely forgotten. His cookbook, however, had a significant impact. Simply put, it became the standard work that cuisine was measured against. The statement made by the structure and choices present in the book – and what was left out – affected judgement regarding taste and made cooking à la mode in France. Though Varenne wrote little that would have been seen as inflammatory – since developments taking place in Italy had already made the old medieval style of cooking unfashionable – his position as the focal point for discussions regarding French cooking obviously made the book controversial. *La Cuisinier français* was a thought-through book, one where choices were made according to Varenne's culinary judgement. In writing the book he thus established a specific set of judgements, a primer in taste.

Although such codifications cannot be seen as absolute, the book still established that a French culinary field existed rather than accepting the then-dominant Italian logic that the French could muster their own judgement when it came to food. Earlier cookbooks had in effect and by necessity been collections of recipes. With little or no amount of radical innovation, this new book established a paradigmatic change. In part this was due simply to the fact that there was enough written on the culinary that a juxtaposition could be attempted. Further, Varenne hit a nerve when he presented his book as a celebration of a new kind of French independence, a clarion call for a specifically French taste and culinary judgment. This was, de facto, a new cuisine and the basis for a new kind of judging refinement.

Antonin Carême as inventor

Nous avons du mal à nous rendre compte aujourd'hui, malgré la belle collection de cuisiniers mégalomanes dont l'époque nous a gratifiés, de l'espèce d'*aura* qui a entouré de son vivant Marie-Antoine Carême, qui se prénomma lui-même Antonin. Il est douteux qu'aucun chef de cuisine, soit avant, soit après lui, ait jamais joui d'un tel prestige. Encore aujourd'hui, le souvenir de Carême reste, parmi les cuisiniers, comme un astre brillant, une comète inégalée. Pour tous les témoins, pour les convives et les amis des convives, pour les disciples et les successeurs des disciples, Carême possédait le je-ne-sais-quoi d'élégance, de tension, de charme, d'insatisfaction, de secret, de fierté, de promptitude créatrice et d'acharnement au travail, ce quelque chose de plus que 'la classe' et où nul de ceux qui le virent ne crut devoir balancer à reconnaître le génie.

Jean-François Revel, cited in the preface to Carême (1833/1994)

As any introductory text book on innovation management explains, innovation is an invention that one has turned into an economic advantage (see Tidd *et al.*, 2001). To control the way any improvement or technological change is broadly understood, some kind of management must be marshalled. Normally this involves matching what new inventions can do with the way in which the market is prepared to adapt to it.

As a result, there has been a notable detachment of the product and the process by which it is managed in this discourse, so that managing innovation is seen as something else than actually innovating. A vulgar version of this told in a way that keeps a strict boundary between technology and economy is the narrative of the genius inventor tricked by a cunning capitalist. In such a view, the invention is an essence and the managing of it is a transformational practice through which the technological object is tied to the market by way of a socio-technical network. It also posits that the creation of technology and the creation of economy are separate issues. This is interesting insofar as the notion of innovations as important parts in an economy came to us through the notion of invention (and not the other way around).

In Schumpeter's *The theory of economic development* (1911), it is obvious that he believes the role of the manager is secondary and that his hallowed entrepreneur is in fact an inventor. The exact role of innovation management thus stands as a contested area, for there seems to be no way to clearly delimit the different aspects of how an innovation is accepted in a society (Bijker *et al.*, 1987). This becomes even more pronounced in the specific area discussed here. It is very difficult to say what counts as a new invention in cooking, as most developments are incremental, and almost all can be understood only in the context of cuisine generally. A strictly technical innovation at least in part can be judged in an instrumental fashion – what it does and how well it does it – but the same does not hold true for *Jambon braisé et glacé à la Piémontaise*, one of Carême's dishes.

This dish, which would probably not impress a modern gourmet, must be understood in the historical and cultural context in which it was served. To caricature a bit: the creation of a new dish can only be done in two ways. On the one hand, you can make a refinement of an existing dish from *La Cuisinier français*, for example, and fit it to tradition or you can develop a new dish that works in the grammar created by a similar work. On the other hand, you can make a whole new dish, departing radically from set rules, and thus innovate outside the edges of the culinary envelope. We refer to this difference as endo- versus exo-innovation, according to whether the innovation tries to conform to a set cultural practice or overthrow it. What follows is a case of radical exo-innovation.

In a number of cases, critique and passionate judgement have been used to create the truth of cooking. The French have seen a number of attempts from the philosophical musings of Brillat-Savarin to the more Rabelaisian Grimod de la Reynière, but there was probably never quite as consummate a character as Antonin (actually Marie-Antonine) Carême. Culinary genius that he was, he saw himself as the saviour of cuisine. In his version of history, he didn't merely rejuvenate a field he saw as degenerated, he represented revolution and rebirth. Trained in a number of specialties, including the art of the patîssier or pastry cook, he entered the culinary field with a fervour. And in the spirit of his age, he saw in cuisine the ideal marriage of art and science and decided to take the union to new levels. After studying at the Cabinet des Gravures, he became accomplished in drawing, and in 1815 he published two books of elaborate illustrations of sugarcraft, *Le Patîssier royal* and *Le Patîssier pittoresque*. He also made his famous statement regarding the art of pastry cooks: '(L)es beaux arts sont au nombre de cinq, à savoir: la peinture, la sculpture, la poésie, la musique et l'architecture, laquelle a pour branche principale la patîsserie'.

Although pastries are no longer the centre of our cooking attention, the patîssier was very important at that time. He was the creator of the grand spectacle of the set table, the pièce montée. Intricate towering setups were the foci of a setting, and Carême mastered them both practically and in theory. They were, in the original sense of the word, follies. Fantastic, often rather gaudy creations that could mimic Roman pillars or some idyllic pastoral scene, they were used to present food and 'make' a table. They were normally placed in central positions, with the most elaborate one at centre stage. Carême excelled in the creation of these pièces de résistances. He was trained in a subfield of cuisine where presentation and image were everything, and his first books are more works of aesthetics than books on gustatory pleasures.

This does not mean, however, that Carême was someone without substance. All accounts point to the fact that he worked extremely hard to master all the disciplines existing in a major kitchen. Having first become a patîssier, he went to work for Talleyrand and learned the art of the cuisinier from a man named Boucher. This process took about 12 years, in addition to his two years as an apprentice patîssier. After toiling in his master's shadow for what must have seemed a lifetime, he emerged in the field in a blaze of glory. Celebrated as the greatest chef of his lifetime, he was called 'the chef of kings and the king of chefs', a characterization that will later be reused to describe Auguste Escoffier and which may also have been used in connection with Taillevent. Living up to the first part of his title, he worked and cooked celebrated dinners for Tsar Alexander I and Britain's Prince Regent, among others.

After finishing his apprenticeship, Carême embarked on his grand project, the development and codification of what was to be known as grande cuisine. In its own way this was the successor to medieval cooking and cuisine l'ancienne that developed in twists and turns out of and as a reaction to medieval cooking. For Carême, this cooking of the 'ancients' was truly important, for it formed the backdrop for the construction of his own culinary judgement.

Antonin Carême was in some ways the last of his kind rather than the first. Perhaps the last truly great chef who worked in private homes rather than as an entrepreneur, he was part of a bygone age, the ancien régime. Aristocratic and elitist, he was not the democratic communicator that Varenne was. Instead, his aim was loftier; he wanted to develop a true cuisine for the ages.

My colleagues can now see undisputed proof of the advances in nineteenth century French cooking for which I have been responsible. I do not claim that this new work should bring an end to further progress in the culinary art: craftsmen who are imbued with the true spirit of science will no doubt produce innovations; but it is my work that will have inspired them.

Carême (1833/1994), translation from Hyman (2001), pp. 71–2

And he did inspire them. He prepared fish and fowl far more simply than had been the custom and emphasized the natural taste of food. He simplified sauces and the way dinners are structured, and he turned away from what he believed was excessively spiced food and the tendency to enrich dishes with a profusion of trimmings.

He also became famous. His *Le Maître d'hôtel français ou Parallèle de la Cuisine ancienne et moderne selon les quatre saisons* was published in 1822, and the *Le Cuisinier parisien*, in 1828; with these he ushered in what he called 'modern' cuisine. Nevertheless, his greatest work, the magisterial *L'Art de la cuisine française au dix-neuvième siècle*, was to be his last.

He died in 1833, the same year the first two volumes of the work were published. His close collaborator Plumérey went on to finish two more volumes after his death. Although it is more or less incontrovertible that Antonin Carême significantly developed French cuisine, it is perhaps more interesting to note *how* he did it. In an insightful article Philip Hyman (2001) refers to Carême's work as a 'Culina Mutata', a mutation in culinary culture. Hyman warns people studying the development of cuisine to pay attention to the ways articulate chefs pass culinary judgement. He comments further:

> (T)he existence of a 'debate' about cookery in print and specifically in cookbooks is, in itself, particularly interesting. It underlines the role of gastronomic controversies in defining cuisine and associates the chef not only with manual skills but with conceptual powers as well. Food, even good food, is not just something one eats: one prefers the old school or the new, one articulates opinions.
>
> Hyman (2001), p. 81

Antonin Carême excelled in the innovation management skill of articulating opinion. His writing was often vitriolic, and he seemed to delight in referring to his fellow cooks as dunces, degenerates or worse. He thus used badmouthing as an innovative way to promote his own innovations.

Carême was also skilled in making radical generalizations about his big project. He presented himself as the originator and main force of 'the modern style'. Such a notion is of course dependent on there being something outdated and classical with which this modernity can be juxtaposed. The problem, which Hyman notes, is that this was not something that existed as much as something that was systematically created by Carême in parallel with the celebrated *cuisine moderne*.

His 'modern style' was presented not only as a development but also as a whole new phenomenon, a pure form of cooking. As an innovation, this juxtaposition is significant. The notion of an innovation is usually perceived as an introduced process, something that can be treated as ahistorical or even breaking with history. The perspective here is more a relational one. What Carême presented were not inventions in any classical sense. He tinkered, he refined, he chose among options and he took things along a specific path. Although he made a number of judgement calls – like proclaiming the correct way to set a grand table or the right sauce for a particular kind of fish – he rarely invented. The curiosity, then, is how he managed to turn his refinements into innovations.

Although culinary criticism existed before him, Carême elevated it to an art form, deftly mixing scientific rhetoric with an almost religious fervour for gustatory sensations. By contrast, Varenne may have broken with the medieval tradition, but he still incorporated parts of it and presented progression rather than revolution. Similarly, la Chapelle, an earlier major chef who held a fairly high opinion of himself as a culinary artist, positioned his own contribution as refinement and rarified judgement but not as the birth of a whole new era. For chefs before Carême, writing on food was a question of judgement and progress, but Antonin summarily dismissed a whole tradition in the name of culinary science. He labelled earlier modes of cooking impure, crass, lacking in style and sufficient understanding, and produced by magic rather than science; he makes every move he then presents, his very oeuvre, an innovation.

Reading a cookbook by Carême is like reading the writings of Karl Marx. Marx trashed bourgeois economists, referring to them as sycophants and cretins; Carême's text is littered with phrases like 'la jactance [boasting] ignorante et prétentieuse'. He referred to the work of la Chapelle as 'ridiculous' and called other chefs 'charlatans'. His disdain for earlier times knew no bounds, and he characterized the work of his predecessors as mistaken and undeveloped at best, barbarian and grotesque at worst. *His* developments, on the other hand, were presented as Herculean feats, for he himself had single-handedly lifted cuisine out of the swamps of the past. The old style of cooking, which Carême seldom pinpoints in any detail, was where monsters lurked, where fish was made to taste like fowl and spices were used in peculiar and suspect ways.

Carême's notion of a *cuisine ancienne* was in many ways a discourse on corruption and pollution. In a way that resembles Mary Douglas' (1966/2001) classic analysis of impurity, he focused on the ways this impurity mixes things he believed should be kept apart. For instance, he railed against the way the 'ancients' used meat as a garnish for fish,

13.2 Title page of *L'art de la cuisine française au dix-neuvième siècle (1833)*

thus creating what for him must have been a monstrous hybrid. He pontificates at length on the necessity of letting fish taste like fish and explains how earlier cooking did nothing to let 'discriminating taste' develop. He went on to attack the way the same earlier cooks used spices and aromatics to create 'unnatural' tastes, and thus they managed the flavour of dishes.

Douglas' analysis of Leviticus showed how notions of impurity were tied to phenomena having or acquiring characteristics across imagined boundaries of classes; for example, a water-living creature with a land-dweller's 'feet' was seen as impure. Carême sought a similar purity in the area of cooking. A fish manipulated to taste like something else was not only bad cooking, but it was also against order and purity. Simply put, it was dirty.

This badmouthing of earlier epochs, which Hyman (2001) traces in detail, can be seen as an integral part of the value-production of cuisine. There is nothing implicit in the notions of innovation or 'creative destruction' (Schumpeter, 1911) that rules out lying about earlier systems in order to introduce a new way of understanding judgement and refinement. Many of the accusations Carême directed at earlier chefs were patently untrue. His claim that he himself had introduced the switch from massive displays of food to more delicate and costly dishes was not only a lie, it was a blatant lie since a similar move was a hundred years old when he wrote of it. This, however, is not necessarily a particularly valid point of criticism. Our moral objections to such behaviour do not disqualify it as an astounding success; Carême's gamble worked. His contemporaries hailed him as a genius, and even today he is referred to reverently in most books on the development of haute cuisine.

What he manages by juxtaposing his own notions of refined food with a made-up *cuisine ancienne* is to transform a set of principles into an innovation by making people believe in his judgement. The exact methods may have been somewhat suspect, but it is obvious that he was highly skilled in managing his project in a way that turned it into an innovation. What is important here is that Carême managed the relationship between the old style and his own new style in a way that made the latter something more than a mere development. By retelling the history of cuisine and presenting himself as a break within its history, he managed innovation into being. Judgement and taste, in this case, were not merely results of schooling, breeding or tradition but were a contested terrain that could be manipulated by lying deftly and pontificating with style. Operating in the fuzzy field of judging gustatory sensations, he understood that refinement and taste were neither fixed nor processes unalterable by individuals but something that could be worked with and engaged in. In his own way, Carême was a postmodern 'imagineer', creating style for business reasons, and his innovation strategy was one where presentation was everything. In an age of science, an age that many still seem to believe was defined by simple economies, he showed how aesthetic judgement lies at the very heart of economics. Although the food he created was at the pinnacle of the culinary arts, he was communicating generally about eating and food economies and showed in the process how the entanglement of nutrition and culture travels through the ages.

By using his power and his judgement, Carême redefined what it is to eat and how good food is to be thought of. In this way the aesthetic judgement of one man affected the development of the civilizing process (Elias, 2000). The exact nature of judgement, however, remains in flux, tentative. All this might seem like a fairly trivial observation, like a minor movement in a highly marginal field. However, it shows us how the seemingly simple notion of 'good food' and 'judgement' must be understood in their historical context, not only in terms of the sociology or history of haute cuisine, but also in terms of the notion of business as well.

The business of food, as well as its economy, is not something that exists apart from the cultural forces that shape what food is and how it is understood. Contemporary management theory tends to afford a place for cultural forces, but the existence of these on a foundational level throughout history is rarely addressed. As Priscilla Parkhurst-Ferguson (1998) and Patrick Hetzel (2003) have discussed, the actions of individual chefs in history have affected not only their own times, but they have also been constitutive of how the culinary field has developed all the way into our contemporary post-industrial age. Thus, the manipulation of judgement evident in the works of Antonin Carême has had a distinct influence that might still exert a specific influence in the multi-billion dollar industry we now know as haute cuisine. And this is not without economic interest.

A structuralism of sauces

Regardless of what one thinks of food and the review that Carême presents, his grand project of a 'modern style' has additional interest for a student of business and economy. What makes him particularly stand out is his highly structured approach to kitchen work. He created a code of practice for kitchens which involved an intricate system of regimented work, a method reminiscent of Frederick Taylor's system but which predates it by a full century. His kitchen was divided into 16 'stations', staffed by a brigade of chefs, cooks and various assistants. Not only did this make the kitchen more efficient, it freed the head chef from a lot of toil and drudgery and positioned him as a creator and overseer more than a *primus inter pares*.

Although hierarchy in the kitchen has probably existed since time immemorial, the cook has usually been classified as a manual labourer. Many of the finest early chefs – Taillevent, Vatel and Menon, for example – obviously worked more as managers and artists than as labourers, but the perception of them was still that of builder and constructor. By introducing structure into the organization, Carême attempted to do through organization what he was doing elsewhere through text. The ordering of the kitchen was, of course, a way to make even more glorious dinners possible, but it was also a way to codify the position of the chef. From having been something akin to a feudal lord, the chef becomes a professor in a laboratory or a captain of industry.

The modernization of the kitchen occurs not only through increasing technological rationality but through the way in which positions in the kitchen are symbolically linked through positions elsewhere in society. Refined cooking may have been one of the first spheres that were heavily organized. Excepting the church and the state, the king's kitchens were likely to have been one of the most institutionalized organizations in medieval life. Although trade and industry were relatively fluid structures which comprised small autonomous units, and larger organizations such as armies were conveyed on an ad hoc basis, the royal kitchen was a constantly operational organization with clear boundaries and an explicit hierarchy. In this sense, it is one of our first modern business organizations.

The medieval origins of cuisine made the organizational culture of major kitchens rather atavistic, however. Physical abuse and harsh working conditions were obviously the norm until the twentieth century. This has changed less than one might think; a certain primitivism still seems to reign in restaurant kitchens (see Bourdain, 2000). Carême's restructuring could thus be seen as part of his overall project of making the art of cooking modern, scientific and ordered.

By arranging his kitchen into manageable units with clear connections between them, Carême could work on creating dishes without worrying about the complexities of preparation in the hustle-bustle of an organically organized kitchen. Growing up in an age which rejoiced in classifications and what must have seemed like a never-ending scientific development, he is likely to have seen similarities between his kitchen and a place of science. The stations were his dissections of cooking, and the instruments such as serving plates he designed himself aided in creating the exactness the age idolized.

Today we tend to see innovative milieus as slightly chaotic and characterized by creative disarray, but this may in fact be a symptom of our age rather than something innate to innovation. For chefs in Carême's age, the workplace was one of confusion and flux, a sorcerer's den of boiling cauldrons, smoke and fire. The ordering of the kitchen may seem like the introduction of that greatest enemy of creativity, Taylorism, but Carême is explicit in saying that this in fact might be the way for cuisine to develop. If we wish to translate this into the vernacular of modern management theory, we could say that even though he was knowledgeable in the post-industrial value production inherent in using presentation and image as important parts of his overall strategy, he was also well versed in Fordist production strategies. The difference is that this took place long before notions such as Fordism and post-industrial economy became possible.

Carême's greatest work may have been the introduction of an order of sauces. Sauces in earlier times had been born of individual preference and a choice among a series of recipes for dressing different kinds of dishes. The scientific mind of Carême, however, came up with a system.

Although Carême's discussion of sauces can be slightly ambiguous for a modern reader – for sauces then were not always the kind we are used to – he in fact established much of classical French cookery by rebelling against the then common thickened variety. The *nouvelle cuisine* that predates his *cuisine moderne*, and which he often refers to as a *cuisine ancienne*, was wont to use all kinds of unthickened sauces, infusions of the kind that regained interest with the 'nouvelle' *nouvelle cuisine* of the 1970s. Carême took this reaction to the bread-based sauces of medieval times and quickly redefined it as a classical idea he had left behind. He instead propagated the use of bound sauces and presented the notion of the 'master sauces' and their lesser variations, 'des grandes et petites sauces en gras et en maigre' (Carême, 1833/1994, pp. 287–402). Although his treatise included 'des ragoûts et garnitures', 'des purées de racines et plantes légumineuses', and 'des essences', this discussion deals only with the sauces that Carême deigned to call true sauces.

(J)e le répète, sans dépenser autant que le vieille cuisine, la cuisine moderne a toute la succulence désirable, et elle a bien plus d'élégance et de variété que l'ancienne. Je le répète sans crainte: la cuisine française du dix-neuvième siècle restera le type du beau de l'art culinaire. (Carême,1833/1994, p. 291)

(N)ous devons toujours marquer des grandes sauces en maigre, ainsi que vous le verrez bientôt, puisque nous voilà très incessamment arrivés à la cuisine du carême. (Et) Vous avez raison, lui dis-je, car ces grandes sauces donnent aux petites plus d'onction et de nutrition: c'est par ces résultats que se caractérise la bonne cuisine. (Carême, 1833/1994, p. 298)

Four master sauces and a series of lesser sauces make up the system. The four master sauces are the espagnol, the velouté, the allemande and the béchamel, emulsions well-known to any modern chef. Together they form the base for the entire system, and more than a hundred variations derive from them. These variations are classified logically into a system and are elegantly presented as the only avenue toward true gustatory pleasure. What Carême did – and it logically follows from his grand project – was codify the use of these variations, deftly building a number of supports for the notion of himself as the creator of the *grande cuisine française*. He maintained he had found the correct way to think about sauces. And further, he claimed French sauces were the finest in the world, based on 'Mes voyages en Allemagne, en Bavière et en Prusse'. Again he makes himself part of a national movement.

Both cuisine and Carême are specifically French and specifically scientific, making it hard to tell them apart. *L'art de la cuisine française* is in these respects both a treatise on the scientific development of a part of economics and a nationalist tract, and there may have been a specific point to this. For although it is the irrefutable judgement of Antonin Carême that creates the modern style – this acme of culinary refinement – the project is a wider ranging one. The systematization of the kitchen, the order of sauces and the created paradigm shift between the old and the 'modern' all coexist as part of an enlightened project in the world brought to the fore by the Revolution. Carême was the dawn of Reason in the kitchen and precursor of a wide range of developments in the economic sphere. The structure of sauces, their 're-engineering', was a microcosm of a rationalization that was to follow in most economic activities.

Carême is a harbinger of a new age, and the sauce is far from an insignificant detail, for every part must fit together in a system, and judgement is a way for this system to develop. No clear dividing line between rationality and aesthetics or between logical decision and judgement exists in these cases, for both guide and create the other. Value creation, in this perspective, is not something merely guided by culinary refinement; it is something that comes into being according to culinary logic, a logic that is both systematic and aesthetic, ordered by science and infinitely permutable.

Cooking the books of culinary history

Commentators on contemporary economics have presented a framework of value production that currently goes from material production to immaterial transformation; 'image', 'ideas', and 'experiences' are modern constituents of the value function, replacing the 'land', 'work', and 'raw materials' of earlier times. This is not only a fallacy, it represents a dangerous ignorance. Much as Antonin Carême created a past where tasteless dunces used their insufficiently refined judgement to produce grotesque food, we now posit a past where our current refined notions of brands and performances did not exist.

Information – that emptiest of words – is now marshalled by the likes of Antonio Negri and Manuel Castells as a *logique moderne*. They quite cheerfully ignore – or criminally neglect – the fact that information and information networks were central value-producing power networks long before the first telegraph line was drawn (see, for example, Schroeder and Borgerson, 2002). Buttressed by an information network unsurpassed in its time, the Catholic Church, for instance, drew much of its power from an information imbalance and successful symbolic management. Similarly, the medieval guilds were in a sense a closed information system, where codified knowledge and symbolic hierarchy were structured and upheld (see Epstein, 1991). Although these depended on fewer sophisticated material effects and perhaps more on sophisticated social technologies, to state that the work done within the system of guilds would have been less networked and less information-dense is analytically sloppy. Even though every age has a tendency to see its own developments as the acme of civilization, studies of and in an age should at least try to see past such glib generalizations.

Refined food, both the *haute cuisine* and the *cuisine bourgeoise*, has always been about image and style. The experience economy that is now presented as a new phenomenon and development has lived quite comfortably in the heat and smoke of the kitchen for a long, long time. Although we lack knowledge about and insight into the earliest forms of refinement in cooking, we can without hesitation report that those aspects now presented as new input into the value-chain have been integral parts of cooking for thousands of years. In other words, the history of cuisine affords us a way to analyse innovation, aesthetics, image and experiences as value creation over long periods of time, rather than as newfangled and still emerging phenomena. The culinary logic present in the thinking and structured style of Antonin Carême can, in its own way, give us a perspective on the notion of late capitalism or post-industrial economy. Although Carême was obviously multi-talented, one of his main skills seems to have been the way in which he could articulate and present judgement and refinement. In a sphere that is ephemeral and whole-heartedly subjective – although Antonin would have contested this last statement – he was a master of positioning. Whether his judgement 'in reality' – wherever that is – was better than Varenne's or la Chapelle's, or whether he actually was any more refined than the ancients he loved to deride, is inconsequential. What is important is that in all his work he could manage these aspects. The culinary sphere, far from being a primitive or marginal economic phenomenon, can in this way be seen as a harbinger of other economic developments. Being related to both the simplest form of economy – the survival of the organism – and the most ephemeral form (image or experience economy) cuisine can stand as a warning counterpoint to simplifying tendencies in thinking about economics. As Marx's plain commodity, the humble sauce, both nourishing and aesthetic, can be 'a very queer thing, abounding in metaphysical subtleties and theological niceties'.

References

Bijker, W., T. Hughes, and T. Pinch (eds) (1987) *The social construction of technological systems*. Cambridge, MA: MIT Press.

Bourdain, A. (2000) *Kitchen confidential. Adventures in the culinary underbelly*. London: Bloomsbury.

Bourdieu, P. (1984) *Distinction. A social critique of the judgment of taste*. Cambridge, MA: Harvard University Press.

Callon, M. (ed.) (1998) *The laws of the markets*. Oxford: Basil Blackwell.

Carême, A. (1833/1994) *L'Art de la cuisine française au dix-neuvième siècle. Traité Élémentaire et Pratique suivi de dissertations culinaires et gastronomiques utiles aux progrès de cet*. Paris: Payot & Rivages.

Douglas, M. (1966/2001) *Purity and danger. An analysis of concepts of pollution and taboo*. London: Routledge.

du Gay, P., and M. Pryke (eds) (2002) *Cultural economy*. London: Sage.

Elias, N. (1991) *The symbol theory*. London: Sage.

Elias, N. (2000) *The civilizing process: sociogenetic and psychogenetic investigations*. Oxford: Basil Blackwell.

Epstein, S. (1991) *Wage labor and guilds in medieval Europe*. Chapel Hill: University of North Carolina Press.

Escoffier, A. (1903/1989) *The Escoffier cookbook – A guide to the fine art of French cuisine* (originally published in 1903 as *Guide Culinaire*). New York: Crown Publishers.

Farmer, F. (1918) *The Boston cooking school cook book*. Boston: Little, Brown.

Flynt, L. (1997) *An unseemly man – My life as a pornographer, pundit and social outcast*. London: Bloomsbury.

Godelier, M. (1965) Object et méthodes de l'anthropologie economique. *L'Homme*, 9 (2), pp. 5–37.

Goody, J. (1982) *Cooking, cuisine and class – A study in comparative sociology*. Cambridge University Press.

Gowdy, J. (ed.) (1998) *Limited wants, unlimited means – A reader on hunter-gatherer economics and the environment*. Washington, DC: Island Press.

Hetzel, P. (2003) Contemporary haute cuisine in France – When French chefs are paying tribute to the past. In S. Brown and J. Sherry (eds), *Time, space, and the market – retroscapes rising*. London: M.E. Sharpe.

Hyman, P. (2001) Culina Mutata: Carême and l'ancienne cuisine. In L. Schehr and A. Weiss (eds), *French food: on the table, on the page, and in French culture*. London: Routledge.

Kurlansky, M. (2002) *Choice cuts*. London: Jonathan Cape.

Lévi-Strauss, C. (1970) *The raw and the cooked – Introduction to a science of mythology*. London: Jonathan Cape.

Marx, K. (1857) Einleitung zur Kritik der politischen Ökonomie. In *Karl Marx/Friedrich Engels – Werke*. Institute of Marxism-Leninism, Central Committee of the Socialist Unity Party. Vol. 13, 7, pp. 615–641. Available online at: http://members.tripod.com/Lonego/Traduzioni/Marx/germantext/karlmarx.htm

Mennell, S. (1996) *All manners of food – Eating and taste in England and France from the middle ages to the present*. 2nd ed. Urbana: University of Illinois Press.

Parkhurst-Ferguson, P. (1998) A cultural field in the making: Gastronomy in 19th century France. *American Journal of Sociology*, 104 (3), pp. 597–641.

Point, F. (1974) *Ma gastronomie*. Wilton, CT: Lyceum Books.

Schroeder, J., and J. Borgerson, (2002) Innovations in information technology: insights into consumer culture from Italian Renaissance art. *Consumption, Markets, and Culture*, 5 (2), pp. 153–169.

Schumpeter, J. (1911) *The theory of economic development*. Cambridge, MA: Harvard University Press.

Symons, M. (2000) *A history of cooks and cooking*. Urbana: University of Illinois Press.

Tidd, J., J. Bessant, and K. Pavitt (2001) *Managing innovation*. 2nd ed. Chichester: John Wiley.

Willan, A. (2000) *Great cooks and their recipes*. London: Pavilion Books.

14
Beautiful business

Ivar Björkman

Grythyttan – from mining identity to repast experiences

This chapter explores the creation of beautyscapes as a driving force in transforming old industrial areas into new aesthetic communities. Sweden's Grythyttan is a beautyscape that specializes in providing the customer with a unique beauty experience.

Grythyttan has a colourful history and is a remarkable example of how a place can be changed from a working class environment to a beauty experience. From its existence as an old mining town with high unemployment to its new life as a dynamic town with appeal to innovative business, Grythyttan is a typical phenomenon in aesthetic society (Björkman, 1998; Jensen, 1999). Its chronicle begins many hundreds of years ago and includes elements of Swedish history and a shift from industry to storytelling. The town's fifteenth-century buildings have been carefully rehabilitated and renovated, all part of their plan to avoid becoming just another boring modern small town.

Grythyttan is characterized by many different features: an inn, an academy for cooks and waiters, research in sensory response in collaboration with different art schools, a 17,000 square-mile museum with a theatre under construction, and various wine and food businesses.

Grythyttan's tale is an old tale. The town has a marvellous knowledge of how to link old and new in an atmosphere conducive to sensory exploration, and in addition, it is the place to go to understand more about how to transform business into a new value proposition that attracts today's customers.

Grythyttan owes a major part of its popularity to Carl Jan Granqvist, a visionary who has helped make Sweden a global leader in food culture. Through networking inside and outside the community, Granqvist, who

14.1   Grythyttan

was born in the neighbourhood, has helped change the whole place from an ordinary industrial area with all kinds of economic problems into an extraordinarily exciting destination. Grythyttan is not just another spa where people go to relax in a pool or to play golf, though. Grythyttan is a concept, and the concept is probably most vividly illustrated in Granqvist himself; listening to him speak about his town gives you the feeling that he *is* the town.

Grythyttan has built its history from within the region to which it has added something new. The narrative is not all fiction, but the moments of fiction are still there. You know you are not in the fifteenth century, yet in part of the town you actually feel as if you were. Letting that feeling take over is dependent on how much you believe the story. The people of Grythyttan see themselves as part of the making of their history and want to avoid just becoming a rerun of their past. They create symbols and rituals underlining their part in the fabrication of their own future history. One example is the copper chest they show visitors. Into this chest they have put different kinds of contemporary objects related to the concept of meal/repast. The overall meaning transforms the contemporary into a history of the future. The inn and the town represent the history. The Sevilla building and its activities represent the present and the future. Another example is the IT project of making old cookbooks available on the Internet. Bringing history into the present and at the same time making way for the future is a formula they work with in order to create the ultimate beauty experience.

Many companies tend to forget this. They look upon their business from the perspective of the present, bookended by the past on one side and by the future on the other. The result is that the customer does not get involved in being part of the transformation process. This, of course, does not mean that Grythyttan 'retreats', for example, with their focus on making history into something attractive for today, are not doing the right thing. Success, indeed, lies in the ability to transform history into a vision for the future. A retreat in a castle, where history plays a major role in creating the beauty experience, reminds the visitor that part of the experience is the fact that the place itself is often the result of visionary thinking. This realization makes it easier to imagine how things were when the castle enjoyed its heyday. At the same time, the place inspires the visitor to dream about his or her own visions as well. This part of the Grythyttan concept is significant for business in general. If a company just talks about *future* customers or *future* employees, it tends to ignore the relationship of the present to the past or the past to the future. If it only talks about history, then of course it has problems making the customer or the employees feel part of the value-adding process.

One very important aspect of creating the beauty experience is the ability to create stories. In the case of Grythyttan, there is not just one story; there are many. One chronicles the history of the place, for example. Another one is the story of Granqvist and his town crew. The story of the Sevilla building is yet another good example. The Sevilla had been the Swedish pavilion at the World Exhibition in 1992, and after the exhibition, officials did not know what to do with it. Granqvist, who visited the exhibition, came up with the idea that he and his partners could buy the building and move it to a place in the Swedish forest that few people had heard about. Voila! The Sevilla was transported to Grythyttan. Today the Sevilla incorporates an academy with lecture rooms, a cookbook library, a cookbook museum, tourist office, restaurant and shop, and the building itself symbolizes the nature of Sweden in many different ways. For one thing, the outdoor floor represents the inland ice covering Scandinavia generations ago.

Grythyttan as a brand involves different kinds of partners: academy, city council, Granqvist, the residents, food industries and wine producers. One indigenous treat, for example, is wine on a cloudberry, a special kind of fruit found in Scandinavia. In addition, one of the leading furniture manufacturers has been around for 50 years, and some of its designs are the same as they were when it started.

Grythyttan stands apart from other towns of its size. Its uniqueness lies in its quality of life generated through aesthetics and knowledge. It incorporates university-level education and research into its aesthetic concept, thereby combining the past and the future into the present; it has quite literally made aesthetics part of the knowledge process.

Embedding beautyscapes

And how does the story of Sweden's Grythyttan clarify the relationship between beauty and business? Is there anything new in the Grythyttan story or is it the same old tale? Today most people live in a consumer society where the purpose of beauty is to seduce. In the commercial world the individual is marketed as a unique formula through a product or service. Throughout the history of industrialized society, everyday life has been peppered with ads that assure people that beauty will make them different and change their life. Today this promise has become even more important than before. The experience and symbolic value of a product or service have increased because we live in a society where a surplus of products and services confuses or even alienates the consumer. In addition, this process creates a longing for original identities (Bauman, 1993), which explains why beauty and business melt together within the field of beautyscapes. One could say that the desire to become part of worlds of fantasy and beauty incorporates a longing for unapproachable meaning which creates new desires.

The term 'beautyscapes', which exists in computer games, movies and television, media, cosmetics, fashion, music, transportation, sports, tourism, restaurants and hotels, interior design and home products, toys and new technology is inspired by sociologist Arjun Appadurais' definition of global landscapes, including ethnoscapes, financescapes, mediascapes and ideoscapes (see Beck, 1998). Beautyscapes engage individuals differently. They can foster sub-cultures with strong social and cultural bonds or they can provide an escape for the individual consumer for a short while.

Four major fields of business specialize in the creation of beautyscapes, and they are to some degree connected to each other: the field of design, which includes enterprises using design as a competitive tool; the field of fashion, which includes clothing, cosmetics and accessories; the field of entertainment, which includes the media, television, literature, games, the movie and music industries; and the field of recreation, which includes tourism, hotels, restaurants and recreational facilities.

More than just emotional rescue

The word 'beauty' has two distinct uses: beauty as sensuous charm, and beauty as aesthetic approval of imaginative works of art. In other words, one refers to the perceptual aspect of the imagination, and the other refers to the appropriateness and intensity of the emotions aroused (Kirwan, 1999).

Beauty is more than just something that arouses emotions, however. Ideals of beauty are normative rules that can repress behaviour. Not being able to live up to an ultimate perception of beauty frustrates individuals and lowers their self-confidence. Not being able to fulfill the ideals of beauty as a successful businessman/woman also results in disappointment. Beauty helps to define morality, social status, class, gender, race and ethnicity.

That said, it is important to remember that social relationships and institutions, other cultural categories and practices, and politics and economics shape these ideals of beauty. These include television images, newspaper stories, music videos and the fashion industry. Interestingly, Amazon.com lists 15 to 20 book titles containing the word 'ugly' or 'ugliness' compared to the word 'beauty', which shows up approximately 4500 times. Most of these books concern the appearance of both women and men and are part of the reproduction process spreading the different ideals of beauty throughout the world. Taking this a step further, Coty Inc. is one of the major beauty businesses collaborating with NASA in making cosmetics for people *out in space*.

Finding the embedding concept

Grythyttan is unique in that it both inspires and extends the meaning of repast to something more than going to a restaurant or to another eating establishment. Using repast as the metaphor for what it is accomplishing not only explains the purpose for its activities but also gives the purpose a wider content. Repast in this case means not only eating but also taking part in conversation. It is during a repast that people meet and discuss things that are not their usual topics. In a sense, repast is a metaphor for a society which encourages people to cultivate themselves, and repast is the concept used to build their beauty concept.

Granqvist himself is an important facilitator in making this happen. He acts as the host who owns everything, but in reality he owns nothing. He worked as a footman in the Swedish royal court and ran his own antique shop. His reputation among Swedes started when he and a colleague did a television show on wine tasting. He now serves as host of a popular television programme in which competitors make a screen guess about a train's destination.

Repast as a theme fits today's society perfectly. Due to rapidly growing globalization, society is on the move. People are becoming part of an aesthetic society strongly connected to an urban lifestyle, a society where relationships of identity and function are changing. Strategies for living are not about constructing an identity any more. Instead it's about navigating among flows of desire and not getting stuck. The rise of an urban aesthetic society affects a population socially, culturally and economically, which also means that markets for concepts like Grythyttan are growing rapidly (Postrel, 2003). Grythyttan represents a mix of nostalgic country lifestyle and its values with more progressive urban knowledge-oriented values. It attracts customers who want to get the feeling of a 'real' identity that supports their desire of not being ordinary.

At the same time that globalization and the rise of a network society are emerging, identity is losing its regional connectedness, and different kinds of social movements are substituting for the loss (Castells, 1999). Possibilities of buying identity have emerged, and it is becoming something people experience rather than being something they use to declare their connectedness. As a result of this modern interpretation, identity is losing its grip. Instead of being something that stops us from exploring new things and situations, it becomes a tool for liberating ourselves, a tool that people just borrow for a little while (Lash and Urry, 1994). In this sense concepts such as Grythyttan fit the market. The creation of beauty – as a short-time identity provider – plays an important role in this concept.

Some might ask whether there is anything in common between the marketing concepts of Grythyttan and Disney. After all, Disney is a part of the experience business too. There is a difference, however. Disney is built upon fiction and storytelling, while Grythyttan, even though it has stories, is for real. Disney is a company, while Grythyttan is a town.

These quick answers are probably oversimplifications of a more complicated picture. Grythyttan is also fiction and in many ways is built on creating great stories. How it differs lies in the way it performs its stories and how it conceptualizes its ideology. Disney is a private company, while Grythyttan is a town with different partners with different interests in the making of their community. As is the case with many little old towns hanging on to their historical atmosphere, Grythyttan tends more and more to be looked upon as part of a Walt Disney concept and is treated as such. It is like the story about the Grecian temples; workers secretly restore the Parthenon by replacing old bricks with new and hiding the old bricks underground somewhere. Tourists visiting the site have no idea of what is going on. While they think they are viewing the real temple, they are actually looking at a copy of it. The difference between Grythyttan and Walt Disney, then, is the belief of what is real and what is not real, not what the reality is in itself.

Criteria for institutionalizing rules of beauty

Institutionalized rules of beauty govern the process of embedding some-thing in a beautyscape. While the prevailing type of ideal depends on traditional concepts of beauty plus cultural, social and technological societal changes, there are also established criteria or rules.

In his book *Beauty in context*, anthropologist Wilfried Van Damme (1996) considers whether or not the aesthetic criteria found in different primitive cultures are similar. Investigating empirical research, he found six beauty criteria in anthropological studies of primitive societies: *skill, symmetry and balance, clarity, smoothness and brightness, youthfulness and novelty* and *fineness and delicacy*. Since these criteria are also used in modern aesthetics and in practice, they would seem applicable in Western society as well.

Van Damme himself might disagree. He appraises his findings by saying the criteria are very questionable and that there is no such thing as 'one ... beauty criterion' to satisfy different cultures. This statement, however, does not mean that criteria are *dis*similar in different cultures. For example, some of these criteria are found in our Western society in how beauty is presented in marketing and product design. In addition, history books of industrial design use these criteria to describe designers and objects (see, for example, Heskett, 1980).

Beauty criteria are differentiators and identity providers within a company. On a corporate level, beauty criteria are often used to underline overall corporate values. All six criteria can be found in all the different features of the Grythyttan concept. To a large extent, in fact, the criteria become the conditions for making repast accepted as repast.

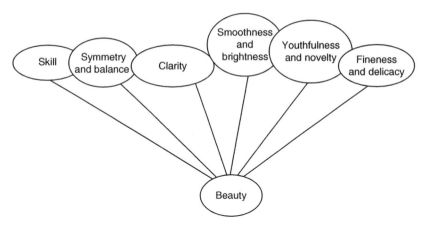

Figure 14.1   Beauty criteria

Skill

How important good craftsmanship or virtuosity is in making a product, service or brand beautiful is a primary consideration. In primitive societies many cultures use good craftsmanship as a criterion for evaluation of aesthetic objects. This criterion is also used in our society in certain business areas like handicrafts and applied arts. In what way skill is valued as a criterion for beauty in other areas varies. In art and design, for example, skill has more to do with virtuosity than craftsmanship.

Skill in the context of art may also refer to special mental or conceptual abilities. This could also be said about people producing ads and commercials. Award-winning marketing often shows a special mental or conceptual quality. It is not enough to feature a beautiful girl or a breathtaking landscape to get through to the consumer. Having virtuosity or special mental or conceptual ability is also very important when it comes to design. Successful design, useful or not, often shows these features. The outcome of skill is often described in terms of quality, and in ads the words 'quality' and 'skill' are often used to underline the beauty of the product or service.

Companies develop and promote different types of skills. A Mercedes carries with it the reputation of having been built by skilled employees; owners claim that the car feels new even after being driven for several years. Good craftsmanship identifies a Mercedes. In addition, 'smart' cars are bestowed with conceptual abilities. Cars without any of these attributes would have a problem being recognized as beautiful. Not being recognized as beautiful does not mean that they will be a problem to sell, but they will have to be strong competitors on price.

In the case of Grythyttan, skill is not only attached to tradition and history but also to the repast concept. Companies use skill in connection with their history, but by using the term 'repast', they create more and deeper expectations. They use skill as a topic that underlines the unusual, something that is tacit by nature. Finally, Grythyttan is also home to an academy, so skill becomes a natural part of education and of course gains emphasis through the process.

Symmetry and balance

The pioneering research of Randy Thornhill, Regents' professor of biology at the University of New Mexico, and Steven Gangestad, professor of psychology at the same university, has shown that beauty may not be entirely skin deep. A number of biological constants transcend culture, ethnicity and advertising campaigns. One of these is bilateral symmetry, which is how well your left side matches your right. Biologists consider bilateral symmetry a marker for developmental stability.

Symmetry and balance are used by different primitive cultures, and while the two terms are often bracketed, they do have their own nuances of meaning. Symmetry designates a rather objective equilibrium between two identical forms or two equal sets of formal characteristics. Balance, on the other hand, refers to a more subjective or less tangible type of equilibrium, as when something feels as if it is in balance. In the

Trobriand Islands off New Guinea, sculptors aim at balance in carving by perfectly weighing their red, white and black lines against each other (Van Damme, 1996).

These two terms are also very common in our own Western history. In late fifteenth- and early sixteenth-century Italy, beauty in good design occurred when the object had a pleasing and elegant appearance and when its members were in due proportion according to the correct principles of symmetry (Clarke, 1998). Symmetry and balance are commonly used in products and services like restaurant menus, car designs, screwdrivers, drinking glasses, company graphic design manuals and advertisements. All of them contain a degree of symmetry and balance by which they are judged according to beauty.

Symmetry is important in communication in terms of how quickly a company symbol is recognized and identified. When observers were asked to judge the pattern of a figure, most people chose not by colour or by brightness, but by the symmetry of the pattern (Fischer, 1999). Symmetry grabs our attention because it appears more attractive. In Grythyttan, the elements of symmetry and balance are very much involved in what they are doing. Judging the quality of a wine, for example, or arranging food on a plate involves these concepts, and hearing Granqvist expound on these topics reinforces the idea of their importance.

Clarity

In some African cultures, clarity in aesthetic systems is defined as 'denoting a preference for recognizable compositions, made up of readily perceptible parts' (Van Damme, 1996, p. 82). In sculpture, the Africans studied favoured defined volumes, sharp renderings of line and mass and a distinct use of colour. These definitions of clarity are also found in other primitive cultures outside Africa.

Clarity is also important in our modern Western aesthetic system in the business world. The use of colour in visual identity, for example, is valued in terms of whether or not the company uses it consistently or not (Schmitt and Simonson, 1997; Longinotti-Buitoni, 1999). The same could be said about product design. A design concept for a product line is valued in terms of its consistency. Companies without clarity in their visual identity and product design are often used as cases of how companies should not act. Recognizable compositions are also highly valued in logotypes. The term 'distinctive' is often used to denote the aesthetic quality of a logotype or a designed product. In the Grythyttan case, clarity would be judged in terms of how successful the repast concept becomes. It is also evaluated by how successful the community is in monitoring the values of companies that use Grythytttan in their marketing.

Smoothness and brightness

The aesthetic importance of smoothness is well established, especially when it comes to judging the attractiveness of the human body. The criterion of smoothness, however, need not always mean shininess or brightness. Its finish may be luminous without polish, or it may be mirror-like and glittering (Van Damme, 1996).

Cosmetics give the impression of smoothness and brightness. Brightness, like smoothness, is often associated with bodily well-being. In some primitive societies, pale colours suggest sickness, age and weakness, yet pale colours are common in fashion ads. In the Mexican town of Yalálag, strong bright colours reflect happiness and good health. In judging the attractiveness of the human body, brightness symbolizes young, healthy skin.

Cultural difference affects what is considered beautiful. In addition, trends play a part in communicating the importance of one criterion or another. If pale colors are 'in' today, they will likely be 'out' tomorrow. New trends are often reactions against established beauty criteria.

Smoothness and brightness are important marketing tools in product lines and services. Companies working with interior design, showroom lighting, tradeshows and shops promote smoothness and brightness in order to make products or services look attractive. In Grythyttan, smoothness and brightness become obvious when an individual enters the Inn. The use of candlelights and natural materials supports the atmosphere of nature. In one sense, it is not smooth, but on the other hand, it *is*, in terms of the underlying feeling of being part of history, surrounded by deep forest.

Youthfulness and novelty

Smoothness and brightness are often linked to youthfulness, especially when it comes to the human body. Youthfulness symbolizes vitality and energy. Part of its meaning also holds a connotation of innovation in art in different primitive cultures (Van Damme, 1996). Youthfulness is also a common aesthetic preference in Western society.

The culture industry consistently revolves around youth. Music videos, movies and television deliver an aesthetic preference guided by youthfulness and novelty. This criterion creates a market and an industry for satisfying the older population's desire to look young.

In what sense novelty is regarded as an aesthetic criterion in Western society depends on its developmental context. In design, for example, novelty can be an aesthetic criterion when it actually brings design into something new. Designer/architects like Eames and architects like Aalto have gained fame and admiration for their development of new techniques to make their products. Society takes its time in accepting new ideas, and sometimes novelty backfires and creates the opposite effect. In Grythyttan, novelty is expressed in their university research and through the innovations that the companies in the area deliver.

Fineness and delicacy

The last aesthetic criteria are fineness and delicacy. While fineness may be interpreted in different ways, it often includes precision and attention to detail, characteristics closely akin to craftsmanship. Delicacy or gracefulness include more elusive qualities, such as elegance. Often fineness and delicacy are found in promotions for exclusive products and services like clothes, cars, boats and different kinds of accessories. Fineness is also important in service industries like hotels and restaurants and is typically used in marketing and communication. The terms 'craftsmanship', 'precision' and 'detail' are also commonly used in ads. 'Elegance' is the name of one of Mercedes-Benz' exclusive design kits. In Grythyttan, fineness and delicacy are very important when it comes to fulfilling the repast concept. In many ways, it is a key criterion. How the service is defined and delivered is crucial in judging the quality of repast.

What is considered beautiful has to do with tradition and accepted concepts about what is beautiful. The perception of what is beautiful, however, is not constant; it changes. For example, the ideals of beauty for women change due to several things: social and political processes in different classes in society, equality between the sexes and overall standards of living and levels of technology. Global processes also influence how the ideals of beauty change within a society.

Surgeons specializing in cosmetic procedures influence our perception of beauty, for we live in a society in which maintaining a youthful appearance is a top priority. The available technology to stop or turn back the clock is more sophisticated than it was 20 years ago, and a legion of drugs and operations stand ready to wage war on age and actually do make people look younger for a while. Pop star Cher appears to be much younger than her 60 years, for example. How much she influences other women's perception of beauty is difficult to estimate, but she proves that people can look much younger than they are. This, of course, encourages others to want to invest in Cher's solution to the age problem.

Having a very 'tight' face as a result of a series of surgeries is actually becoming an ideal of beauty in Western society. While many took note of Michael Jackson's early plastic surgery, today what people focus on is how short-term his surgically induced youthful appearance has been. Jackson has become a symbol for the thousands of people having a number of facelifts.

A logical conclusion, then, would be that the ideals of beauty today comprise not one but several different standards. This is certainly the case when it comes to how beauty is used in marketing. In one magazine alone, a reader is exposed to several different ideals relating to different periods in the history of beauty, and today, ideals representing different periods in aesthetic history exist for only a moment.

Institutional mapping of beautyscapes

What, then, makes a beauty ideal a beauty ideal? Influences outside a company have great power in the shaping of beauty ideals. These include social and cultural movements, the media, advertising agencies, trend consultants, fashion, sports and the music industry (Seabrook, 2000). Their efforts are displayed in the kind of beauty ideals the consumer takes in when watching commercials or the movies or when selecting products and services. McDonald's is an example of a service industry highly involved in these processes. Another is the sports industry, which is also actively involved in promoting its ideals of beauty.

Company management often tries to tailor their company to a very specific and well-known beauty ideal. Ikea, for example, has a specific beauty ideal reflecting the preferences of owner Ingvar Kamprad. The same could be said about The Body Shop and Alessi. The beauty ideal is part of the corporate culture.

Certain clues reveal the kind of beauty ideals a company has and what it wants its employees, visitors and customers to promote. These clues can be picked up in interior design, architecture, dress codes, product design and marketing and identity programmes. The ideals of beauty make more or less sense depending on how well the beauty programme is implemented and how it is used in the organization. It also makes more or less sense depending on whether or not the artifacts symbolize the overall corporate culture.

In conclusion

The connection between beauty and business is not new; it is a union that has been around throughout the history of business. What is different is the attention the merger is getting today and how it can be an initiative for changing the direction of a whole region. Knowing the tools for leveraging the value from mining to repast expectations is important in Western society. Companies or regions do not write their own beauty history but instead rewrite themselves into an existing history. They are also at an advantage if they know how to spot a map of a beautyscape and are able to insert themselves in it and relate to it. These maps entail intricate ideals and complicated institutions, and recognizing and relating to the existing criteria are necessary in order to understand the coordinates on institutionalized maps. Grythyttan, for example, has the ability to adjust to these taken-for-granted criteria. They follow these rules by the book and this has led them to success.

Another way of explaining the success of Grythyttan is to say that ongoing globalization affects the reproduction of beauty ideals and the creation of beautyscapes. On the one hand, the opportunity to consume new identities gives individuals greater possibilities of accepting differences and fostering tolerance than is in evidence today. On the other hand, there is also a tendency for people to lose their sense of identity because they are able to fulfill so many desires. This does not mean that they will lose their sense of identity completely; instead they will develop ephemeral desires, and this does not necessarily become a bad thing for society (Lipovetsky, 1994). Going to Grythyttan would then be part of fulfilling one weekend desire among 51 other weekend desires, and this is good for all other beauty concepts around the world.

People are striving to find an identity and concurrently striving to preserve identity as well (Baumann, 1993). While cultural and social identity have played important roles in modern society, modernity means that people have to change, for modernity not only provides people with an opportunity to change, it forces them to do so (Castells, 1999; Warhol, 1975). The need for preservation is based on a belief that a modern society should be well organized, stable and predictable and that time is linear and cumulative. The best strategy for living in this kind of society is to save for the future and to act as if the reward will come after you have performed your duty. In this so-called modern society, identity has played an important role in describing where we come from in terms of country of origin and level of social class. As a result, however, it has also made way for opportunities to create new identities, to abandon cultural heritage and to replace it with a new identity in the market, complete with new ideals of beauty.

In history, beauty has often been perceived as something unattainable, a luxury not necessary for survival (Maquet, 1979). The market today is overloaded with ideals of beauty that range from urban beauty to a country look or Victorian style and ethnicity. These ideals are constantly shifting, and we simply absorb them in our routine living experiences. While the average human being does not take them too seriously, these ideals do offer opportunities for people to realize their visions for the future. They are both identity and experience providers for the consumer (Schmitt, 1999).

At the same time, the globalization process makes it difficult to separate different lifestyle themes seen from a geographical standpoint. Universal beauty criteria are becoming more widespread throughout the world. The globalization process and mass production also create a need for cultural belonging and uniqueness. There seems to be a growing belief that somewhere there is an original and that an object can be described as having certain 'physical' qualities.

Products and services that explore uniqueness and cultural belonging are becoming more and more important in the global market, however. Anthropologist Marcel Mauss (1954) points out that capitalism can grow only if the geographical market for capitalism grows. If every individual in the world has the same standard of living, and people are satisfied about having more or less the same products and services, capitalism would tend to die. Today nearly every market is under the flag of capitalism, and markets are growing from within. The capitalist system has developed a technique where cultural differences are still to be explored and marketed. The industrial society associated with mass production is becoming more and more transformed into beautyscapes characterized by images of uniqueness and individual choice. Suddenly, 'Made in Sweden' – which everyone believed was not important anymore – is adding a unique value all its own.

References

Bauman, Z. (1993) *Postmodern ethics*. Oxford: Blackwell.
Beck, U. (1998) *What is globalisation?* Cambridge: Polity Press.
Björkman, I. (1998) Sven Duchamp or – expert on aura-production. Dissertation. School of Business, Stockholm University.
Castells, M. (1999) *The information age*. Vols 1–3. Oxford: Blackwell.

Clarke, G. (1998) 'La più bella e meglio lavorata': beauty and good design in Italian Renaissance architecture. In F. Ames-Lewis and M. Rogers (eds), *Concepts of beauty in Renaissance art*. Aldershot: Ashgate.

Fischer, E.P. (1999) *Beauty and the beast. The aesthetic moment in science*. New York: Plenum Trade.

Heskett, J. (1980) *Industrial design*. London: Thames and Hudson.

Jensen, R. (1999) *The dream society*. New York: McGraw-Hill.

Kirwan, J. (1999) *Beauty*. Manchester University Press.

Lash, S., and J. Urry (1994) *Economics of signs and space*. London: Sage.

Lipovetsky, G. (1994) *The empire of fashion: Dressing modern democracy*. Princeton, NJ: Princeton University Press.

Longinotti-Buitoni, G.L. (1999) *Selling dreams*. New York: Simon & Schuster.

Maquet, J. (1979) *Introduction to aesthetic anthropology*. Malibu, CA: Undena Publications.

Mauss, M. (1954) *The gift. Forms and functions of exchange in archaic societies*. Glencoe, IL: Free Press.

Postrel, V. (2003) *The substance of style*. New York: Harper Collins.

Schmitt, B. (1999) *Experiential marketing*. New York: Free Press.

Schmitt, B., and A. Simonson (1997) *Marketing aesthetics*. New York: Free Press.

Seabrook, J. (2000) *Nobrow. The culture of marketing, the marketing of culture*. New York: Alfred Knopf.

Van Damme, W. (1996) *Beauty in context. Towards an anthropological approach to aesthetics*. Leiden: Brill.

Warhol, A. (1975) *From A to B & back again*. London: Pan Books.

Conclusion

15

Aesthetic leadership and its triadic philosophy[1]

Pierre Guillet de Monthoux, Claes Gustafsson and Sven-Erik Sjöstrand

Detecting leadership between management and administration

Many people sensed it as they strolled beneath the saffron sails of the Christos' 7503 Gates in Central Park, but making sense out of this type of experience requires a bit more than just a walk in the park. Our textual excursions into the worlds of art, business and mixed art and business presented here under the sponsorship of the Fields of Flow programme illuminate the aesthetics at work in such experiences.

One thing is sure: this mixture of art and business competence will continue to enrich socio-economic life and give greater voice and support to a leadership already intuitively doing the right thing. Each of our cases demonstrates that aesthetic leadership is here to stay. It is neither fad nor fashion, nor will it be forgotten in harsh recessions when cost-cutting axemen holler 'Hunt, Kill and Eat.' Aesthetic leadership is not a luxury for wealthy managers; it is an absolute necessity if we want to have a dynamic economy catering to human needs and desires. The empirical chapters of our collection show how aesthetic Flow generates dynamics in socio-economic life. In addition, these writers point out that Fields *without* Flow call for aesthetic leadership to regain their vitality and energy.

What aesthetic leadership contributes to art firms and other organizations is clarified by analysing the setting in three steps: defining the general problem, isolating its general solution and describing the perspective or philosophy needed by the aesthetic leader in the situation.

Problem: dualism

Our cases provide concrete examples of how *dual dilemmas* tend to dominate minds and actions, and these dichotomies cause problems, stalemates and conflicts. When it comes to running a firm, for example, we might be trapped between management and administration, between markets and hierarchies, and agonize over the best solution for this dual dilemma. In the final analysis, the remedy is found not by flipping a coin but by actually dodging the dualist trap.

Solution: aesthetics

Examples from the cases show how aesthetic options can transform deadlocking dyads into dynamic *triads*. The solution is aesthetic, but two different routes to the solution emerge, one adopted by business, the other by art firms. The aesthetic leader must encourage business to discover its inherent aesthetics, to recognize that aesthetics is everywhere. In art, the aesthetic leader must acknowledge that aesthetics is but one of many options, that there are many practical conditions to be considered before we get an artwork.

Philosophy: triadic action

The cases help define aesthetic leadership as the ability to organize muddled realities into triads of *fields*. The aesthetic leader has to make others see and discriminate among different fields. Leaders also have to facilitate *flows* connecting fields, for even though the fields are different and have to be faced differently, they are not independent of each other. Aesthetic leaders have to work as triadic philosophers.

Traps of dual dilemmas

Body/mind

The organization of a factory has often been criticized as the managerial decapitation of organizational bodies. In a kind of vulgar Cartesian dualism, Frederick Winslow Taylor and other scientific management advocates severed industry's work hands from its planning head. Since then an army of planning minds has trotted from engineering and business schools into boardrooms and offices. To them the concrete body did not count, only the abstract mind. This body/mind dualism certainly helped organize factory work, but during the twentieth century when the model was diffused to all possible and impossible fields of human activity, the dualistic carving up of almost any activity into the *work* or *planning* that some call 'managerialism'[2] has been censured over and over again.

Once this dualistic point of view is accepted, something important is abandoned. Not only have workers been typecast as waiters of manufacturing machines, professional managers also feel alienated from the concreteness of organizational life. This explains the attraction of the 'bodily turn' today taken by researchers in organizational aesthetics as they rediscover and reassess the importance of the concrete embodiment of action.[3] Emma Stenström's Weight Watchers case reflects this new body consciousness and at the same time illustrates how deep-rooted the dualism is. It even stops us from tackling the real problem.

One important success factor of Weight Watchers might well be a kind of nostalgia for pre-industrial embodiment where mind and body were still one. People joining the programme seem to be professionals with lives marked by a managerialism that makes them dream of regaining touch with their bodies. They feel they live in abstraction and look for ways to become concrete.

The means by which Weight Watchers successfully markets embodiment seem paradoxical, however. Dealing with a desire rooted in an excess of management, Weight Watchers offers new managerial techniques of control, monitoring and calculation. This demonstrates the dual dilemma in a nutshell; attempts to escape simply reinforce control. How could you ever escape planning by making careful plans? Furthermore, in the despair following the failure to gain freedom, deadlocks in the worst of cases may turn into disasters.[4]

Stenström's case of a body business competing with diet methods in health markets is an illustration of such dual dilemmas. Weight Watchers avoids corporate jargon but provides their customers, called 'members', with new managerial methods for comparing and ranking foods, for monitoring weight, for calculating BMI[5] scores and for defining 'success'. In Weight Watchers' business plan, the tools and measurement standards are integrated means for making the body 'slim' in terms of an ultimate operational goal. Slimming is an enterprise, a competitive project measured by the BMI scores. Weight Watchers' activities are instrumental in the loss of weight, and its main product is a toolbox for the scientific management of the means for reaching this overall slimming end.

Again the dilemma surfaces. Stenström remarks that very few Weight Watchers who reach goal – that is, attain their target weight – manage to maintain this ideal weight for a five-year period. The slimming technology of the Weight Watchers organization has meagre efficiency;

weight-watching bodies cannot be controlled by the Weight Watcher mind. And yet the organization is resoundingly successful. Could it be then that members of the programme want to 'be beautiful', but it has little to do with 'being slim', despite Weight Watchers' marketing claims that this is what it is all about? Within a dual scheme, such speculations find little support. To really understand what makes up the success of Weight Watchers, we must step out of the body/mind dualism. This is what makes the Weight Watchers enterprise slightly pathetic. It strives for something that will always remain tacit in the terms of its business jargon.[6]

Project/institution

In her reading of art school textbooks for filmmakers, Jenny Lantz reveals another aspect of dualism-dominated theories of management and what can happen when creativity is taught as management. She finds that textbooks constantly pit producers against directors when presenting filmmaking as a profession. This echoes Pierre Bourdieu's (1986) influential definition of the dual dilemma of capital as either economic or cultural, totally ignoring the positive touch in Sven-Erik Sjöstrand's (1997) dichotomy where good management emerges out of a Janus-faced tension.[7] Lantz shows how filmmaking studies morph into combat lessons for corporate struggles between creative projects run by individual directors and greedy institutions where film-industry producers reign supreme. Individuals trying to market their ideas to the industry become caught in a project/institution dualism.

Lantz illustrates the static nature of such dualism. Directors and producers become readymade prototypes of the creative and capitalist classes. They act out their roles in a sort of dualistic class struggle with producers cast as nurturing breadwinners and directors as courageous and visionary. Producers support projects in hopes of making film industry blockbusters. Directors spend their careers designing and realizing projects expressing brilliant ideas that are innate and original. Greedy and narrow-minded producers struggle with creative directors; a calculative capital-based rationale wrestles with a constructive and creative one. Industry representatives stagnate in a kind of conservatism geared primarily to cost-control and rationalization, while artists become bold dreamweavers and business developers. Lantz's textbook authors side with directors and feel they should possess enough power to impose their will on disrespectful producers, those who threaten to interfere with their creative process. Only a courageous, heroic director opportunistically manipulating the prejudices of the industry gets hold of the money. Armed with market information about what 'arty' trends are currently 'in' or about the right way to seduce a 'media-wise' audience, they always win over production-oriented producers. Even on the academic level, then, on the learning curve of the art school classroom, a dual dilemma emerges. On the one hand sit the film projects, and on the other, a film industry institution conserving values concerning successful art and audience tastes.

The dualist drawback Lantz points to is a strong gender bias where successful moviemaking turns into a kind of homo-social boxing match between action-oriented males. Furthermore, not only does this dualism exclude women, but it also reduces invention and creativity to a minimum. Lantz notes how textbooks recommend that students devote time in art school to teambuilding and experimentation. Once in business and caught between the calculative rationales of projects and zero tolerance for failure in institutions, little time or space is left for creation in the deadlock of a project/institution dualism, however.[8] And this is what artists really fear: the systematic elimination of playfulness in the name of efficient projects and profitable institutions.

Change/control

Katja Lindqvist's chapter evokes the image of what has become a classical icon of dualism: Dionysus/Apollo. Nietzsche's uncompromising aesthetics turned this classical dyad into a symbol of the destructive tragedy where creative forces clash with intellectual powers. Dionysus was god of creative energy while Apollo was the protector of cool calculators, clever tricksters and smart traders. To Nietzsche and the Nietzscheans, these two divinities were irreconcilable, for there are no bridges between commerce and culture, no positive flows between art and management. The cool, controlling Apollo and the wild, enterprising Dionysus hang out in Lantz's and Marcus Lindahl's studies as well; Lantz treats what belongs to art, and Lindahl writes about industrial engineering. Most filmmaking is full of the practical details of logistics, costs and technical choices, all of which provide golden opportunities for interference by project management rationales in the process. Lindahl verbalizes the tension permeating an industrial project on an Indian building site operating under the controlling regulations of Wärtsilä, the Finnish power plant provider. The Apollonian views how each should perform her task, while the Dionysian everyday reality is a battlefield of muddling-through for mission-oriented project teams. As is the case in most traditional industries, a bureaucracy of rules seems to reign in Wärtsilä's power plant corporation. Inside this institution the building of each plant is run as a project coordinating the purchase and assembly of goods and work from up to 20 subcontracted suppliers. Project managers in a temporal organization with short-term goals sometimes clash with institutions administered by the rulebook.[9]

In Lindahl's industrial case we get an engineering version of the dual dilemma of how project-planning, oriented towards future change, clashes with a corporation's traditional institutionalized rules and regulations. The means–end logic of projects cannot cope with economically unacceptable slowdowns or standstills, and institutional memory of past solutions lacks the urgency and force necessary for practical solutions. Lindahl's engineers are confronted with the limits of their dual doctrines. To get things going, they must go outside the dualism. To be able to concurrently handle a tricky situation *and* save both their projects and institutions, engineers have to do something different and, dualistically speaking, 'strange'. By improvising, they leave administrative repertoires and management lessons behind and, by defining improvisation as 'exceptional', are able to return to their dual safe base once the mission is accomplished. The mere fact that Lindahl's case of Finnish industrial engineering takes place in India does indeed add a flavour of exoticism to the exceptional. Escaping dualism is an expedition into challenging territory that will remain uncharted by management and administration.

Stefan Meisiek's study provides an account of a different but frequently used way of coping when things do not work out. Managers of the homecare organization in the chapter by Meisiek spin on the horns of a dilemma: they want change, but at the same time they need to maintain institutional control. Like Stenström's case, Meisiek's example casts doubt on the validity of managerial-effect measurements of the action they initiate. Just as joining Weight Watchers does not necessarily lead to sustainable slimming, calling in the DaCapo theatre to produce higher job-satisfaction in the workforce-audience or improve communication between home care workers and clients is not a slam-dunk either. Things in Wärtsilä, Weight Watchers and the homecare organization get going by acting outside the dual framework. Although one speaks of 'change projects', these cases are not examples of projects in strict managerial terms. That is why both managers fail to measure their effects, and administrators cannot control them. At the same time, Meisiek's account illustrates how outside competence makes it possible to escape institutional control, at least briefly. We witness something besides change and control, something that from a dualist position makes things move in almost mysterious ways.

Price/value

Erik Piñeiro's contribution is about technical development squeezed between market valuations and managers pushing down the costs of programming. Managers pressure programmers through their harsh control of the time and money allotted each project. Piñeiro displays how counterproductive this type of management is, according to programmers. The effects of management's slapdash planning, sloppy customer specifications and frequent redefinition of program designs make quality work impossible. Though frustrated, programmers still dream of well-planned projects providing elegant solutions to well-defined problems. They deplore the price/value squeeze that has made more of a mess of the computer industry than of 'good old civil engineering'. Piñeiro's programmers are convinced that if customers had the slightest hint of how sloppily programs were conceived they would never invest in the expensive software. They would start to question the value of the goods they pay for and turn to honest crafters for better products. The fact that managers act as middlemen who cleverly market the bad quality caused by their own cost-rationalization explains why buyers believe that mediocre software gives value for money. A union of producers and consumers will solve the dilemma and discourage technical development hampered by destructive price/value dualism.[10]

Science/tradition

Bertil González Guve's chapter on the managerial task of judging investment risk is set in the world of a Swedish investment bank. Drawing on his tenure as an investment analyst, Guve convincingly argues that investment assessment is a constant escape from the dualism of scientific calculus and tradition-based consensus. Lantz showed how management textbooks present filmmaking as projects run according to institutional values, and management books in corporate finance tell a similar story about calculus-based decision-making for consensus. To Guve, science/tradition is a dual facade in the sense that neither managerial methods nor routines or customs of an administrative tradition can account for how judgements are made in real situations. Neither scientific management nor administrative traditions offer the complete truth. Lantz sensed this lack, and Guve now proposes a different way of understanding judgement as a creative process.

Helena Csarmann's and Alf Rehn's chapters treat ways in which individual actors handle and manage dualisms in order to make things move despite these deadlocks. Csarmann cites Werner Stengel and his complex roller-coaster designs, while Rehn presents the classic French chef Antonin Carême, an early inventor of *haute cuisine*. Both are creative entrepreneurs operating in surroundings strongly dominated by dual perspectives. The intense and ephemeral thrills of rides and of gourmet pleasures that Stengel and Carême base their businesses on defy any dualist understanding. They are still able, however, to fuse their business ideas with both the values of regular institutions and the technical means to reach projected ends. The hero of each success story depends on science and tradition in the form of engineering and safety standards for constructing roller coaster rides and the history and habits of cuisine. Science and tradition are indeed necessary, but what dualisms stand for is hardly sufficient to make things happen and provide sparks to unleash the energy of enterprise.

Ann-Sofie Köping's and Jeanette Wetterström's chapters point out how putting on an opera performance or a classical concert takes technical skills akin to those involved in running industrial projects. It necessitates an active adaptation to highly institutionalized values. Köping's account of creativity in symphonic music escapes the usual psychological idealization of creativity as something personal and subjective, and she acknowledges the roles of controlling institutions and planning musical projects. From early childhood, the musician becomes intimately involved with the never-ending work of practicing. Furthermore, a musical career has to be strictly managed. Making music takes disciplined techniques and physical training. One interprets prescribed scores on standardized instruments according to institutionalized conventions. Orchestra work as well as music consumption follow routines that have become internationalized and taught globally. In concert halls all over the planet musicians are seated according to the same strict order and drilled to perform a concert with as little as one or two conducted rehearsals. This indeed meets the managerial expectations of commercially viable projects, that is, something instantly tradable and ready for the market without further developments or amendments. Köping surprisingly illustrates how the dual perspective of scientific management and carefully administered traditions fit symphonic music making even better than most industrial organizations. In practice, culture as well as commerce is subject to the science/tradition dualism. They also share the need to transcend management and administration by way of some sort of playfulness perhaps. Musicians as well as programmers achieve quality only after they go beyond dualism.

Matter/form

The suspicion that the dualism has to be extended to a triad is actually at the heart of aesthetic philosophy. Behind both Ivar

Björkman's account of Grythyttan and Wetterström's historical tale of opera management one discerns an echo of the classic dilemma of aesthetic philosophy according to Immanuel Kant: the shortcomings of matter/form dualism (1986). In Björkman's chapter we are introduced to Carl Jan Granqvist, a culinary guru who has created his own art firm, Grythyttan, by navigating between poles of material cooking and forms of service. According to Wetterström, opera undergoes historical development and shifts from being a material manifestation of the King's legal power to a formal expression of state economy. One may hypothesize that, in the former case, matter and form is about goods versus services; in the latter, about law and economics.

Wetterström identifies how over three centuries operatic enterprise has moved from being embedded in the institutional body of the Swedish kingdom to becoming a cultural project in state public policy. In the earlier period, the art of opera was rooted, or better, incorporated, in the courtly institution; this endowed it with value legitimated by the King's body. The monarchy rested on visibility, and theatrical events helped underline the order where audiences fit in as subjects under the King's Law.[11] An administration according to the law of the kingdom gave way to management in tune with an economic model. Issues of performance and efficiency slowly slipped into the public discourse of art, supplanting the earlier considerations of courtly traditions and customs. In other words, a long pendulum swing between matter and form resulted in a 'new era' in which legal-regal arts administration was gradually replaced by state economic arts management.

Escaping through aesthetic options

Aesthetics in business

Marja Soila-Wadman's story shows the aesthetic options that seem to provide a way of coping with dual dilemmas. She paints a vivid picture of how film workers – that is, technicians and actors – cooperate smoothly in highly interactive processes where a director's role is less heroic creator than facilitator of 'collaborative art'.[12] On the backstage of filmmaking, Soila-Wadman experiences a physical concrete process in time and space. She discovers zones of desire and intuition and feels intense emotional relationships among its film workers. Inside the team, Soila-Wadman observes a concrete reality hidden to outsiders, one that exposes a dual perspective of the kind shown in Lantz's presentation of 'classroom filmmaking', according to leading US textbooks. Soila-Wadman relates a story of feelings and emotions where cooperation seems to depend on aesthetic communication with all senses at play.

Compared to this blood-sweat-and-tears movie-shooting event, Lantz describes a dry project/institution dualism that is barrenly antiseptic and anaesthetic. Only to a small extent can differences between the US entertainment industry and Euro independent moviemaking account for the contrast between Lantz's and Soila-Wadman's chapters.

The real difference depends on which perspective is embraced. Lantz illustrates the traditional dual focus. Outsiders look upon creativity as locked up in a black box. Soila-Wadman opts for an aesthetic perspective experienced by insiders participating in events taking place and in time somewhere between technique and the planning of projects and institutions.[13]

Stenström makes a similar discovery as she stumbles on the hard facts of the desire of Weight Watchers members for something hardly reducible to a body/mind dualism. There is something different and alien to the dual outlook, and herein lies the aesthetic option in her case. It reveals itself as the customers' desire for the personal transformation implied in becoming a body. The aesthetic option attracting people to Weight Watchers manifests itself as a powerful longing that might, but does not have to, become apparent in successful careers and relationships. Stenström tells about people craving for life-transforming experiences of 'being a body and being seen as a desired and admired being'. From the dualist perspective, becoming is too ephemeral and fleeting to ever be captured or measured.[14] Although it cannot be squeezed into a dualist perspective, becoming is nevertheless very concrete to the real people joining the Weight Watchers organization. What really makes a business like Weight Watchers tick and thrive is not what the dual perspective makes us see. It is the aesthetic option that generates its energy.

Acknowledging that financial management textbooks fail to provide a solid understanding of how investment analysts make their judgements, Guve recalls his aesthetic option from his experience in banking. Besides the science/tradition dualism legitimating logical-decision methods and socio-logical habits in banking, Guve remembers the gut feeling that gave confidence to the judgements he made on projects in the bank. Judgement is a key concept in aesthetic philosophy; therefore, Guve's discovery of an aesthetic option in financial operations is not farfetched. He argues that financial judgements are not reducible to the dualism of managerial decisions and administrative habits.[15] Instead, he claims, judgements are directly dependent on confidence in the projects assessed. Guve suggests we might learn more about how bankers evaluate projects by comparing them to critics judging art than by comparing them to scientists or traditionalists. He contends that financial judgement is a matter of aesthetics and will remain so as long as bankers are human beings, regardless of increased sophistication of methods or models for decision-making. For those who do not accept aesthetics as a powerful option in their professional life, the confidence necessary for moving ahead to action will never materialize.

Lindahl's findings, based on his field observations at the Indian power plant construction site, illustrate how efficient industrial engineering imposes 'exceptions' on both regular planning and project management. Exceptions are not made primarily to change things or because something unexpected has happened. They are produced when things slow down and momentum is lost. The point of exceptions is to make special room for action between and outside of change and control.[16] By labelling the actions undertaken on his industrial site as exceptions or improvisations, Lindahl implicitly considers the third option as an aesthetic one.[17]

In Piñeiro's netographic study[18] of Internet chats, programmers present themselves as the hidden artists of the computer industry, although they feel like exploited old-time factory workers. Instead of enslaving the producers in ugly sweatshops, however, the true quality of their products is hidden from customers by binomial machine codes. If producers and consumers were to unite, the managers–exploiters and their price/value manipulations could be bypassed, and the beauty of quality could again shine over the software market.[19] The aesthetic option would then be visible to all, not only to the programmer-artists alone.

Our cases prove that inside accounts from industry and business show aesthetics as a part of everyday reality.[20] Empirical research can discover the aesthetics inherent in economic organizations. Careful observation and sharp documentation have to wipe away the thick layers of dualist dust covering aesthetics in offices, workshops, stores and other sites of business and industry now masquerading behind rationalist rhetoric.

That was how Piñeiro, himself an ex-hacker and computer engineer, tracked down a hidden community of programmers voicing their aesthetics on the Internet. The web became a third art space for their quality option. Thanks to inside access, Guve and Lindahl were able to detect the existence of the aesthetic options of judgement and improvisation. Stenström sensed that a third aesthetic reality of becoming might be needed to grasp the attraction of the Weight Watchers organization. Soila-Wadman discovered an inside aesthetic event through a crack in the same dualist wall that surrounds filmmaking as seen from the outside managerial perspective Lantz exposed in her chapter.

Options in art

What, then, is the place of aesthetics in art and in business? Certainly a sharp distinction can be noted between the two areas. Contrast Piñeiro's case with Meisiek's case, for example. Business, as in software production, has to rediscover its hidden aesthetics, while art firms, such as the DaCapo theatre, must realize that aesthetics is just one of three options.[21] It seems as if 'serious' business firms are legitimized by suppressing the importance of any relationship with the arts, even to the point of denying the existence of an aesthetic dimension. You really have to be familiar with what goes on inside a business organization to identify its aesthetics. In art, on the other hand, it's all about aesthetics. An art firm parading as a rational business might lose its cultural credibility. In this sense, art is like business turned outside in.

Many of our cases show how art firms put aesthetics upfront and leave managerial and administrative aspects – vital for their survival and development – cloistered backstage. Just think of the architectonic bracketing in the white cubes of museums or in the black boxes of theatres. Or imagine the rather elaborate division of labour in art firms that isolates the creative cocoons from worldly concerns and delegates menial tasks in projects and institutions to art technicians. In the past, many successful dancers, musicians and actors spent their careers embedded in projects and institutions, cajoled by art managers and arts administrators discreetly serving fine arts in the dark of the backstage. In the arts today, however, there is more interaction with managerial and administrative domains. This has resulted in an attitude adjustment for both the artist and the business professional. Business realizes that it needs creativity, and artists admit that isolation ruins the zest and actuality of their art. Firms do not see the point of being mere factories or trades, and artists want to avoid becoming dusty and losing relevance. As art and business approach each other, artists will realize that aesthetics, although still primordial for their enterprises, is nevertheless just one of three possible options.

In the chapter about the homecare organization, Meisiek observes the effect of such developments on the Da Capo theatre. The company is brought into a setting where neither institutional control nor straight management consulting projects for change seem helpful. Those running the homecare organization obviously felt that their methods and routines had fallen short of coping with the real problems. Managers felt the need for aesthetics as a third approach beyond the dual techniques. While this development might disappoint theatre lovers who believe in pure art for it means looking upon aesthetics as one of three perfectly legitimate modes of action, Da Capo does not pose as pure art. The company does not pretend to operate in isolation separated from the institutional systems of norms nor does it take over the job of a management consultant specializing in change projects. Da Capo wants to make its contribution to society by taking part in doing things peculiar to puritanical art lovers. There is no absolute freedom for art, and Meisiek's chapter criticizes implicitly the naïve idealism that craves total liberty from all real constraints.[22] Saying farewell to pure idealism means facing the fact that aesthetic options must cohabit with and negotiate their relative freedom with commercial projects as well as industrial institutions. The contemporary challenge of art, which is the reason why art is in demand out there, is to propose true and viable solutions without reproducing class structures or infecting people with the false consciousness of mass entertainment.[23] Meisiek shows how the Da Capo theatre goes about handling this challenge by making room for a critique as a third aesthetic option between the change/control dualism already dominating the homecare organization. A critique that helps the transition from dyad to triad is radically different from project change and institutional control. It must neither slam the door on the dyad nor turn into its tool of 'maintenance and lubrication' (Mangham and Clark, 2004, p. 848). The fact that consultants bring theatre to their client firms indicates that the aesthetic option fills the space left empty when consultants and bosses become aware of their limited powers. That Da Capo accepts this reality shows how they also see limits to aesthetics; aesthetics is just an option.

The place of aesthetics as one of three options is clarified by Wetterström's learned remark on the third position of art in modern society. She notes that Kant's definition of aesthetics as the education of a faculty of judgement was important to the shift in outlook on art. Before Kant, aesthetics was a visualized and thus materialized part of a royal institution, and after Kant it was seen as a formal project of the socio-economic state. After Kant, opera-going, as well as all other art attendance, was considered a philosophical schooling in aesthetic judgement, defined as something distinct from both psychological sense perceptions and cognitive structures of thought. Aesthetics after Kant, who was himself a fan of triads, became defined as philosophical play between matter/form.[24] There were hardware matters undeniably suited for a strict scientific treatment, and there were also formalities for human conduct that Kant recommended to moral reflection. If one knew the limits of the two domains, as the administrators and consultants in the homecare organization did, one could detect a third realm, the place of aesthetic judgement. In modern Western societies then the third aesthetic option has its territory mapped out by no less a person than Immanuel Kant.

In the same way that the appropriate place of Kant's aesthetics is best understood in consideration of his work, Köping shows how a concert emerges out of a creative process equally surrounded by two realms. Symphonies need technical projects of music making and institutions supporting the values of so-called classical music. Musicians have the responsibility of doing their homework, that is, practicing individually, before they collaborate with their conductor in interpreting a score. Köping's careful account rediscovers the fact that concertgoers tend to forget this dualism. Music making is not all art; aesthetics simply has its rightful position as residual between the two other dimensions.

Thanks to functioning projects and regulating institutions, good orchestras are able to play correctly all by themselves. That is why conductors like Witold Lutosławski and Gennadij Rozhdestvensky unanimously declare they never correct, command or instruct their orchestras. Control or change is obviously taken care of by projects and institutions outside the creative processes of rehearsals and performances. Instead, leading the aesthetic option consists of coaching and facilitating creativity in subtle and unobtrusive ways. While the aesthetic leader is neither a manager nor an administrator, it would be imprecise to go so far as to call her a visionary. The aesthetic leader must be a realist and an understanding and respected guest who cultivates and finely tunes relational skills of peer groups embedded inside dual organizations.[25]

Köping's insights into conducting also shed light on Lindqvist's chapter on the success and failure of curating. The curator emerges as kind of dualistic go-between that is invited as a 'guest' by projects and institutions. It is as if museums and art shows are so enthralled by dualism that they can only envision the third realm as something foreign or alien to regular organizing. On the other hand, artists also tend to ignore or neglect dual managerial realities. Maybe such benign neglect lies behind the failure of parachuting artist Pippilotti Rist in as curator of Expo 01. The need was for an aesthetic leader, but instead a poor artist found herself in the midst of quasi-political meetings and managerial discourses she was probably unaware of and certainly was unable to make sense of. Maybe she became overwhelmed and was carried away by the dual destructive struggle between Dionysus/Apollo. Maybe too Nietzschean an outlook prevented her from opting for Eros as a third way out of the dual dilemma.

Rist's explicit complaint about 'lack of respect' underlines the importance of generosity and hospitality in the third aesthetic option; after all, this is where Eros, god of love, openness, and creativity, reigns. To establish and defend such havens of generosity and islands of hospitality from the invasion of managers and administrators seems to be a crucial task for aesthetic leaders.

Artists must resist self-flagellation as a doomed Dionysus in a Nietzschean tragedy. Leadership must make them discover Eros, for from Lindqvist's point of view a successful curator should neither be a wild Dionysian nor a controlling Apollo. From Eros and aesthetic leadership – and here Lindqvist's findings are supported by both Köping and Soila-Wadman – she must learn to surrender to generosity. Once we acknowledge that art is dependent on and at the same time different from the managerial-administrative dualism, we detect its realm as a third space of hospitality, a place for gifts. It is certainly no coincidence that conductors, directors and curators are treated not as managers or administrators of art workers but as the invited guests of orchestras, theatres and museums. On the other hand, they should not be antagonistic to managers and administrators, for they must be able to cooperate while still maintaining the special atmosphere and relationships inside the third field of aesthetics.

The triadic philosophy of aesthetic leadership

Organizing fields

The cases thus make it possible to discern a special kind of aesthetic leadership concerned partly with facilitating flows and partly with organizing fields. Let us investigate the second task first. For aesthetic leaders, organizing means mapping and maintaining the three distinct fields (see Figure 15.1). Acknowledging the aesthetic option turns dyadic perspectives into triadic perspectives. As real life is blurred and seamless, we need leaders to sort out the different fields. Findings from the 13 cases help us patch together key features from each field into ideal-types we call the management, administration and aesthetics fields.

The management field

This field is marked by material concerns and likes to present itself as scientifically precise and accurate. Its main discourse takes the shape of

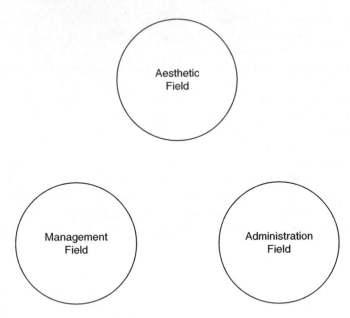

Figure 15.1 Three distinct fields

shoptalk about projects and management methods. The management field is change-oriented and considers itself an ideal arena for Dionysian pleasure seeking. In this field, restless entrepreneurs feel at ease; here is the home of those who espouse the freedom of markets and who constantly nurture adventures for new biz-dev projects. Here professionals offer techniques, and management consultants find buyers for their new models and recipes. They like to be considered skilled technicians.

The field is strictly future oriented and strives towards determined goals. What counts is measured effects, hard facts and quick pay offs. This is certainly not the place for speculation or vague memory. Science and precision are highly regarded and serve as models for economic calculations of reasonable courses of action. On this field we are likely to find Weight Watchers struggling with their diet, Wärtsilä field engineers, and those managing software programmers. Also in this field are musicians preparing a concert or the technical staff of an art museum setting up an exhibit. Here we find action-oriented managers with a preference for monetary transactions and little respect for bureaucracy.

The administration field

The film industry producers, investment bankers, Wärtsilä bosses, home-care workers or art space administrators would probably find themselves at home in the administration field. This is the field for institutions. Here abstract form and thought are much more highly regarded than are mundane matters. Finding guidance requires one to look for values in tradition and always have an eye on the past. That is why we might find both admirers and interpreters of old established art forms like opera or symphonic music on this specific field. Here is also the place for stoic statesmen with a cool Apollonian outlook on things. One cultivates one's mind and contemplates forms for the wise regulation of action and the control of its costs. The discourse of this field is about justice and equality. Small-talk interprets and preserves values in the consensual bedrock of the taken-for-granted. The most respected discipline is the Law, and one carefully designs organizations to fit predetermined tasks. Human interaction is looked upon as guided and governed by principles and norms. This is the place for administrators who prefer to see themselves as guardians of the public sphere of society.

The aesthetics field

The third field is the one thriving on aesthetic options. Here one prefers poetry to shop- and small-talk. This is the place where judgement is made beyond calculus and consensus, where one experiences the intensity of becoming a timeless presence separating past and future. This is a field where a critique offers clues to meanings of quality. Here is the ground for play and improvisation among collaborative artists. If the first field was one suited to economists, and the second suited to jurists, this third is a playground for creative philosophizing, where one coins unique aesthetic concepts like the 'repast' of Grythyttan in Björkman's chapter. In each of our cases we find signs of an aesthetic field. It exists in both art and business, although it might be hidden or suppressed in business, like the beautiful code of good software or the aesthetic judgements of investment bankers.

The aesthetic field needs a place, a theatre for its events. It is closely connected to the two other fields, for as our investigations show it is defined by what they are not. Although supported by projects and institutions, the aesthetic field produces events of a quality hard to translate into commercial prices or conventional values. In this field, gifts and generosity reign, while managers seek profit and administrators control costs. To managed change and formal organization for control, it adds improvisation in an atmosphere of playful becoming. By so filling the gap between the two other fields, it both bridges and buffers the fields of management and administration, but its definitional vagueness, this in-between position, leaves this aesthetic field utterly vulnerable. It is a soft and gentle field dependent on the protection of Eros. The curators, directors and conductors encountered in our cases perform this function. In contrast to the managers and administrators, however, their competences seem hard to pinpoint. They are the custodians of brittle beauty and ephemeral sublime quality, and as Soila-Wadman puts it, their main task is relational. Moreover, the identity of the aesthetic leader is not self-made but upheld by peer groups in aesthetic fields. This is well illustrated by Köping's account of how an orchestra 'makes or breaks' its conductors. The day the aesthetic field drops a conductor, a curator, director or choreographer she lapses back into her roles as a musician managing projects, conservator of an institutionalized art-tradition, actor of the theatre company or one of the dancers in the corps de ballet.

Facilitating flows by triadic action

We have seen how dualism cons business into thinking it has only two legs and one foot in each of the first two fields. In the illusion of being completely dependent on the third only, it may live in the short haul but certainly not survive the long one. Business sometimes pretends that art is only about self-expressive acting-out and has nothing to do with either managing projects or administering institutions. Artists think business is nothing more than successfully making money.[26] Our cases have proven how wrong these assumptions are. We have seen that both art and business must be in touch with all three fields in order to survive and develop.[27] Next after identifying and maintaining the three fields comes the crucial job of managing the flows between them. The fields have to be brought together without altercation; otherwise, we will again be caught in the dual dilemmas that triadic organizing sets out to avoid.

Aesthetic leadership has the responsibility of connecting the three fields while still preserving their sovereignty. Successful aesthetic leadership must assume all three fields to be of the same importance; one must not consider them as being on different hierarchical levels[28] or accept any arguments claiming the superiority of any one field.[29] The field-connecting role of aesthetic leadership is symbolized by the triangle in Figure 2 below.

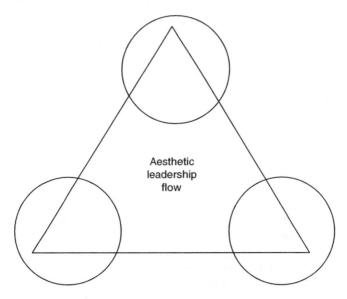

Figure 15.2 Connecting the fields

The cases written up by Björkman, Csarmann and Rehn concretize aesthetic leadership and help to avoid continual references to it in the abstract. Björkman explores how the small village of Grythyttan was transformed under the leadership of Carl Jan Granqvist, a Swedish television wine connoisseur and antique dealer turned entrepreneur and regional developer. When consumers look for beauty rather than goods and services, it requires aesthetic leadership in addition to having a feel for management and administrative thinking.[30] To Björkman, aesthetics is the key to understanding how Granqvist's leadership mobilized a sleepy God-forsaken municipality into a much talked-of venue.

Granqvist positioned Grythyttan in between a gourmet restaurant and a department of the local university. At the beginning he worked as the manager of the restaurant as well as serving as an eloquent inspirer of local government and the regional university administration. The university college also contains a shop for local foods, a wine cellar and a library of famous cookbooks. Granqvist does not simply offer good eating or sell local products, however. Björkman's case exemplifies how Granqvist has carved out an aesthetic third position between goods and services in Grythyttan. This was achieved by the clever invention of a new concept: 'repast'. Repast is the positioning tool for a third aesthetic option where Grythyttan, under the leadership of Granqvist, sculpts meals into the gestalt of an aesthetic event.[31] For a repast, say Granqvist and his zealots united in a newly founded *Repast Academy*, is much more than a gourmet meal. It is a concept covering the shaping of relationships between guests in an aesthetic event. It is led, conducted and directed by a perfect host and master of aesthetic ceremonies ... like Carl Jan Granqvist himself.

Granqvist as a leader has found the third field on the map. He claimed it as land of aesthetics and characterized the territory by his 'repast' concept. The aesthetic option would never have survived on its own, however. It had to be supported by both projects and institution. The local university agreed to establish a repast-based education, and repast research has been successfully negotiated into the state educational system. The restaurants offer repast packages, making meals appreciated as social ceremonies.

Granqvist himself remains in the third field. Lacking educational credentials, he is not qualified for a formal university position. He has also left his post as manager of the inn where it all started some 20 years ago. Had it not been for Granqvist, the three fields would have been unconnected.[32] Thanks to him, Grythyttan today thrives on the energy flowing between the aesthetic, management and administrative fields.

Csarmann, in her studies of roller-coaster manufacturer Werner Stengel, and Rehn, who first addresses *haute cuisine* and then the classic French chef Antonin Carême, offer interesting information about how aesthetic leaders manage flows between all three fields.

Csarmann focuses on how Stengel connects the aesthetic field he has himself discovered and developed to the field of technical projects. Stengel GmbH, Stengel's firm, scientifically turns thrills into skills; in fact, they are captured in engineering routines involving about 200,000 pages of technical DIN standards and proceedings. Standardization makes it possible for the engineers to calculate cost-based prices for the most complex kinds of roller-coaster assignments. The core service rendered – the thrill – has thereby been translated into science. The success of Stengel GmbH rests on turning fearfully sublime rides into algorithms of G-force and 'heart line spins' for maximum safety. Aesthetic options have flowed into intricate sets of causal reasoning for continuous testing of hypothetical means–end relations.

While Csarmann focuses on the flow from the aesthetic field to that of science and projects, Rehn emphasizes flows where aesthetic inventions are negotiated into worlds of institutional values. Rehn shows the effort spent by Carême in writing and illustrating books of culinary criticism, all the while describing his own art as modern, fashionable and refined. Carême thus contrasts his own culinary thinking with what he categorizes as a miserably outmoded craft of medieval cooking. In order to enhance the value of his own subjective contribution, he designs an orderly system of sauces for the purpose of organizing culinary discourse in his own favour. By this clever inscribing of his individual dishes in a culinary tradition, Carême rewrites the rules of the discourse to his own advantage. Rehn shows how Carême turns his culinary inventions into innovations by embedding them in the institution of cuisine.[33] The aesthetic leader Carême rewrites the norms supporting institutionalized culinary discourse that regulated the administration of cooking of the time, while the leader Stengel translates new roller-coaster thrills into acceptable technical standards. The former fixes flows between the fields of aesthetics and administration, while the latter seems to focus the flows from aesthetics to management.

Grankvist, Stengel and Carême are successful aesthetic leaders of fields of flow. Their management rests on their mastery of the three different characteristics of each of the three fields. From strong bases in their aesthetic fields, they connect, influence and vitalize the two others.[34]

The overall empirical lesson learned from our thirteen cases is that *all three fields* must be in flow. Aesthetic leaders never let any single field dominate or overflow the others. Project management, institutional regulation and aesthetic sensibility must cohabit in mutual respect. If a field should drop out of the flow, aesthetic leaders must rescue it and replace it in the flow. Each field has sources of its own and cannot be outsourced as when we hire a consultant to run our projects, a nightclub to stage our events or refer vaguely to culture instead of getting in real touch with institutions. A theatre lacking an artistic team, one with only technicians and administrators, only project and institution, will be an empty shell. An orchestra without a conductor generating concerts will not be a real orchestra. When managerial dualism threatens to take over, restaurants go for open kitchens, filmmakers produce 'the making of movies', and programmers go for an 'open source system'. By putting their own work on show as the automobile industry does in Formula One races, they hope to regain touch with their own aesthetic fields. That is what aesthetic leadership is about, and that was what insures the charm, beauty and sublime experience of Gates and other installations in art as well as business: triadic philosophy in Fields of Flow!

Notes

1. P. Guillet de Monthoux and S.-E. Sjöstrand, using a study of American artist, director and designer Robert Wilson, claimed that firms under aesthetic leadership might be labelled Philosophy Firms. See Guillet de Monthoux and Sjöstrand (2003).
2. Managerialism is often seen as corporate cannibalism that focuses on instrumental jargon and monetary measurements for any human action. It presents any subject as manageable and controllable. For criticism of managerialism, see Hjort (2003) or Deetz (1992).
3. See Strati and Guillet de Monthoux (2002) special issue of *Consumption Markets and Culture* 5 (1), *Æsthetics and Management – Business Bridges to Art*.
4. Many fictional narratives offer extreme dramatizations of such disasters. The novel *American Psycho* or the movie 'Fight Club', for instance, reflect how deadlocks inevitably reproduce the dualism in corporate capitalism. They argue that violence and crime result when bloodless corporate professionals desperately attempt to get in touch with their bodies and escape their managerial existences in which they are completely engulfed. Nice people control and discipline their evil bodies by sport, workout or safe family sex. They master and minimize the unknown mysteries out there but are unable to grasp them, given the dual dominance. This is the tragic mood David Lynch has become famous for explaining. Such fiction itself, of course, serves the dualism by showing that destruction comes out of the incapability of going beyond dualism. The message is clear: outside the dualism there is nothing!
5. BMI = Body Mass Index.
6. Knowledge may seem tacit only if we limit ourselves to the dual outlook. Matters of existence cannot be reduced to measurements and planning. Nevertheless they can be treated by a philosophical or poetical approach outside the dualism.
7. While Bourdieu seems to claim that one has to choose to be either cultural or commercial, Sjöstrand implies that the two sides can be reconciled. A true reconciliation, as we are arguing here, can *never* occur within a dual system where 'tertium non datur'. It takes a third position to overcome the dual dilemma.
8. One visible consequence of such commercialism of creativity where time devoted to experiments is minimized is that much artwork seems to be grounded on the art school experiments of artists. In retrospect we can find that the school work done by such famous filmmakers as David Lynch, Roman Polanski and Andrei Tarkovsky contain visual key elements of their coming productions in the way PhD dissertations seem to contain the subsequent research of scientists. In other words, creativity has to be coped with somewhere else. Where and how always remains a mystery in the dual perspective!
9. The dualist outlook, of course, raises the difficult question of what comes first: projects or institutions? Are institutions shaped as sediments of bygone successful actions? Or are they governing principles providing a firm foundation or constitution for single actions taking place within their jurisdiction? If we toy with Greek mythology, we have to acknowledge that projects and

institutions, symbolized by the Dionysus–Apollo dualism, are two distinctly different entities, each with traits of its own. We see how a dualist perspective prompts a question with a solution as little in view as the hen–egg query.

10. Piñeiro's programmers echo an idea fundamental to classical political economy from Adam Smith to Karl Marx. The price paid for a product is its market price. This market price is caused by circumstances in the situation of exchange. Exchange value, however, fluctuates and passes. But, so say classical economists, market value apart, there is also a natural value. The natural value is more fundamental, essential and stable. It seems like Piñeiro's programmers want to make the natural value of software, its real quality, transparent to buyers so that they can criticize market values. Then consumers will become aware of quality and be able to discern good from bad software. They will know what they are really paying for.

11. In Meisiek's chapter, there is an interesting parallel to Wetterström's account: organizational theatre today resonates in the courtly theatre of yesterday. What difference is there between playing in castles or corporations?

12. Austin and Devin (2003) take an explicit interest in what they call 'collaborative art', or the art of artists working in teams in organized processes of production. It seems as if most contemporary art is of a collaborative kind and that the lone artists are hard to find in today's art worlds. Music, theatre and dance are overtly collaborative arts, but today, painting, sculpture and poetry are equally brought about by people working in what, due to the fact that art is the fruit of the cooperation of coordinated work, might be called 'art firms' (Guillet de Monthoux, 2004).

13. It is obvious that the filmmaking Soila-Wadman accounts for represents only one bit of the whole making of a movie. The shooting is carried out separate from the cutting, for example, and so are the financing, the marketing, the casting and all other processes that might be accounted for in precisely the project and institutional terms of efficiency and value Lantz presents. Still the shooting cannot be said to exist independently of the other phases of filmmaking.

14. The powerful aesthetic experience Weight Watchers members hope for is not really 'transcendental'. It is not a matter of reaching some blissful ideal state. *Becoming* is more like what the American art philosopher Arthur C. Danto dubs a 'transfiguration' of the commonplace. Joseph Pine, the experience economy guru Stenström quotes, once pointed out to Project Flow researchers that the next step after experience economies will be a 'transformation economy'. He argued that we will soon realize that experiences have a limited attraction. The 'been there-done that' effect soon sets in. Then, says Pine, we will shift to consuming what promises to constantly transform us. It may be relatively simple things such as training us to become better golfers; soon, however, it will be about continuously changing our existence. When shifting from being to becoming, business will go from operating in private and public sectors to what Pine calls the 'personal' sphere. Pine thus offers still another way of suggesting that we crave a third aesthetic option to get things and people moving.

15. Using Max Weber's triadic model, Romain Laufer sees three modes of legitimating action: the scientific, the traditional and the charismatic. Laufer uses the model to understand how the mainstream of legitimization has been

meandering between the three, while we tend to see the three operating simultaneously in projects, institutions and aesthetic action, with each using its own mode of legitimization. See Laufer and Paradeise (1990).

16. There is a growing interest in training professionals in staging exceptions in which they can subsequently find room for improvisations. The Negotiation Project at Harvard Law School, for instance, explores the role of 'improv' in negotiations and what one could learn from jazz musicians and actors. One is confident that the success of negotiation rests not only on good models and stable institutional settings; it is also essential to educate a feel for the aesthetic option too.

17. Play between Matter and Form is the classic definition of aesthetics provided by Friedich Schiller's interpretation of Immanuel Kant's aesthetic philosophy of the third Critique. The concept of play, central to aesthetic philosophy, is very close to Lindahl's *improvisation*. For an introduction to classical aesthetics in connection to management, see Guillet de Monthoux (2004).

18. 'Netography' is a term covering the widespread use of web chats as empirical research data.

19. The programmers' reasoning accounted for by Piñeiro seems to perfectly follow the model of classical political economy where middlemen – grocers, overseers, landlords – were the ones responsible for 'market failures'. The programmers' blueprint for good *quality* software actually goes from a triad (programmer artists, project managers, and buyers on the market) to a dyad. They, as did most classical economists, seem to believe that doing away with the third party – that is, the go-between middlemen distorting the balance – will solve the problem. For an account of political economy and its view on middlemen, see Guillet de Monthoux (1993).

20. The point of the aesthetic sociology of organizations developed mainly by Antonio Strati is to make researchers help members of organizations regain touch with the poetic, beautiful and sublime reality of working life. Beyond the dualist perspective, supported and fossilized by logical empiricism, a truly empirical perspective must be replaced. For aesthetics is a phenomenon of reality and not an ideal. The aesthetic option is out there and far less idealistic than the dualisms that tend to obscure it.

21. Two studies from Fields of Flow researchers Björkegren (1996) and Guillet de Monthoux (2004) serve as further empirical bases for this argument. Björkegren explains that many businesses actually base their commerce on aesthetics; they have to acknowledge their aesthetic dimensions. Guillet de Monthoux claims that all art involves often hidden and overlooked managerial aspects motivating the use of the term 'art-firm'.

22. In an article on theatre-in-a-factory in a special issue on so-called organizational theatre, Iain Mangham and Timothy Clark (2004) find little empirical support for the slightly outmoded idea of theatre as a change agent. They seem to find it hypocritical that actors and theatre companies refer to art revolutionaries like Augusto Boal when selling their shows to firms. This kind of disillusionment with art as a revolutionary panacea is probably based on a completely erroneous idea of what contemporary art and artists aspire to in practice and expect to achieve. The kind of criticism artists realistically hope to offer is of a much more subtle kind, and if we don't face this reality,

we might throw out the baby with the bath water due to false expectations and a lack of experience with art in society. Art certainly has effects but not of the kind either management scientists or critical organization studies scholars fancy.

23. See Böhme (2003) pp. 71–82. In his revision of critical theory, Böhme strips it down to a warning that art and aesthetics might not lead to the freedom some claim. Böhme's concession is that nothing proves that commercial or industrial elements in art making necessarily end up in instrumental aesthetization or kill auras by technical reproduction.

24. Guillet de Monthoux and Sjöstrand (2003) drew on this fact by calling aesthetically led firms 'philosophy firms'. For bringing aesthetics into organizing, introducing a third field makes it possible to let reflection affect operations in a way akin to what Kant means by aesthetic philosophy. See chapter in Czarniawska and Sévon-Berg (2003).

25. In Oliver Williamson's (1975) book on markets and hierarchies, a third form, the peer-group, is mentioned but rapidly skipped over. Bill Ouchi introduces a serious consideration of a third organizational mood by talking about clans next to bureaucracies and markets. Sven-Erik Sjöstrand brought his early problematization of both Williamson's and Ouchi's models to the Flow project. Alf Rehn also developed a netographic study of how software developers avoid managerial capture of innovation by offering their creations as gifts. François Dosse showed how empirical studies of new industrial organizations have forced social scientists to shape new ideal types beyond classical dualisms to account for their findings. In their book about recent comparative industrial organization in France and the US Robert Salais and Michael Storper found it necessary to use an interpersonal model next to commercial trade-projects and industrial institutional models. Marcel Henaff argues that gifts signal a specific social system at work, not to be confounded with exchange or contract-based models. To Henaff the gift-system (absolutely not to be seen as a gift-*economy*) has the ability to forge social systems of strong personal networks within which market exchange and its depersonalized standardization can be embedded. This third way could be observed in modern technological developments, as in Piñeiro's chapter and in Mauss' classical study of how natives conduct *both* Kula, that is, gift socialization, and Gimwali, that is, trade by exchange, *in parallel*. This third kind of organization that today is being rediscovered (the cooperative is, for instance, an old organizational form sharing many features with this new gift-system) in many fields of production has, however, long been observed and officially recognized in art organization. Eve Chiapello calls the personal relations based on mutual respect fundamental to the third kind of organizing *agape*, friendly love. See Ouchi (1980); Rehn (2001); Salais and Storper (1993); Dosse (1997); Henaff (2002); and Chiapello (1998).

26. Still we know that the most important institution for modern capitalism is business failure and bankruptcy and that art often is defined as an exercise in action-sublimation.

27. In her book *Artistes versus Managers* (1998), Eve Chiapello emphasizes the convergence of art and industrial firms exemplified by a study of the art-like ways in which Renault chose to organize the manufacturing of the Twingo car. Another example is Dirk Luckow of Siemens Kultur Program and Mike

Meihré of Dornbracht AG who, during a Project Flow seminar in Berlin 2001, said that meanings of products today are no longer acquired in the market setting but in cultural contexts. This seems to be one of the main factors explaining why corporations seem to support art projects they can land in an official art space, instead of going for trade fairs or advertising campaigns.

28. Traditionally it would be easy to claim that the administrative field encompasses the two others. But states and government are not, if they ever have been, immediately accepted as macro systems ruling over the fields of management and aesthetics. It would be as questionable to postulate the reign of the management field over the others as to claim the absolute superiority of aesthetics. Societal facts support our view of all fields being more or less on the same level. States interact with corporations, and art and aesthetics are allied with both public and private interests. Fields can be intertwined in networks, rhizomes or plateaus, rather than ordered by levels of importance. Little can stop aesthetic leaders; the fields are ready for flux!

29. For instance, the administrative field may claim its universal values to be preconditions for any organization, the managerial field may claim its superiority over administration by economic argument, and the aesthetic field might refer to truth or religion as proof of its superior powers.

30. Björkman's opinion seems close to that of Virginia Postrel (2003). She sees aesthetization as a liberating consumer movement fuelled by small powerless producers making little profit competing on perfect markets by radically cutting costs of beauty goods – all in the best interests of consumers. For a recent opposing picture suspecting that cultural industries limit our capacity of aesthetic interpretation, instead of liberating it, by programming consumers' minds via 'temporal media objects', see Stiegler (2004b). A third position is given by Böhme (2003) in his assessment of the contemporary relevance of critical theory for understanding today's aesthetic industry.

31. The repast seems to cover the meal as a participatory performance, and Grythyttan University trains its students in various forms of historical meals like the picnic, the funeral, the traditional banquet and the Greek symposium. Grythyttan seems to try to find forms of meals that generate an ideal social interactive dialogue; they speak of repast and democracy. So the repast is not a good nor is it a service but rather what Stiegler (2004a) calls a 'temporal object' similar to a film or a music piece offering a set form conditioning people to join in. Stiegler, who may be branded an aesthetic idealist, is very critical of such managed aesthetics; he thinks it kills the singularity, or subjective individuation, that true art should support.

32. A restaurant, a single managerial unit, might exist in settings ruled by administration, namely the local government. Perhaps the innkeeper would buy the services of some event-maker, for instance, a DJ arranging an occasional disco in the restaurant. But the outsourcing of aesthetics to separate event-makers and a purely administrated relation to local government is hardly enough to generate flows between the fields. Aesthetic leadership is about making the fields interact, not only about exchanging services and making payments.

33. In Gilles Deleuze's (1998) reading of Hume, one may find the idea that the subjective creativity of leaders like Granqvist, Stengel or Carême, perhaps

thought frivolous, branches out in two directions: the experimental hypothesis testing, based ultimately on belief in connections between means–ends or cause–effects, and the invention of serious artificial institutions that can harbour and administer our frivolous whims and desires. The subjective element is therefore playful but also serious and organizing. Its playfulness, frivolity or whatever word is chosen indicates something Deleuze calls *vivacity*, that is, what makes both projects and institutions alive and well. The liveliness implies also that humans tend to jump to false conclusions and make their own rules and values 'overflow' into realms unfit and even unintended. Maybe here this Humean idea approaches a Nietzschean will, a force giving a direction in time, that is, a motivation that can replace the metaphysical idea of a transcendental blueprint that reality is attempting to fulfill. At this point Deleuze also notes the great difference between Kant's transcendental philosophy and Hume's idea of the passions in relation to our understanding of aesthetic action: that is, what pushes us to move forward and realise our project.

34. Rob Austin and Lee Devin spend much effort in their book *Artful making: what managers need to know about how artists work* precisely defining artful making so that it escapes the verdict of being just some unserious anything-goes playfulness. People working in projects and institutions have to open up to flows from aesthetic options. The trick seems to be to define it without completely translating it into project management or institutional control-terms, to communicate without losing the zest of aesthetics!

References

Austin, R., and L. Devin (2003) *Artful making: what managers need to know about how artists work*. Upper Saddle River, NJ: Prentice-Hall.

Björkegren, D. (1996) *The culture business: management strategies for the arts-related business*. London: Routledge.

Böhme, G. (2003) Contribution to the critique of the aesthetic economy. *Thesis Eleven*, 73 (May) pp. 71–82.

Bourdieu, P. (1986) *Distinction. A social critique of the judgement of taste*. London: Routledge & Kegan Paul.

Chiapello, E. (1998) *Artistes versus managers, le management culturel face à la critique artiste*. Paris: Mètailié.

Czarnaiwska, B., and G. Sévon-Berg (eds) (2003) *Northern lights: organization theory in Scandinavia*. Stockholm: Liber.

Deetz, S.A. (1992) *Democracy in the age of corporate colonization: developments in communication and the politics of everyday life*. Albany: State University of New York Press.

Deleuze, G. (1998) *Empirisme et subjectivité*. Paris: PUF.

Dosse, F. (1997) *L'empire du sens*. Paris: la Découverte, pp. 180–91.

Guillet de Monthoux, P. (1993) *The moral philosophy of management from Quesnay to Keynes*. Armonk, NY: M.E. Sharpe.

Guillet de Monthoux, P. (2004) *The art firm: aesthetic management and metaphysical marketing*. Palo Alto, CA: Stanford University Press.

Guillet de Monthoux, P., and S.-E. Sjöstrand (2003) Corporate art or artful corporation: the emerging philosophy firm. In B. Czarniawska and G. Sévon-Berg (eds), *Nordic light: organization theory in Scandinavia*. Malmö, Sweden: Liber.

Guillet de Monthoux, P., and A. Strati (eds) (2002) *Aesthetics and organization* [Special issue]. *Human Relations*, 55 (7).

Henaff, M. (2002) *Le prix de la vérité, le don, l'argent, la philosophie*. Paris: Seuil.

Hjort, D. (2003) *Rewriting entrepreneurship. For a new perspective on organizational creativity*. Malmö, Sweden: Liber Ekonomi.

Kant, I. (1986) *The critique of judgement*. Oxford University Press.

Laufer, R., and C. Paradeise (1990) *Marketing democracy*. New Brunswick, NJ: Transaction Books.

Mangham, I., and T. Clark (2004) Stripping to the undercoat: A review and reflection of a piece of organization theatre. *Organization Studies* 25 (5), pp. 841–51.

Ouchi, W. (1980) Markets, bureaucracies and clans. *Administrative Science Quarterly*, 25 (March) pp. 129–41.

Postrel, V. (2003) *The substance of style*. New York: Harper Collins.

Rehn, A. (2001) Electronic potlatch. Dissertation. Stockholm Royal Institute of Technology.

Salais, R., and M. Storper (1993) *Les mondes de production*. Paris: Éditions de l'école des hautes études en sciences socials.

Sjöstrand, S.-E. (1997) *The two faces of management. The Janus factor*. London: Thomson.

Stiegler, B. (2004a) *De la misère symbolique: l'epoque hyperindustrielle*. Paris: Galilée.

Stiegler, B. (2004b) *Philosopher par accident*. Paris: Editions Galilée.

Strati, A., and P. Guillet de Monthoux (eds) (2002) On aesthetics and management – business bridges to art, special issue of *Consumption Markets and Culture*, 5 (1).

Williamson, O. (1975) *Markets and hierarchies: analysis of antitrust implications*. New York: Free Press.

Index